CHURCHILL & ATTLEE

CHURCHILL & ATTLEE

THE UNLIKELY ALLIES
WHO WON THE WAR

DAVID COHEN

Biteback Publishing

First published in Great Britain in 2018 by
Biteback Publishing Ltd
Westminster Tower
3 Albert Embankment
London SE1 7SP
Copyright © David Cohen 2018

David Cohen has asserted his right under the Copyright, Designs and Patents Act 1988 to be
identified as the author of this work.

ISBN 978-1-78590-317-5

10 9 8 7 6 5 4 3 2 1

A CIP catalogue record for this book is available from the British Library.

Set in Adobe Caslon Pro

Printed and bound in Great Britain by
CPI Group (UK) Ltd, Croydon CR0 4YY

MIX
Paper from
responsible sources
FSC® C020471

For Reuben, whom I miss and mourn every day, and for his brother, Nicholas, who gives me great joy

CONTENTS

ACKNOWLEDGEMENTS

This book would not have come to fruition without the encouragement of many people. I first discussed the idea with Jeremy Robson, who put it forward to his colleagues at Biteback. My agent and friend, Sonia Land, liked it too. I have been more than well served by my publishers, especially Olivia Beattie and Bernadette Marron, who edited the copy. Maria Andrews helped with much research and fact-checking and was marvellous. My long-term friend Jennifer Fraser read the first draft.

I am also extremely grateful to Lord Hunt of the Wirral, who spoke with his colleague Earl Attlee, who has generously granted me permission to use Attlee's poems. I am profoundly sorry my late son, Reuben, could not comment on the manuscript, as he so often made my work better; his mother, Aileen La Tourette, also suggested many improvements.

Anne Blackman provided me with very useful information on Attlee. And I am grateful also to Steve Ely, whose notion on when a personality is formed, originally devised to study Ted Hughes, I have applied when examining Attlee and Churchill. I am also very grateful for conversations that have led to ideas – and, in the case of Simon Ward, practical help with his photocopier. Much help came also from David Blackman, David Carr Brown, Julia Ross, Sabbagh Curran and Chris Wallis.

Attlee was an avid keeper of letters, memos and papers, all of which are now housed in a collection at the Bodleian Library in Oxford. I found much useful material stored in boxes 4, 6, 13, 20, 21, 22, 23, 32, 69, 72, 86, 69, 124, 128 and 142. The Churchill Centre at Churchill College, Cambridge is a veritable treasure trove of material on the great Prime Minister, and I visited it extensively while carrying out research. I must thank the librarians at both institutions, who were immensely helpful and readily offered their assistance.

This warm thanks extends to the librarians at the British Library, especially the rare books team (this seems to be the only spot in the library where one can photocopy). And also to the Tower Hamlets Local History Library and Archives, which was very useful on Attlee.

There have been many fine biographies of Churchill; Sir Martin Gilbert's is pre-eminent and I have relied on it at many points. Roy Jenkins's *Churchill* is a fine work, too, and while some of it is controversial, Boris Johnson's book has the fizz of the champagne Churchill so enjoyed.

Attlee's *As It Happened* is a major source for his childhood and youth. Kenneth Harris's biography has many details, as has Peggy Attlee's biography of Attlee's brother Tom. John Bew's *Citizen Clem* has been widely admired and rightly so. Churchill's biography, *Lord Randolph Churchill*, remains the best source on his father.

Celia and John Lee's work on the Churchills remains highly illuminating on Lord and Lady Randolph's marriage. It contains the many letters in which they nagged their son to do better and work harder. Their work reveals much family history including Churchill's relationship with his brother, Jack.

PROLOGUE

Winston Churchill wrote his only short story two years after the Second World War ended. In *The Dream*, his long-dead father appears. Churchill tries not to be frightened by this apparition which begins to cross-examine him.

What has he done with his life? When Lord Randolph died in 1895, Churchill was not a promising young man. Has he done better since then, his father demands to know.

'I was a major in the Yeomanry,' Churchill replies. His father is not impressed by the middling rank. Glancing around Churchill's studio in Chartwell's fine grounds, he admits, though, that his son has obviously been 'able to keep himself going'.

Churchill tells his father he has four children and five grandchildren. Lord Randolph then turns to the world situation. 'Have there been any wars since I died?' he asks, and if so, was Britain victorious?

'Yes, we won all our wars,' Churchill responds.

In telling his father that he became a major, Churchill was hiding much of the truth about his military career. By 1947, when he wrote the story, he had been a lieutenant-colonel in the army, not to mention

First Lord of the Admiralty and Minister of Defence. At one point, Lord Randolph admits he is surprised that his son is so well-versed on the subject of war. 'I never expected that you would develop so far and so fully. Of course you are too old now to think about such things, but when I hear you talk I really wonder you didn't go into politics … You might even have made a name for yourself.'

Churchill never tells his father that he became an MP, let alone that he served as Prime Minister and steered Britain to victory in the Second World War. Interpreting Churchill's reticence is tempting, but not simple. A famous son writes a fiction, in which he conjures up his less famous father, who was usually disappointed in him. The son fails to tell his father much about the triumphs he has achieved. Keeping quiet, which did not come naturally to Churchill, obviously reveals something about his feelings; he loved his father dearly, but perhaps he did not totally trust him. Perhaps he also wanted to spare his father's feelings because he had succeeded far more than Lord Randolph had done.

Clement Attlee was less conflicted when it came to his father, Henry Attlee, but he was reluctant to discuss their relationship. Attlee discusses the loss of his father in his autobiography, *As It Happened*, but is brief, including little detail, and refrains from discussing his private sense of loss. In his notes, however, Attlee was extremely tender; his father had always been kind and broad-minded. Upon Henry Attlee's death, Clement gathered three glowing testimonials from his father's colleagues, but, ultimately, Attlee chose not to publish any of them. He never explained why he did this.

INTRODUCTION

The likelihood of two Prime Ministers sharing the same governess seems low, yet this was the case for two of Britain's greatest Prime Ministers: Winston Churchill and Clement Attlee.

The governess in question was a Miss Hutchinson, who described Churchill as a 'strong-willed little boy'. Churchill was not particularly fond of his governess and complained to his mother that she was 'so stiff and stern'. Miss Hutchinson left the Churchills when Winston was six years old, and later went to work for the Attlee family, where she taught Clement until he was old enough to start school. 'She could never have thought that the two little boys were destined in turn to be Prime Minister,' Attlee marvelled in his autobiography, *As It Happened*.

During the 1945 election campaign, contrasting depictions of the two political leaders were quickly established by the press. Churchill was seen as the lordly smoker of Havanas and 'Clem' a pipe-smoking man of the people, whose wife drove him from meeting to meeting and pressed his trousers herself. Following Labour's victory in the 1945 election, Churchill told Attlee that a British Prime Minister could hardly meet Comrade Stalin and Harry Truman, the new President of the United

States, without a valet – he even went so far as to insist on lending Attlee his own man.

At the annual Attlee Foundation lecture in 1897, Attlee's former private secretary, Sir David Hunt, recalled this anecdote and told the audience that Attlee had remarked: 'The Russians were most surprised, but the Americans were simply flabbergasted when I came back with the same private secretary that Winston had gone away with.' Hunt added that Attlee ultimately took Churchill up on his offer and brought the proffered valet with him. In his diary, Churchill's assistant private secretary, John 'Jock' Colville, wrote that Attlee told him it was 'the first and last time he ever had a valet'.

Churchill's willingness to be of assistance to his Labour counterpart was not entirely surprising given his respect for the man. In the 1950s, Colville posed a question to the Prime Minister: which Labour leader did he feel had been the most helpful during the war? Colville had expected Churchill to plump for Ernest Bevin, who had persuaded the trade unions to drop many restrictive practices, but although Churchill liked and admired Bevin, he chose Attlee without hesitation. Attlee had shouldered much responsibility and had always been loyal to the government.

On 3 February 1955, both men were at Buckingham Palace when Churchill spotted the 72-year-old Attlee 'quivering'. Attlee soon fainted into the arms of Churchill, who, with the assistance of Attlee's wife, placed the unconscious man on a couch. Despite being nine years Attlee's senior, Churchill lamented, 'Poor Attlee, he is getting old,' and ordered complete silence about the incident. As comrades-in-arms, the men were loyal to one another.

Churchill is an enduring figure of much interest, immortalised in literature and film. According to the British Library catalogue, there have been over 100 biographies of Churchill, and he is the central figure of numerous films, including the recent Oscar-winning *Darkest Hour*. There is extensive writing on his paintings, his bricklaying, and more than one book focusing on his passion for cigars.

In his intriguing biography of the British Prime Minister, Sebastian Haffner, a German journalist and author who fled Nazi Germany in 1938, described Hitler and Churchill as two duellists. Haffner was fascinated by the paradox that a 'grand seigneur' led a coalition that included 'several men of the Labour movement'. He believed that Churchill was a man of two disparate personalities, the statesman and the generalissimo, a leader who believed that 'jaw jaw was better than war war'.

John Lukacs's *The Duel: The Eighty-Day Struggle Between Churchill and Hitler* also presents the two men as warriors. The struggle began on 10 May and ended on 31 July, Lukacs writes. On 19 July 1940, when the duel between Churchill and Hitler was at its most intense, Hitler delivered a lengthy speech that presented a 'rational' case for peace. Churchill made no response to this, not being, as he told Jock Colville, 'on speaking terms' with Hitler.

Upon first reading, *Sir Winston Churchill: Master of Courage*, by Princess Marthe Bibesco, appears to be built entirely on fluff. The book reveals how the princess and Winston, as she refers to him affectionately, would have intimate conversations where he would confide in her. The majority of what Bibesco writes is unworthy of serious reflection, but she does make one interesting point: Churchill possessed an 'essential childishness'. Perhaps 'childishness' is an exaggeration, but Churchill was known to be extremely playful, a quality which served him well following his devastating election loss in 1945.

After this defeat, Churchill decided he would go to France and Italy to restore himself, and resumed the use of a false name that he had operated under during the war: 'Colonel Warden'. Churchill persuaded Prime Minister Attlee to involve himself in this subterfuge, which carried on for several months, and Attlee was quite happy to indulge Churchill.

Attlee has been the subject of eight biographies, including John Bew's excellent *Citizen Clem*, which argues that Attlee has been 'underappreciated'. Bew has a point, certainly in terms of films. The Labour leader does not appear in *Dunkirk*, which is absurd, as he was asked by Churchill to draw up plans for the evacuation, while *Darkest Hour* opens with an angry speech in the House of Commons – a speech Attlee never made. For the rest of the film, he appears only as a muttering figure in the background, while the Earl of Halifax and Neville Chamberlain plot how to remove Churchill from Downing Street. Film-goers would never guess that it was Attlee who provided Churchill with crucial support in May and June 1940, when many politicians had still hoped to make peace with Hitler.

Attlee may not have left a long-lasting impression, but many leading Tories, including Harold Macmillan and Margaret Thatcher, admired his integrity. The most remarkable tribute to his leadership came in 2004, when Ipsos MORI conducted a poll of 139 historians and political scientists to determine the most successful Prime Minister of the twentieth century – Attlee came first. Since Churchill liked horse racing, let's say that he lost by a short head.

Despite the many biographies, not one has focused on examining the forty-year-long relationship between Attlee and Churchill. Even Roy Jenkins, who has written biographies of both men, did not devote much space to why they managed to collaborate well. Historians seem to have taken that almost for granted. This book concentrates, therefore, on what made collaboration between the men possible and how it worked.

It tries to identify what divided and what united them – policy, personality and principles. It is not a joint biography, so there is relatively little on some key moments, such as the Battle of Britain, in which Attlee only played a small part.

The book follows a largely linear timeline, although on occasion theme takes precedence over chronology. 'Leadership Qualities' is thematic, as is a small section on collaboration at the end of Chapter 7. Both shed light on how the two men achieved so much without losing their separate political identities.

CHAPTER 1

THE ROGUE ELEPHANT
AND THE MOUSE

In ballet, a dance performed by two people is known as a *pas de deux*, literally translated as a 'step of two', and in many ways this is a fitting description of Churchill and Attlee's relationship. In *Citizen Clem*, John Bew argues that their *pas de deux* started as a mating dance, with both men circling each other warily before deciding to commit to each other in good faith. There is some truth to this, but they were also, though metaphors can be pushed too far, comrades-in-arms.

It is rare for rival politicians to work together well over a long period of time. Nelson Mandela and F. W. de Klerk argued over the timing of Mandela's release from prison, and their relationship did not improve once Mandela was freed from Robben Island. French history offers one all too human example; after the 1986 French National Assembly elections ended in stalemate, the socialist President François Mitterrand was forced to nominate the conservative Jacques Chirac as Prime Minister. During what was called the cohabitation, the two men soon fell out; cohabitation proved to be more conflict than collaboration.

The most surprising political collaboration of all is perhaps that of two leaders whose communities had been bitter enemies for three centuries. The Protestant Reverend Ian Paisley and the Catholic IRA leader Martin McGuinness seemed likely to curse each other to their graves. That they could work together at all, let alone well, is extraordinary. In 2007, when Paisley became First Minister of Northern Ireland and McGuinness his deputy, British officials were astonished when these enemies of thirty years asked them to leave the Northern Ireland Assembly's complex. Despite their differences, the two men discovered they could collaborate. In December 2007, the pair charmed President George W. Bush. 'Up until 26 March this year, Ian Paisley and I never had a conversation about anything – not even about the weather,' McGuinness told Bush. Remarkably, Paisley, who routinely denounced the Pope as the Antichrist, soft-soaped centuries of hate as nothing more than 'squabbles'. Protestant and Catholic were now on the same side. 'There will be a fight for peace. You have to fight for peace. And we are dedicated to that,' Paisley told Bush. No one has yet explained how suspicion and hatred turned into friendship. The media began calling Paisley and McGuinness the 'Chuckle Brothers', because they cracked so many jokes together.

When Paisley retired, McGuinness gave him two poems, one by Seamus Heaney and one that he had written himself. Paisley's widow, Eileen, said that during her husband's final illness in 2014, McGuinness texted frequently to check on him. 'It gave Ian a lot of happiness as well to know that he had left that impression with [him]. His friendship with Martin McGuinness had meant something very special to him,' she said. After Paisley's death, McGuinness said, 'Despite our differences, I found him to be a charismatic and powerful personality. He always treated me and those who worked with me with respect and courtesy. The peace process and I have lost a friend.'

Churchill and Attlee were never the Chuckle Brothers, but they worked well for a number of reasons, quite beyond the critical need to unite against the Nazis. Although Attlee wrote about his happy childhood, he chose to gloss over some serious problems, including his mother's determination not to involve the family with outsiders. This isolation affected Attlee more than his siblings. In *As It Happened*, he admits that he 'had always been painfully shy'. Churchill's childhood had been difficult, but he was more inclined to bare his soul on the subject. *The Dream* suggests that, even at sixty, Churchill was still trying to understand and please his father. He had always adored both of his parents, but while he could be critical of his father, he thought his mother 'a fairy princess: a radiant being'.

McGuinness believed that for a collaboration to succeed, differences must be respected. Attlee and Churchill always differed on two issues: India and socialism. Socialism was 'a philosophy of failure, the creed of ignorance and the gospel of envy', Churchill told a crowd in Perth on 28 May 1948. It only led to the equal sharing of miseries. 'There are two places only where socialism will work; in heaven where it is not needed, and in hell where they already have it,' he remarked acerbically.

Socialism, on the other hand, was a 'living faith' for Attlee. In 1937, he rejoiced that 'I have been a socialist agitator for thirty-seven years'. In *The Labour Party in Perspective*, he took the orthodox view: 'The evils that capitalism brings differ in intensity in different countries, but the root cause of the trouble once discerned, the remedy is seen to be the same by thoughtful men and women. The cause is the private ownership of the means of life; the remedy is public ownership.'

Despite Churchill's virulence towards socialism, he and Attlee shared more political similarities than one might expect. Both men were reformers who proposed the abolition of the House of Lords. Despite, as he noted in *As It Happened*, being once described by Colonel Vigne, with whom he played bridge as they sailed to Gallipoli, as a 'damned democratic socialist tub-thumping rascal', Attlee, like Churchill, was a staunch monarchist. They were united by their hatred of communism; Churchill likened the comrades to 'baboons', while Attlee described them as 'gratuitous asses'. 'I stuck up for the socialists in Washington. I always got on with Attlee,' Churchill wrote.

Churchill first joined the Cabinet in 1908, when he was appointed President of the Board of Trade. He soon argued in private for a coalition between the Liberals and the Tories, so the idea of pulling together in the national interest was not a taboo for him. Just two years later, Churchill was appointed Home Secretary. In this capacity, he helped push through domestic reforms that Attlee's government built upon after the Second World War.

Meanwhile, in 1911, Attlee was employed by the government as an 'official explainer', a role that involved touring Essex and Somerset on a bicycle and telling audiences congregated in village halls about a specific reform, the National Insurance Act. Churchill had played a large role in shaping it, as well as much of the other reforming legislation in 1910 and 1911, including the Coal Mines Act and the Labour and Shops Act.

By the time the Second World War started, Liberal leader David Lloyd George and Churchill had learned about collaboration and worked well together. A chapter of Roy Jenkins's celebrated biography *Churchill* is titled 'The Sorcerer's Apprentice at the Board of Trade'. The sorcerer refers to Lloyd George; the apprentice Churchill. The two men forged a working relationship that lasted some forty years and generally stayed loyal to each other.

It was not plain sailing for Attlee, who had to juggle four mighty egos: Hugh Dalton, Herbert Morrison, Stafford Cripps and Ernest Bevin. The first three were convinced that they would have made more successful Labour leaders. Attlee also had to contend with Harold Laski, a gifted economist, but a man who possessed little talent for politics.

Roy Jenkins regarded Lloyd George as the most talented politician of the early decades of the twentieth century, yet he was not considered by Churchill to be a rival, as he was his senior. The most important figure Churchill had to deal with was his father, and his memories of him. Lord Randolph Churchill had once enjoyed a glittering political career. It is apparent from reading *The Dream* that Churchill's relationship with his father was crucial for him, not just as a young man but even when he was the saviour of Britain. Lord Randolph was a complex and flawed man and father. He could be stunningly rude. At his club, he once found himself cornered by a bore, so he summoned a waiter and instructed him to listen to the end of the man's story as he was too irritated to hear another syllable. On 3 August 1886, Lord Salisbury appointed him Chancellor of the Exchequer and Leader of the House of Commons. Lord Randolph did not imagine that William Henry Smith, the puffed-up ruler of a number of railway kiosks, who had become Secretary of State for War, would dare object when he proposed a cut to the £31 million defence budget.

Dear Lord Salisbury,

The approximate Estimates for the Army and Navy for the next year have been to-day communicated to me by George Hamilton. And Smith. They amount to 31 millions – 12 and a half millions for the Navy, 18 and a half millions for the Army … The total 31 millions for the two Services, which will in all probability be exceeded, is very greatly in excess of what I can consent to.

When Smith did object, Lord Randolph was certain that Salisbury would support him. On 20 December, he wrote to Salisbury, who replied two days later, warning how damaging his resignation would be. Lord Randolph interpreted this response as an acceptance of his resignation. He then proceeded to write a letter of farewell to the Prime Minister, following which, he went to the theatre.

Lord Randolph left a performance of *The School for Scandal* at the end of the first act, and told his wife he was going to his club. Instead, he strode to the offices of *The Times*, handed the editor the letter of resignation he had written to Salisbury, and told the editor to print it. His wife knew nothing of the unfolding drama till she came down to breakfast the next morning and read the paper.

'Quite a surprise for you,' Lord Randolph told her. Lady Randolph was hurt and later reflective. She wrote, 'In vain I tried to console myself with the thought that happiness does not depend so much on circumstances as on one's inner self. But I have always found in practice that theories are of little comfort.'

Lord Randolph had expected that his threat to resign would force Salisbury to beg him to reconsider. This did not happen. Churchill wrote that 'he delivered himself unarmed, unattended, fettered even, to his enemies; and therefrom ensued not only his own political ruin, but grave injury to the causes he sustained'. His father was never again a politician with real influence. 'A man can never recover his lost position,' Churchill stated in his biography of Lord Randolph. Writing the book forced Churchill to confront some difficult personal issues. He ducked some too, especially the scandalous aspects of his mother's behaviour, but he ducked fewer than many other sons of famous fathers.

Like Lady Randolph, Queen Victoria learned of Lord Randolph's resignation from *The Times* and was offended not to have been told beforehand.

Former Prime Minister Herbert Asquith's daughter, Violet Bonham Carter, said that Churchill worshipped at the tomb of the unknown father. Lord Randolph was not just unknown to his son; it could be argued he was unknowable even to himself, as many of his actions were so impulsive and inconsistent. He constantly railed against Gladstone and the Liberals, and referred to them in a speech as 'these plunderers of classes, these destroyers of property, these friends of the lawless'. Yet Gladstone occasionally dined with the Churchills and Edward Marjoribanks, the Liberal Chief Whip, did so regularly, as he was Lord Randolph's brother-in-law.

Despite Lord Randolph's open dislike of them, Winston Churchill left the Tories for the Liberals in 1904, and stayed on their benches for nearly twenty years. The son analysed his father, and then both praised, but also defied, his memory. Perhaps Attlee and Churchill would not have worked so well together if Churchill had been a lifelong Tory.

Paisley and McGuinness may have been political enemies, but they were both natural warriors. Churchill also fell into that camp, and had always held aspirations of achieving major office; Attlee as a young man, on the other hand, was not overtly ambitious. Their personalities were radically different. Churchill was largely regarded as an extrovert; he loved talking, and would often talk about himself. An uninhibited man, Churchill was not afraid of showing his emotions, and was seen crying in public on more than one occasion. The man who came from an upper-class background did not have a stiff upper lip.

Attlee, however, was painfully shy; his reserve a classic characteristic of the introvert. He was not much given to self-revelation, let alone to crying in public. In *As It Happened*, he wrote that he was brought up with 'great reverence for [his] seniors, who, it seemed to us, had attained a standard of virtue which we could never hope to approach'. Discipline and discretion were the tenets of Attlee's upbringing, and they would shape his behaviour as an adult. As a colleague, he did not begrudge Churchill the limelight.

Over time, though, Attlee's personality changed. He himself said few thought him even a starter, and there has been a debate about who belittled Attlee as 'a sheep in sheep's clothing'. The historian Denis William Brogan asked Churchill if he had used the phrase. Churchill responded that he had, but not in reference to Attlee. He had skewered Labour Prime Minister Ramsay MacDonald as the sheep and mocked him because he wanted to go tiger hunting unarmed.

Hugh Dalton, who became Chancellor of the Exchequer under Attlee, came up with a different animal analogy, referring to Attlee as 'a little mouse'. Another critic dubbed Attlee 'a modest man who had much to be modest about' – this, too, has often been wrongly attributed to Churchill. Beatrice Webb, who seemed to judge everyone she met, was caustic. To her, Attlee 'looked and spoke like an insignificant elderly clerk, without distinction in the voice, manner or substance of his discourse. To realise that this little nonentity is the Parliamentary Leader of the Labour Party ... and presumably the future P.M., is pitiable.'

Another famous joke made at Attlee's expense, which has again been attributed to Churchill, echoed Webb's lack of regard for the Labour leader. It went like this: 'An empty taxi arrived at 10 Downing Street, and when the door was opened, Attlee got out.' Upon hearing the joke, Jock Colville noted, Churchill was unamused.

Mr Attlee is an honourable and gallant gentleman and a faithful colleague who served his country well at the time of her greatest need. I should be obliged if you would make it clear whenever an occasion arises that I would never make such a remark about him and that I strongly disapprove of anybody who does.

Attlee had had a fine military record in the First World War, Churchill added. Although Labour had a strong pacifist element, and Attlee himself supported the No More War movement, the Labour leader maintained a keen interest in the military. Churchill respected Attlee for his expertise in the area and allowed him to co-chair meetings of the Defence Committee during the Second World War. In 1940, Churchill was not regarded as a supreme military strategist, with historian B. H. Liddell Hart even deeming him a 'rogue elephant'. The Tories, too, saw Churchill as something of a wild card, given that he had sat on the Liberal benches for a number of years.

Collaborations have many strands and one was that both men shared a love of words. Over the past 200 years, a large number of Prime Ministers have written memoirs, but Churchill and Attlee also wrote fiction, a much rarer beast. Disraeli, of course, wrote sixteen novels including *Sybil*, *Coningsby* and *Tancred*, but he is the great exception. Churchill authored one novel, *Savrola*, while Attlee also tried his hand at fiction, penning a satirical short story about the Bullion family.

Attlee also loved poetry, with his boyhood favourites including Tennyson and Kipling. His own poetry, although never published, eloquently expresses his innermost thoughts and feelings. In later life, Attlee wrote a poem reflecting on his election as Prime Minister in 1945:

> Few thought he was even a starter,
> There were many who thought themselves smarter.
> But he finished PM
> A CH, an OM,
> An Earl and a Knight of the Garter.

This nifty verse suggests that Attlee's confidence blossomed over the years. Shy and timid as a young man, it is unlikely that he would have written something so bold then. The contrast and parallels between Churchill and Attlee are interesting – a master of English prose and a lover of poetry who could turn out a good light verse and more. We shall see later how Churchill learned to write so well when he was a pupil at Harrow.

Two men are key sources in trying to understand Churchill, because in different ways he confided in them. Brendan Bracken, an Irish journalist who founded the *Financial Times*, worked for Churchill from 1923 and eventually became his Minister of Information. Stanley Baldwin described Bracken as Churchill's faithful *chela*, the Hindu word for disciple. Churchill's other key confidant was Charles Wilson (later 1st Baron Moran), a doctor and chair of a Home Office committee on how to prepare London hospitals for war casualties; he also served as President of the Royal Society of Physicians. He became Churchill's personal doctor after Churchill became Prime Minister in 1940. Bracken told Moran that in order to truly understand Churchill, one had to study his childhood. In his youth, Churchill found that unflattering comparisons were occasionally drawn between him and his younger brother, Jack (many of which are discussed in Celia and John Lee's *The Churchills: A Family Portrait*). Attlee did not have the same pressures to contend with; he grew up in a tight-knit family, where he and his brothers were not made to feel as if they were in competition with one another.

As Prime Minister, Churchill was often anxious about his position and was eager to be seen as successful, perhaps a hang-up from his childhood. This desire may have been the motivation behind why, in 1942, he called for two votes of confidence in his administration. Attlee defended Churchill vigorously in the House and only twenty-five MPs voted against the government.

Attlee could question Churchill's ideas without threatening his primacy. As a result, he could coax, criticise and even influence Churchill's behaviour. On one occasion in 1942, while Churchill was in America meeting with President Franklin D. Roosevelt, Attlee decided to make amendments to the Allies' war aims so that they would be more in line with his own socialist views. Churchill did not complain.

Comparing politicians can also sometimes lead to the apparently eccentric. Height is an important theme in Boris Johnson's *The Churchill Factor*. Johnson appears to accept the psychological theories of Alfred Adler, an Austrian doctor and founder of the school of individual psychology, who thought that power, not sex, as Freud believed, was the primary motivator for human behaviour. If you were short, you had to compensate by becoming powerful. Johnson draws from this theory, suggesting that Churchill hated Hitler because the Nazi dictator was taller than him.

Nevertheless, Johnson may have a point when it comes to the two Britons: Churchill was 5ft 6in. tall and Attlee was much the same height. The fact that neither man towered over the other may have helped them work well together, perhaps.

Churchill would probably have dismissed Johnson's ideas about 'short man syndrome', as he had never regarded himself as diminutive in stature. Churchill had been a stylish young man. In the 1972 film *Young Winston*, based on Churchill's *My Early Life*, actor Simon Ward is a model of elegance. Attlee has not been played by a major star. The Labour Minister of Education, Ellen Wilkinson, wrote, in an introduction to Cyril Clemens's biography of Attlee, *The Man from Limehouse*: 'The cleverest publicity man could not turn the new British Prime Minister into a glamour star. Quite simply, he wouldn't let them. He has a quiet, sarcastic little smile for the stunt merchant.'

Although short man syndrome may seem far-fetched, Churchill did suffer from depression, which is often referred to as his 'black dog', though he had little time for psychologists or psychiatrists. In 1942, he wrote, 'It would be sensible to restrict as much as possible the work of these gentlemen.' He did not want the breed 'to quarter themselves upon the Fighting Services at the public expenses'. He denounced psychiatry as 'charlatanry'.

Lord Moran's two-volume biography of Churchill offers a number of analyses of Churchill's personality. It is always worrying when an author gives verbatim quotations of long private conversations, as is the case in *Churchill at War*. Moran may be embellishing, and this should be kept in mind when he quotes Brendan Bracken, telling him, 'You and I think of Churchill as self-indulgent; he has never denied himself anything, but when a mere boy he set out to change his nature, to be tough and full of rude spirits.'

Bracken added that Churchill was 'a despairer. Orpen, who painted him after the Dardanelles military disaster, called him a man of misery.' (William Orpen was a successful painter and chairman of the Chelsea Arts Club.) During Churchill's years in the political wilderness, between 1929 and 1939, Bracken reported that Churchill would say 'I'm finished' at least twice a day. Out of government, he was 'wretched' because he had little to do. 'Why, he told me that he prays for death every day,' Bracken ended dramatically.

At the start of his *Painting as a Pastime*, Churchill comes close to describing depression himself: 'Many remedies are suggested for the avoidance of worry and mental overstrain by persons who, over prolonged periods, have to bear exceptional responsibilities and discharge duties upon a very large scale.' Travel, rest and exercise could help, he pointed out. He then quoted an unnamed American psychologist who had said that worry 'is a spasm of the emotion; the mind catches hold of something and will not let it go'. Churchill continued that it was 'useless to argue with the mind in this condition. The stronger the will, the more futile the task.'

For Churchill, the crisis came when he had to resign as First Lord of the Admiralty, after the Dardanelles fiasco. The loss of responsibility and power left him stunned. 'Like a sea beast fished up from the depths, or a diver too suddenly hoisted, my veins threatened to burst from the fall in pressure. I had great anxiety and no means of relieving it.' He loved action, but he was now in a position where he was unable to act. Reading was no escape in such extreme circumstances; the remedy for Churchill's ills was to be found in painting. 'To restore psychic equilibrium we should call into use those parts of the mind which direct both eye and hand.'

It will be argued later that Churchill himself, as well as Moran and Bracken, were inaccurate in claiming he suffered from depression. There is no doubt, though, that Churchill often needed his wife, colleagues and subordinates to pull him out of his moods.

Attlee wrote little about any personal struggles. He had learned to stay calm while dealing with the controversies and feuds in the Labour Party during the 1930s. That sense of calm helped him to keep Churchill's black dog at bay. In her contribution to *The Man from Limehouse*, Ellen Wilkinson observed that Attlee's sensible speeches often defused tense meetings. She said, 'I have seen 200 angry men, after such a speech, leave a room wondering what they had been making such a fuss about.' Joseph Kenworthy (later 10th Baron Strabolgi) began his political career as a Liberal, before joining Labour in 1926. He met Attlee for the first time in 1922, and stated that Attlee's 'strong and calm character was a very great asset to Winston Churchill during the war, when he had the difficult task of coping with the temperamental and sometimes erratic Winston'.

Attlee's interest in psychology was widely shared in 1915. The trauma of the trenches in the First World War highlighted the importance of psychology and psychiatry. Early on, British soldiers serving on the

Western Front began to report they suffered from tinnitus, headaches, amnesia, tremors and extreme sensitivity to noise. Ten per cent of British officers and 4 per cent of enlisted men had 'nervous and mental shock' without having any head wounds. In 1915, Charles Myers, a co-founder of the British Psychological Society, wrote about the condition in *The Lancet*. Shell shock, as it came to be known, baffled doctors and was a source of great interest for many, like Attlee, who were fighting at the time. Today, the condition is recognised as post-traumatic stress disorder.

Attlee, an avid reader, would hardly have missed the debates on shell shock. It may well be the case, though he never publicly acknowledged it, that he believed psychology might help him deal with his shyness. There is another explanation. While lecturing at the London School of Economics, he met pioneering social psychologists, including Graham Wallas. Attlee's first book, *The Social Worker*, published in 1920, shows he was familiar and at ease with the latest psychological theories. In a speech he made in the Commons in 1940, he stressed the need to study the psychology of the Germans because they had a different mentality and then asked how a halfpenny increase in postal charges would affect the psychology of letter and postcard writers.

When Attlee became Churchill's deputy, he appointed the economist Evan Durbin, a rather forgotten socialist, as his personal assistant. Durbin joined forces with the psychoanalyst John Bowlby, well known for his theories of how children bonded with their mothers, to edit a book on ways to prevent wars. This book has been largely neglected, partly because of the popularity of *Why War?*, Einstein and Freud's correspondence on the same subject published in 1933.

Attlee also brought John Strachey into the coalition government and then, in 1946, made him Minister of Food; Strachey would become Secretary of State for War in 1950. Strachey's cousin, James Strachey, translated Freud's work into English and witnessed the battles that raged in British psychoanalysis, sparked by the jealousies between Freud's daughter, Anna, and the innovative Austrian psychoanalyst Melanie Klein. James Strachey referred to it as the 'Battle of the Ladies'. Attlee's cousin, Wilfred, was a GP in Eton and worked with Dr Ronald Fairbairn, a psychoanalyst and father of the rather volatile Tory MP, Nicholas Fairbairn. Despite his being surrounded by people with ties to psychoanalysis, none of the biographies of Attlee make much of his connections with it.

Attlee was never a jealous man and this is evidenced by his unstinting praise of Churchill during the war. 'No one else could have done what he did,' Attlee wrote. When Attlee was critical, he behaved discreetly; Jock Colville, in *The Fringes of Power*, recalls that Attlee once typed an unflattering memo to Churchill himself, so that it would not leak. In 1952, loyalty prevented Attlee from attacking Churchill personally after London was mired in a thick smog that was dubbed the 'pea-souper'. Initially, Churchill's government had dismissed the idea that this 'fog of all fogs' was killing Londoners.

Attlee and Churchill were able to joke with one another, if the following anecdote is not legendary. It is claimed that Churchill once entered the gentlemen's lavatory in the House of Commons and, upon spotting Attlee, chose a urinal as far away as possible from the Labour leader.

'Feeling standoffish, Winston?' Attlee asked.

To which Churchill replied, 'That's right. Every time you see something big you want to nationalise it.'

This bantering in the gents suggests that humour formed part of a complex relationship and helped the two men to work together exceptionally well. If they had not done so, the world would have been darkly different.

CHAPTER 2

THE STRONG-WILLED BOY AND THE 'PENTING' CHILD, 1874–1895

Winston Spencer-Churchill was born on 30 November 1874 in Blenheim Palace, which had been built to reward Churchill's ancestor the 1st Duke of Marlborough, John Churchill, for his military triumphs. The duke defeated the French at Blenheim in 1704, while his brother, Charles, commanded the English fleet. One of the most brilliant generals on the French side was also related to Churchill; James Fitzjames was the illegitimate son of Arabella Churchill, Marlborough's sister, and King James II, the last Stuart King. Churchill's four-volume biography of Marlborough was one of his best books. His ancestor had led a coalition under Queen Anne for six years from 1702, so Churchill knew they could work.

On one occasion, Churchill sat down to dinner with his son, Randolph, and upon finishing the meal he commented on how pleasant it had been. He also could not help but remark that, over the course of one meal, they had spent more time together than he had ever spent with his own father. Although Churchill was exaggerating, it is undeniable that Lord Randolph was an inconsistent father. He would sometimes neglect his son and criticise him in a way that was not unusual in the 1880s and 1890s; Edmund Gosse's classic *Father and Son* focuses on Gosse's turbulent relationship with his father, a staunchly religious man and strict parent. But although tensions between father and son were not uncommon during the period, Churchill's relationship with Lord Randolph was perhaps unusually complicated.

It soon became apparent, not long after Randolph started school at Eton, that he was a stubborn boy. When he got bad reports, he would write long letters to his parents justifying his results. He also appears to have felt invulnerable at times. Randolph and some fellow Etonians once stole strawberries from a local farmer, but while most of the other boys had the good sense to scarper, Randolph was caught in the act. Churchill once observed in Parliament that many working-class lads were sent to Borstal, or prison, for doing nothing worse than what high-spirited toffs did at Eton or Oxford. In 1818, pupils had rioted at Eton when the headmaster, Dr John Keate, tried to impose a curfew.

One of his contemporaries at Eton, the future Liberal Prime Minister Lord Rosebery, described Lord Randolph as 'Always tense and highly strung … he seems to have had no knowledge of men, no considera-tion of their feelings, no give and take.' But Roseberry continued that 'in congenial society, his conversation was wholly delightful. He would then display his mastery of pleasant irony and banter; for with those playthings he was at his best.' Churchill would be far more playful, and usually a lot kinder, than his father.

After completing the 'Grand Tour' of Europe in 1873, Lord Randolph met a beautiful American girl, Jennie Jerome, during Cowes Week on the Isle of Wight. 'If Montaigne is to be believed, this period of extreme youth is love's golden moment,' Churchill wrote of his parents' relationship. Randolph had never been in love before, and 'the force and volume of the tide swept him altogether off his feet'. Jennie Jerome was smitten too, and they decided to get married only three days after they had first set eyes on each other. Both sets of parents were appalled: the duke had hoped for a better match for his son, while Mr Jerome, who had made a fortune out of some risqué schemes in New York, was worried that Randolph was after Jennie's money. Parents had, Churchill wrote, huge power over their children in the 1870s. In Oscar Wilde's *The Importance of Being Earnest*, first performed in 1895, no one can marry unless Lady Bracknell gives her permission, despite her being a mere aunt. Randolph and Jennie Jerome should have accepted that they could not wed, but both were strong-willed characters.

Churchill gives a touching account of how the couple simply insisted they would get married. When they told their disapproving parents, there were unromantic complications: how much money would Jerome settle on his daughter and how much of that would Randolph promise to give his wife? Jerome was right to be worried, as the couple would constantly fritter away their cash. When the 1874 general election was announced, the Woodstock seat fell vacant – a seat the Churchills regarded as theirs by hereditary right. Randolph was asked to contest it, and the marriage could not take place until the election was over. He wrote to Jennie: 'Ever since I met you everything goes well with me – too well; I am afraid of a Nemesis.' The feared disaster did not come; Randolph duly won Woodstock.

The couple were married on 15 April 1874, at the British embassy in Paris. Churchill was born on 30 November, thirty-three weeks after the wedding. There has been some debate as to whether his impulsive parents slept together before they married. Historians Celia and John Lee have calculated that Churchill was born 228 days, or just over seven and a half months, after the marriage, so the marital proprieties may well have been observed.

The strawberry-stealing incident was just an early sign of Randolph's gift for getting into trouble. In 1875, he became embroiled in a scandal involving his elder brother, Lord Blandford, the lover of the married Lady Aylesford. The Prince of Wales branded Blandford a blackguard and challenged Randolph, who had sided with his brother, to a duel. Randolph refused to fight, excusing himself on the grounds that he did not want to be responsible for killing the heir to the throne. Prime Minister Benjamin Disraeli appointed Lord Randolph's father as Lord Lieutenant of Ireland, and Randolph went with him to Dublin to act as his secretary. Once the Prince of Wales disapproved of you, it was impossible to show your face in London society. However, Lord Randolph was an ambitious young politician, and he often had to travel to London to take part in debates in the House. During these visits, Lord Randolph's vivacious wife was left alone and Lord Randolph, too, would be alone in the capital. Both parties had opportunities to be unfaithful.

In February 1882, Lady Randolph noticed a marked deterioration in her husband's health and this, coupled with Lord Randolph's perceived marital indiscretions, provoked his detractors to spread nasty rumours which implied that Lord Randolph was suffering from syphilis. His medical condition was also discussed in Irish writer Frank Harris's scurrilous autobiography, *My Life and Loves*, in which Harris claims definitively that 'Randolph had caught syphilis'. Even Churchill and his immediate family sometimes appeared to believe that Lord Randolph had died of the disease. Churchill biographers Celia and John Lee, however, are less convinced and accuse Harris of unwarranted malice.

Concerned about the family's reputation, Churchill's nephew

Peregrine asked Dr John Mather to investigate Lord Randolph's medical records. Over a century on, and following a two-year examination, Mather concluded there was no evidence that Lord Randolph had contracted syphilis. The Churchill Centre and Museum suggest a 'left-side brain tumour' would be more consistent with his symptoms. Neither of his sons, the Churchill Centre says, 'was born with the infections that resemble secondary syphilis, nor did they have late hereditary syphilis, commonest between the ages of seven and fifteen, manifested by deafness, partial blindness and/or notched teeth'. Syphilis often causes impotence, but Jennie gave birth to their second son, John 'Jack' Churchill, in 1880, five years after Randolph started seeing Dr Clayton. Whether it was syphilis, impotence or a brain tumour, from the early 1880s onwards, Randolph was prone to sickness.

As a small boy, Churchill would often catch a glimpse of society's most famous men and women, who were regularly invited to the family home. Churchill might not have enjoyed much of his parents' attention but, by his teenage years, he had met at least five past and future Prime Ministers – Gladstone and Disraeli, Balfour and his uncle, Lord Salisbury, and Lord Rosebery.

Between the ages of two and six, Churchill lived in Dublin. Churchill's mother, whom he likened to a fairy princess, spent lavishly and would often be busy with princes and politics. She had little time to devote to her son, but she was not all that different from most upper-class parents of the time. In her *Book of Household Management*, Isabella Beeton stressed the need for parents to choose a competent nanny, because children would spend far more time with their nanny than they would with their mother. Churchill's parents chose well; Mrs Everest, whom Churchill would affectionately refer to as 'Woom'.

Mrs Everest was so competent that she even managed to cut

household costs, which was extremely useful given that the Churchills were often in debt. A relative of Mrs Everest's worked as a warder at Parkhurst Prison on the Isle of Wight and, in July 1880, she took the then six-year-old Winston to Ventnor for a cheap holiday. Mrs Everest's cousin told the young Churchill stories about prison mutinies, and described how, on occasion, he too had been attacked.

Churchill later wrote that 'It was at "Little Lodge"', his home while living in Ireland, 'that I was first menaced with education.' Education meant the addition of a governess to the Churchill household, and Miss Hutchinson was engaged to teach young Winston. In preparation, Mrs Everest took Churchill through *Reading Without Tears*, but, although he was making good progress, he had not mastered the book by the time Miss Hutchinson arrived. Unfortunately, the governess also wanted Winston to be good with numbers. Churchill, however, struggled with figures and found that they 'were tied into all sorts of tangles and did things to one another which it was extremely difficult to forecast with complete accuracy'. But the terrifying Hutchinson 'attached enormous importance to the answer being exact'. To his dismay, Churchill's mother nearly always sided with Miss Hutchinson. When he was seven years old, Churchill was packed off to boarding school. He was nervous, but also 'excited and agitated by this great change in my life'. After all, everyone had assured him that their schooldays were the happiest of their lives.

In *The Young Winston Churchill*, John Marsh writes that

Winston spent most of the short journey [to St George's Ascot] groping tearfully in the darkness for three half crowns, which, after his mother had handed them to him, he had let fall on the straw-covered floor …Winston's heart was heavy as an old four-wheeler carried him and his mother through the dark November afternoon from Ascot station to the school.

Churchill tried to be brave when his mother left, but the problems started at once. A master told Churchill to learn all the declensions of the Latin word for table, *mensa*. Although Churchill had never studied Latin when the beak – Marsh writes these chapters rather in the manner of the Billy Bunter books, so it seems apt to use this term – later quizzed him, Churchill, who always had a good memory, performed well. Then Churchill asked the beak: 'What does O table mean, sir?'

The beak replied that it was the vocative case. 'You use it in talking to a table,' he added. Winston stared at him as if the beak had lost his marbles. 'But I never do talk to tables,' he stated innocently, only to be warned that he would be punished if he was impertinent. Punishment at St George's was vicious, even bloody. Lady Randolph had left her son at a school where the masters were addicted to beating their pupils, sometimes until the boys bled.

Literary critic and journalist Thomas Ricks has argued there are parallels between Churchill and author George Orwell – and that these started with their experiences at preparatory school, where both were treated brutally. In his essay 'Such, Such Were the Joys', Orwell describes being beaten after wetting the bed while boarding at St Cyprian's. Orwell recalls fervently praying to God, hoping against hope that he would not commit the offence again, but his prayers go unanswered. Sent to the headmaster's office for being a 'dirty little boy', he is thrashed with a riding crop.

Churchill and Orwell were highly intelligent and the cruel treatment they endured at school seems to have instilled in them a hatred of bullies. In light of recent psychiatric research, this is not so surprising.

The child psychiatrist Sir Michael Rutter studied the extent to which children who have been powerless and beaten or seduced become abusers when they are older; he asked what makes some children resilient and others less so. Intelligence is a major factor, he decided, because clever children can make more sense of why they are being ill-treated. That fact, according to Rutter's 2007 paper 'Resilience Competence and Coping', allows them to overcome ill-treatment better than their peers. Churchill himself wrote,'How I hated this school and what a life of anxiety I led there.'

Put up and shut up was what boys were expected to do. Marsh notes that the young Churchill 'said little to his parents who were in any case busy about their own affairs'. If Winston had opened his heart to them, they would no doubt have 'thought he was romancing', Marsh added. He failed to point out that Churchill wrote a number of letters to his mother, begging her to visit her devoted and loving son – she was usually too busy. In her *Reminiscences*, Lady Randolph describes one high-society jamboree after another, as well as the piano duets she played with Prime Minister Arthur Balfour.

Churchill's parents were unsympathetic, partly because they were self-obsessed, partly because they did not know the truth about the school, and partly because their son's reports were usually less than complimentary. Lady Randolph wrote to her husband that 'as to Winston's improvement, I am sorry to say I see none – he can read very well, but that is all ... The first two days he came home he was terribly slangy and loud. He teases the baby more than ever. It appears he is afraid of me.' Celia and John Lee add that Lady Randolph 'might well have pondered why Winston had become afraid of her', and why he teased his baby brother. It never dawned on Churchill's mother that it all might have something to do with how he was being abused at school. Churchill summed up his experiences of school as 'an unending spell of worries that did not seem petty then'. The floggings at St George's were more severe than anything boys suffered in a reformatory, Churchill wrote.

In 1884, Churchill fell ill. The family doctor, Dr Robson Roose, suspected a weak chest at first, but upon closer inspection he noticed marks on Winston's bottom that indicated the boy had been beaten savagely. As a result, Dr Roose suggested that Lord and Lady Randolph enrol their son at Brunswick School in Brighton, run by the Thompson sisters, who seemed to have little interest in beating their pupils. Churchill began to do well in many of his subjects; he came top of his class, perhaps most surprisingly, in mathematics.

The new school might have provoked less anxiety, but that could not be said of his father. As ever, Lord Randolph was hardly consistent. When Churchill was nine and a half years old, his father gave him a copy of *Treasure Island*, which was immediately 'devoured'. But the gift of the book did not make up for the fact that when Lord Randolph was in Brighton for a political meeting, he neglected to visit his son. When Churchill found out, he was incredibly hurt. 'The neglect and lack of interest in him shown by his parents were remarkable, even judged by the standards of late Victorian and Edwardian days,' stated Churchill's own son, Randolph.

Even at the kindly school in Brighton, there were still some upsetting incidents. On 17 December, Charlotte Thompson wrote to Churchill's mother to say that he and another boy had been involved in a fight 'about a knife a tutor had lent them for their work. The drama passed quickly, but Winston received a blow inflicting a slight wound in his chest.' Dr Roose was summoned and found that Churchill was 'not much hurt'. Lady Randolph, meanwhile, was unperturbed by the news, and made no plans to visit her son at school. She was quite happy to wait a few days for Dr Roose to bring Winston to town to see her.

When Churchill was only nine years old, Lady Randolph met one of the great loves of her life, Count Karl Kinsky, an Austro-Hungarian diplomat who cut a dashing figure with his distinguished moustache and impeccable riding skills; he even won the Grand National steeplechase on Zoedone in 1883. Kinsky often visited Lady Randolph at home, but took care to do so only when her husband was away. Moreton Frewen, a louche character who had married Lady Randolph's sister, Clarita, called Kinsky 'the best Austrian that ever was'.

Lady Randolph's passion for Kinsky made her anxious at times; stemming, in part, from the fact that he was younger than she was. In 1886, she even turned to her mother-in-law, the Duchess of Marlborough, for support, despite the two women never having been particularly close. The two letters that the duchess wrote back were kind and wise, but also critical. She warned Lady Randolph against being vindictive, writing, 'I *pray* [that] you do not breathe thoughts of revenge against *anyon*e. It will bring you no blessing.' Lady Randolph should instead focus on her children and the new cook: 'If I were you I would not, if it killed me, let the heartless lot you live with generally see there was "a shadow of a shade of a shred" wrong'. Lady Randolph did not heed her advice, at least as far as looking after the children was concerned.

The Churchills often struggled to make ends meet. On more than one occasion, Lord Randolph could not afford to pay society doctor Oscar Clayton's fees, so, in an attempt to fortify his bank balance, Randolph tried to sell four of his horses – only two of which reached the reserve price. Nevertheless, Randolph sometimes sent his sons a part of his winnings on the turf, though he expected them to show proper gratitude. It seems unlikely that, by the time he had reached the age of twelve, Churchill would have been completely unaware of his parents' emotional and financial problems.

Despite everything, Churchill proved fiercely loyal to his father. In 1887, while still at Brunswick School, he was taken to see a pantomime that featured a sketch mocking Lord Randolph. Upon witnessing the crowd hissing at the spectacle, Churchill burst into tears before turning to berate the man seated behind him. Churchill snapped: 'Stop that row, you snub-nosed Radical!' Lady Randolph wrote to her husband, who was in Morocco, informing him of the incident and Lord Randolph sent his son a sovereign for being so fiercely loyal.

By the mid-1880s, Lord Randolph had been forgiven by the Prince of Wales, who came to dinner with his wife. Lady Randolph provided a splendid banquet. Before they sat down to eat, Princess Alexandra told her, 'We haven't played Bach for a long time.' The duet they played whetted the Prince's appetite so much that he selected not just one, but both of the soups on offer. Small wonder, then, that Lady Randolph would refer affectionately to him as 'Tum Tum'. After this successful evening, the Churchills were restored to London society.

By 1888, Lord Randolph had decided on which public school Churchill should attend. One might have expected Randolph to send his son to Eton, but he did not think Winston bright enough for his old school. Harrow was chosen, but Churchill found studying for the entrance examination a struggle. Lady Randolph scolded that Winston worked fitfully, so he could not sit his exam for Harrow, and that 'you make me very unhappy'. His father threatened to send him to a tutor and his mother chided, 'I think you repay his kindness very badly.' Winston's ten-year-old brother, Jack, seemed much more of 'a starter', and was always top of his class. Finally, though, Churchill passed the Harrow entrance examination.

When he arrived at Harrow in 1888, Churchill was especially taken by the huge swimming pool, which seemed to him more like a river. In his first days there, he pushed sixth former Leo Amery into the pool, and Amery duly returned the favour. Amery ultimately proved forgiving; he edited the school magazine and published Churchill's first writings, though he insisted on cutting out some criticisms of the school. Fifty-two years later, Amery made a crucial speech in the House of Commons, questioning why British military intervention in Norway had failed. Amery called for Chamberlain to resign as Prime Minister and paved the way for Churchill to replace him.

Churchill never mentioned that the Prince of Wales invited Lady Randolph to his country house parties, which involved more than just hunting and shooting, and where husbands and wives exchanged partners. But there was an etiquette surrounding all the decadence, which remained hidden under the blankets, as it were. Everyone attending the parties knew and abided by the rules; the fun must not end with scandal in the divorce courts. The question is: when did Churchill realise his parents' marriage was far from perfect, and that his mother had a scandalous reputation in London society.

In 1890, four years after he resigned, Lord Randolph sailed down the Nile and was awed by the tombs of the Pharaohs. He was making a point when he wrote to his wife that he had become 'a true philosopher, nerve calm, health good'. That Lord Randolph needed to be philosophical was something both he and his wife were well aware of. Count Karl Kinsky had been transferred to the Austrian embassy in London and was living on an estate near Lady Randolph, who did not keep him away from the children. In 1890, Kinsky gave Churchill his first gun, and set up a target range for him and his brother Jack. Kinsky also introduced Churchill to the German Emperor, Kaiser Wilhelm II, whom Churchill would confront in the First World War twenty-four years later.

Given the failure of his own marriage, it is surprising that Lord

Randolph should have chosen to strike a pious note when the Prince of Wales's son died in 1892. Albert, Duke of Clarence, was thought to be gay and it was rumoured that he had died of syphilis, though the official story was that he succumbed to the more respectable influenza. 'Perhaps this grief may bring them [the Prince and Princess of Wales] together more and put a stop to importunate affairs,' Randolph wrote. By then, his own marriage was close to collapse and, only a few months later, he admitted to his friend, Nathaniel Rothschild, that his wife was living with Freddy Wolverton, a close friend of the Prince of Wales.

Attlee's education can be described as less dramatic. In 1892, he was sent to Northaw School in Potters Bar, and being away from home encouraged the retiring boy to come out of his shell a little. The Bible was taught in detail at the school, and Attlee once distinguished himself in a scripture examination. It shows how little he revealed of himself that this success even sparked talk of him having a religious vocation; no one in his family knew that Attlee was not the devout Christian they believed him to be. Nevertheless, he knew the Bible so well that he had 'a meticulous knowledge of the kings of Israel'. Cricket was the real religion of the school, though, and the two passions sometimes became entwined as the boys invented cricket teams in which the kings of Israel featured. Israel was always captained by the top batsman, Jehu, 'on account of his driving prowess', which somehow never got mentioned in the Old Testament. King David, who slung the stone at Goliath with such deadly accuracy, should have opened the bowling. Attlee did not show much cricketing prowess himself, being a good fielder, 'nothing of a bowler and a most uncertain bat'. For Attlee, cricket remained an enthusiasm all his life.

When he was fourteen, Churchill had one success that impressed his headmaster at Harrow: he recited to the school all 1,200 lines of

Thomas Macaulay's *Lays of Ancient Rome*. Macaulay's first line is heroic, as Horatius and two friends hold a bridge against the Etruscans, giving the Romans enough time to destroy it; the enemy are left stranded on the other side of the River Tiber. Churchill was already passionately interested in military history; he had been given toy soldiers for his seventh birthday, and his collection had grown to some 1,500, all neatly organised into battalions. 'The toy soldiers turned the corner of my life,' Churchill said. When Lord Randolph saw them, he asked if his son 'would like to go into the army'. For once tactful, Randolph did not add that the army might be a good choice because Winston did not seem intelligent enough to go to Oxford, as Randolph himself had done.

Churchill waxed lyrical over his English teacher at Harrow, Robert Somervell, referring to him in his memoirs as 'a delightful man'. Somervell was a stickler for English grammar; he took 'a fairly long sentence and broke it up into its components by means of black, red, blue and green inks … It was a kind of drill.' Churchill never got on with Latin, and even less so with Greek, but he 'got into my bones the essential structure of the ordinary British sentence – a noble thing'. Harrow gave him the tools to be a writer. In *My Early Life*, Churchill allowed himself some irony at the expense of his father's old enemy, Gladstone, who was a fine Greek scholar. Gladstone apparently read 'Homer for fun, which I thought served him right'.

A bomb was the oddest incident of Churchill's schooldays, and an early illustration of his love of risk and action. John Marsh claims there was an empty mansion in Harrow's grounds, and a well which was choked with debris. Churchill decided that the debris must be blown up to save the well. He never explained how he managed to gather together the material he needed to make a small bomb; he may have stolen explosives from the school's cadet corps' stores. He then lowered his bomb into the well, lit the fuse and retreated to a safe distance. The bomb initially failed to go off, so Churchill went back to find out why. The bomb then exploded, scorching his face. A lady in a nearby house rushed out and cleaned up Winston. She herself was no sneak, but unfortunately for the young Churchill, someone else betrayed him. Winston confessed to his mother that there had been 'a deuce of a row' about this bomb, and the headmaster had birched him.

Churchill wrote that he had been a coward at Harrow, and described himself as a 'runt' at the school. Some biographers have suggested he was keen to prove something to those who had bullied him at school – but two events suggest that he was never overawed by fellow pupils.

Firstly, he was made head of fags; his first official appointment, he noted. Fags were junior boys who were forced to act as servants for the most senior students. The second event that showed he was no coward concerned his old nanny, Mrs Everest. Servants were not expected to visit pupils at Harrow, but when Mrs Everest arrived there, Churchill 'not only greeted her with a smacking kiss', according to Marsh; he then 'took her arm through his and paraded her up and down the high street, ending by taking her into the tuck shop for tea'. Churchill's final verdict on Harrow was much like a naughty schoolboy's taunt. 'I am all for the public schools, but I do not want to go there again,' he said.

Attlee had much fonder memories of school, as we shall see. His family life was also more stable; he grew up in a home that was a model of middle-class respectability. The family was perhaps more pious than most, as Sunday was a day of strict observance. A consistent presence in his children's lives, Henry Attlee proved neither a controlling patriarch nor an emotionally distant father. He lived to a routine and left his house in Portinscale Road in Putney every morning to commute to his solicitor's office in the city; Attlee sometimes walked with his father to the station. Unlike many late-Victorian parents, Henry did not impose his own views on members of his family; there were even political discussions over dinner, as Henry was a Liberal and his wife Ellen a Conservative. The family kept bound copies of the satirical magazine *Punch*; Attlee liked the cartoons especially and his brother Laurence thought they formed an early part of Attlee's political education.

The gulf in social class between Blenheim Palace and Putney was great, but the Attlees were nevertheless a fairly affluent family. Socialism did not come to Attlee as a result of material deprivation; as well as the governess, Miss Hutchinson, the Attlees kept three servants. Attlee was proud of his family history. The Attlees had once been important bakers and had made enough money to buy a large manor house, Comarques, in the Essex village of Thorpe-le-Soken. Henry's career was successful; he became president of the Law Society in 1907 and Lieutenant of the City of London.

Attlee's mother was devoted, but at times difficult. Ellen was the daughter of Thomas Simons Watson, secretary of the Art Union of London, which produced reproductions of famous pictures and sold them at affordable prices. The oldest child in a family of seven daughters, Ellen helped to bring up her younger sisters after their mother had passed away. She proved something of a disciplinarian as a mother, and perhaps this owed to having spent much of her youth looking after her siblings.

'She was essentially a family woman and had, I think, a certain jealousy of the family showing independence and seeking friends outside the family circle. This attitude tended to make us self-conscious and shy,' Attlee wrote in what seems to be a rare attempt to explain his shyness. He was aware his siblings were far less reserved than he was. He wrote even less about his mother than about his father, perhaps because he did not want to be critical of her. In *With a Quiet Conscience*, Peggy Attlee wrote that Tom, Attlee's brother and her father-in-law, often had such bad dreams that he woke up and ran to his parents' bedroom.

One surprising piece of evidence suggests that Attlee's childhood was not an entirely happy one. Attlee's sister, Mary, said he suffered from 'violent fits of temper'. When in one of these furious moods, Attlee would sometimes bury his head in a chair to hide from his mother, which could indicate that he was afraid of her, or perhaps that he was ashamed of his behaviour. Then he would say that he was sorry, which the family called Clem 'penting' – or repenting. His mother apparently trained him out of these furies, and neither Attlee nor his siblings ever explained what had caused the violent fits. Attlee also often fell ill, and it is likely that there was more stress in the household than Attlee ever admitted to.

Being unwell, Attlee was first educated at home by his mother and Miss Hutchinson. Lessons started with the Bible. Attlee complained in his autobiography that he was always on church parade, but church bored him; he believed religion to be 'mumbo jumbo'. Although it might work for many of those Attlee liked and admired, 'it meant nothing to me one way or another'. In his typical laconic way, he did not comment further on this point. Like Churchill, Attlee was also taken on holiday to the Isle of Wight, and while he was there, one particular incident would reveal that the Attlees could be snobbish. Attlee was walking on the rocks with his brothers and sisters when someone shouted in a cockney accent, 'Look at those little kids walking on the rocks.' Attlee's brother, Bernard, judged the comment to be the 'essence of vulgarity', and Attlee himself noted that 'we thought it a very fine retort'. He accepted the class distinctions of the time. He read voraciously, but his reading did not make him question much. 'The capitalist system was as unquestioned as the social system. It was just there,' Attlee wrote.

From Northaw, Attlee went to Haileybury, a school which specialised in training boys for the imperial civil service. Pupils studied the colonies that they expected to be administering one day, including, of course, India. At Haileybury, Attlee met Owen de Wesselow, who would become a friend for life. As an adult, de Wesselow became interested in psychiatry and studied at the Pitié-Salpêtrière Hospital in Paris, where Freud had studied in 1895.

Attlee was familiar with psychological ideas, but never wrote about any personal conversations he had had with his father. Discretion was the rule in his family. Churchill, on the other hand, was sceptical about psychology but more willing to be personal. His father did not often confide in him, but the rare occasions when he did became treasured memories. One autumn day, Winston shot at a rabbit that was running across the lawn of an estate where the Churchills were guests, startling Lord Randolph.

Randolph recovered himself and reassured his son, and Churchill then had 'one of the three or four intimate conversations with him which is all I can boast'. Old people like him, Randolph confessed, were not always considerate of the young because they were so absorbed in their own affairs. He told Winston he was glad he liked shooting. Churchill listened, spellbound, as his father spoke in 'the most wonderful and captivating manner' about school, the army and his son's future. Churchill was 'amazed at his intimate comprehension of all my affairs'. In this mood, Randolph confided, 'Do remember things do not always go right with me. My every action is misjudged and every word distorted. So make some allowances.'

Although Randolph thought his son too dim for Oxford or the Bar, he allowed him to visit the House of Commons to listen to debates. Churchill saw Gladstone speak and wrote that 'the Grand Old Man looked like a great white eagle'. One moment in the House impressed the teenager deeply. Gladstone, leader of the Liberals, and Joseph Chamberlain had been colleagues until 1886, when Chamberlain left the party to found the Liberal Unionist Party, triggering a political rivalry between the two men. After Chamberlain's son Austen had made his maiden speech, Gladstone followed, but before dealing with the subject of the debate, he looked at Chamberlain and said 'it was a speech which must have been dear and refreshing to a father's heart'. This tribute, Churchill wrote, 'swept aside for a moment the irreparable enmity of years'. Chamberlain was much moved.

The 670 MPs were a tight-knit crowd. In his 1895 *Psychologie des Foules* (*The Crowd: A Study of the Popular Mind*), Gustave Le Bon points out that in a crowd,

> a man descends several rungs in the ladder of civilisation. Isolated, he may be a cultivated individual; in a crowd, he is a barbarian – that is, a creature acting by instinct. An individual in a crowd is a grain of sand amid other grains of sand, which the wind stirs up at will.

Watching from the public gallery, Churchill was already ambitious enough to imagine the day when he would join his father in the House as an MP.

Attlee's family did not mix in either exalted or permissive circles. His own school career lacked drama, but there were no signs of the fits of temper he had experienced at home. In his autobiography, Attlee passed briefly over his time at school. Yet school had always mattered to him; he kept all his reports, even though they were mediocre. He was never more than an average pupil.

For all their differences, Attlee and Churchill shared one characteristic:

neither shone at games. Nevertheless, they both played polo – Churchill astride a horse, Attlee on a bicycle. Bicycle-polo was an eccentricity that had been invented in County Wicklow in 1891 by the editor of *The Irish Cyclist*, Richard Mercredy, and Attlee's father often played the game with his children. If Attlee and Churchill ever discussed their childhoods and experiences at school, no record of such discussions has been found.

Lord Randolph's health was now beginning to fail. Lord Rosebery said that 'by 1889 Randolph no longer had the nerve of his prime'. Attlee was not forced to witness any decline in his father's reputation, and his childhood continued to be less eventful than that of his Conservative counterpart. As he grew into his teens, Attlee became interested in politics, but more in personalities than in actual policies.

The magazine *Punch*, which Attlee read, caricatured the politicians of the day. Attlee himself could be very cutting about politicians, and also very funny; arguing about politics was a form of self-expression. 'It struck us all – it made him quite a character. And though he was shy and tongue-tied with outsiders, he wasn't backward in coming forward within the family, the study and in class,' his brother Laurence noted.

At Haileybury, Attlee slowly became more confident. In 1901, he spoke at the school's debating society. With some confidence, he opposed the motion that museums and picture galleries should be open on Sundays. His headmaster's final report noted: 'He is very self-opinionated, so much so that he gives scant consideration to the opinion of others.' It seemed that the little mouse was beginning to find its voice.

Churchill struggled to gain acceptance to Sandhurst, partly because he was so poor at mathematics, and Sandhurst required him to slay 'a dragon called the Differential Calculus'. Dragons are creatures of legends, of course, and Churchill once wrote mythically, 'I had a feeling once about mathematics that I saw it all – depth beyond depth was revealed to me – the Byss and the Abyss.' The pun solved no equations, of course.

After Winston had failed twice to get into Sandhurst, an exasperated Lord Randolph sent his son to Captain James, a well-known tutor in Earl's Court Road. The cramming worked, with James's methods so effective that Churchill would later write that 'no one who was not a congenital idiot could avoid passing thence into the army'. When he did finally scrape in, Churchill boasted of his success, but his father roasted him in a letter. 'I am rather surprised at the tone of your exultation,' Randolph wrote. Getting into Sandhurst was nothing to be proud of, he pointed out, as Winston had 'come up among the 2nd and 3rd rate class who are only good for commissions in a cavalry regiment'. The diatribe continued. 'Never have I received a really good report of your conduct in your work from any master or tutor … Always behind-hand, never advancing in your class, incessant complaints of total want of application'. Despite all 'the abilities you foolishly think yourself to possess'.

Lord Randolph wrote to his mother, the Duchess of Marlborough. 'I cannot think highly of Winston's [result]. I have told you often & you would never believe me that he has little [claim] to cleverness, to knowledge or to any capacity for settled work.' Randolph catalogued his son's 'total worthlessness as a scholar' and his 'great talent for show-off exaggeration'. Sometimes, children under stress will react by being reckless in order to prove themselves. A dramatic example of this occurred in January 1893. Unable to afford anywhere else, the Churchills stayed in Bournemouth with Randolph's sister, Lady Wimbourne. During a boisterous game, Churchill found himself trapped on a bridge, with his brother at one end and a cousin at the other. Attempting to escape, Winston climbed over the railings of the bridge and leapt for a nearby pine tree.

'I looked at it, I computed it, I meditated,' Churchill wrote, and then added, imitating Hamlet: 'To plunge or not to plunge, that was the question.' He plunged, but failed to make the safety of the pine tree – and crashed about thirty feet to the ground. Randolph was so concerned that he rushed back from Dublin, collected a good surgeon, and went to his son's bedside. Churchill lay unconscious for three days.

I have pointed out that psychology captured the public's interest during the First World War. In the 1920s, this interest continued. The great American humorist James Thurber poked fun at psychoanalysis regularly in the *New Yorker*. He also co-authored the magnificent *Six-Day Bicycle Riding as a Sex Substitute*. Who needed Freud? Psychobabble bloomed.

There was solid work, too, however. B. F. Skinner, one of the great psychologists of the twentieth century, began a series of experiments on rats and pigeons, the findings of which could explain the motivation for Churchill's recklessness: his father's dismissive behaviour. Skinner showed that the most effective way to get rats to learn how to perform various tasks was to give them intermittent rewards. In one set of experiments, they received the reward of a pellet of food just once in 100 runs. Skinner presented some evidence that children reacted the same way. Lord Randolph, with all his inconsistencies, was a very intermittent father. Skinner would have been unsurprised to find that, although he bore much criticism from him, Churchill loved and proved intensely loyal to his father.

Churchill exhibited the same fierce affection for his mother, but he was more critical of her and also worried about her well-being. In the early 1890s, she travelled to Monte Carlo alone, and her jaunt made the London newspapers, which reported that a thief had stolen her purse. Her eighteen-year-old son was unconvinced that this was the real reason for her being short of money, and wrote to his mother, begging her to stop gambling. He had started to realise that she was not just a radiant princess. His parents' debts, and their frequent anxieties about money, affected Churchill deeply. When he began to earn money as a journalist, he was always careful to negotiate the best fees he possibly could.

In *My Early Life*, Churchill recounts his speaking debut not as a triumph, but a comic failure. In 1894, during his final term at Sandhurst, Churchill got wind of a purity campaign, spearheaded by a Mrs Chant (a member of London County Council), who aimed to shut down music halls. Outraged by the idea of a purity campaign, and learning of a group called the Entertainment Protections League that had been formed to combat Mrs Chant's plans, Churchill decided to write a speech and deliver it to the league's members. He travelled from Sandhurst to London on a half-day holiday and, although he could not really afford it, decided to take a hansom cab from Waterloo to Leicester Square.

Churchill had imagined he would be greeted by a large contingent of the league, eagerly cheering his robust defence of the right to sing, dance and be merry. To his dismay, he discovered that only one person – the founder of the league – had turned up to welcome him. Churchill strode out of the room, 'with a magnificent oration surging in my bosom', and only half a crown in his pocket. He needed a good dinner to console himself. Walking down the Strand, he located a pawnbroker's shop and, in exchange for a fiver, pawned the gold watch his father had given him. When he found out, Lord Randolph reacted furiously. Churchill never pawned anything again, but then he never again found himself facing an audience of just one.

By now, Lord Randolph was much weaker. 'What can be more painful than to feel the whole apparatus of expression slipping from him?' his son wrote. When he spoke in the House, Randolph's hands shook visibly. Loyal as ever, Churchill wrote that the quality of his father's speeches showed there had been no decline in his intellectual powers.

Aware he might not have long to live, Lord Randolph decided to leave his unsatisfactory son enough money to lead 'a respectable life', even if the boy did not deserve it. In a letter dated 9 August 1893, Randolph wrote: 'I am certain that if you cannot prevent yourself from leading the idle useless unprofitable life you have had during your schooldays & later months, you will become a mere social wastrel ... and degenerate into a shabby unhappy & futile existence.'

The rebuke from his dying father stung, but, as was often the case, Randolph proved inconsistent in his behaviour. In his last years, he also took his son to the Empire Theatre, to the races and to Tring to meet the Rothschilds. He was pleased that his son was 'nice-mannered. Sandhurst has done wonders for him.' Yet Churchill wrote that 'if I ever began to show the slightest idea of comradeship, he was immediately offended'. Once, when Winston suggested he might help his father's private secretary write some letters, Randolph 'froze me into stone'.

In 1930, when *My Early Life* was published, Churchill could say confidently that he knew this behaviour by his father had been merely a passing phase; if Lord Randolph had lived for another four or five years, 'he could not have done without me'. It led Churchill to offer his own psychological theory that 'a boy deprived of his father's care often develops, if he escapes the perils of youth, an independence and a vigour of thought which may restore in after life the heavy loss of early days'. C. P. Snow, famous for bridging two cultures, the humanities and the sciences, suggested that Churchill sometimes had poor judgement, but also moments of great insight.

In late June 1894, Lord Randolph embarked on what his family feared could be a final voyage, visiting America, Japan and China. Lady

Randolph's relationship with Karl Kinsky had ended, and perhaps because she sensed that her husband was dying, she decided to accompany him on his trip. Typically, the pair did not bother warning their two sons that they were about to leave the country. The first Churchill knew of the trip was when a cyclist messenger, without explaining why, told him he must go to London. Routinely the authorities at Sandhurst refused a request for special leave, but Lord Randolph telegraphed the Secretary of State for War, asking for his son to be allowed to come and see him off. Randolph looked 'terribly haggard and worn with mental pain' when he took leave of his sons. 'He patted me on the knee in a gesture which however simple was perfectly informing,' Churchill said. Lord Randolph was, and knew he was, 'under a sentence of death'. His death was anticipated and the couple took some macabre luggage with them: a lead-lined coffin.

While his parents were away, Churchill tried to get as much information as he could about his father's health. In November, the Churchills reached Yokohama in Japan. Churchill wrote to his mother on 8 November 1894, informing her that Dr Roose had told him Lord Randolph's hand was often numb and that there was little that could be done. His mother should 'try and look on the bright side of things', Churchill said, and begged her not to fall ill herself. On 24 November, Churchill again met Roose, who showed him a telegram: Lord Randolph's condition had deteriorated.

Lady Randolph wrote in a letter to her sister, Clara: 'You cannot imagine anything *more* distracting & desperate than to watch it & see him as he is & to think of him as he was.' Worse still, Kinsky had just sent a telegram informing her of his engagement to a much younger woman, the Countess Elisabeth Wolff-Metternich zur Gracht. Jennie Jerome, whose father was new money American, could hardly compete with a descendant of the Austrian Foreign Minister who had tangled with

Napoleon. She shared her heartache with her sister Leonie, writing, on 31 October, 'I have sacrificed to him the one real affection I possessed … I feel absolutely mad … it hurts me so I have been paid out for all my iniquities.' She added in a later letter, 'I care for him [Kinsky] as some people like opium or drink.' Lady Randolph had lost her lover and her husband would soon follow. Her sons knew all about her passion for Kinsky by then, and Jack wrote to his mother asking, 'Is it too late to stop it?' It was, of course, far too late to prevent the marriage.

When his parents returned from their trip, Churchill's father said he had perhaps six months left to live.

'And then?' Churchill asked.

'Westminster Abbey.' Lord Randolph envisioned a splendid burial.

Early on 24 January 1895, Churchill ran across a snowy Grosvenor Square to his grandmother's house, to be by his father's side in his final moments. 'His end was quite painless. He had been in a stupor,' Churchill wrote.

Crowds accompanied the coffin to Westminster Abbey for the funeral, but Lord Randolph had arranged to be buried at Bladon near Blenheim Palace. Churchill mourned for his father, and for the bond that would never develop between them as he grew into manhood.

Churchill wrote his short story, *The Dream*, after a conversation at dinner. His daughter Sarah pointed to a vacant chair and asked her father who he would most like to see sitting there. Churchill picked his father.

In *The Dream*, Lord Randolph appears in his son's studio, as Churchill is trying to copy a damaged portrait of his father. Lord Randolph flatters his son by mentioning Winston's photographic memory: 'You recited the twelve hundred lines of Macaulay without a single mistake.' Churchill says 'his voice and facial features were utterly expressionless', but it was probably the nearest to a compliment that he could have hoped for from his father. 'Winston knew only too well that Lord Randolph's disappointment, anger and loathing towards him was deeply embedded.' These harsh words demand an explanation; the obvious one is that Churchill could not bring himself to reveal his own achievements, which surpassed those of his father. He wanted to spare Lord Randolph feelings of jealousy – even in a work of fiction that his long-dead father would never read.

Winston tells his father that the socialists have changed: they nationalised many industries but there was never a revolution in Britain. In fact, the socialists have become rather 'bourgeois', Winston says. Their attitude to the monarchy is an example; once they attacked the institution, but now they viewed it 'not only as a national but a nationalised institution'. The less-radical radicals were even attending parties at Buckingham Palace, though they drew the line at formal dress. 'Those who have very extreme principles wear sweaters,' Churchill adds.

'How sensible,' Lord Randolph observes.

When his son explains that Lord Salisbury is still Tory leader, Lord Randolph replies, 'He must be a Methuselah.' Churchill points out that this particular incarnation of the Salisbury line is the grandson of the man who destroyed his father.

Details in the story reflect the awe in which Churchill still held his father over fifty years after Lord Randolph's death. His father takes out a match box 'from his watch-chain, which was the same as I was wearing. For the first time I felt a sense of awe.' Churchill rubs his brush in paint to make sure everything is real, but he still shivers.

His father asks if Russia is still a danger. Churchill has fun telling him that the Tsar is no longer a Romanov, but someone who is much more powerful. Comrade Stalin, who was only briefly Churchill's comrade-in-arms, would have liked that.

France and Germany are both shattered, Churchill explains, which triggers memories of a trip to Paris when he was nine years old and he asked his father about a Strasbourg monument. When Lord Randolph discovers that France now rules Strasbourg, he reflects that the war 'must have been as bloody as the American Civil War and must have cost a million lives'.

His son puts him right, telling him that in the last war 'seven million were murdered in cold blood, mainly by the Germans'. Europe now lies in ruins and another, even more terrible war may be looming, Winston adds. Churchill was writing when he feared the atomic bomb might destroy the planet.

Lord Randolph is stupefied and says: 'Winston, you have told me a terrible tale.' Churchill, however, never tells his father of the glorious part he played in the terrible tale.

Jock Colville suggested in his memoirs that, if Lord Randolph had lived longer, he would have handicapped his son's career. It is impossible to know, but the loss of a father when a child is young seems associated with that child's later political success. Lucille Iremonger's *The Fiery Chariot: A Study of British Prime Ministers and the Search for Love* reveals that nearly half of the British Prime Ministers up to 1970 lost their fathers while they were young. American Presidents have done so too, or had to endure absent or violent ones; both Ronald Reagan and Gerald Ford's fathers were alcoholics, while Bill Clinton's biological father drowned, and Barack Obama has written much about his missing father.

Despite the sorrow he felt over Lord Randolph's death, Churchill passed out twentieth in the list of the 130 Sandhurst cadets. In March 1895, he was gazetted to the Oxfordshire Hussars. He deeply regretted the fact his father had not lived for two more months to see this take place.

Lord Randolph's death was not the only one that Churchill had to contend with that year. Although his beloved nanny, Mrs Everest, had been let go by the family in 1893 (perhaps due to financial constraints), when Churchill heard that she was seriously ill, only a few months after his father had passed away, he rushed to north London to be by her bedside. Mrs Everest could still recognise Churchill, but gradually she became weaker and 'death came very easily to her'. Churchill believed that she had led such an innocent and loving life that she was not afraid. 'She had been my dearest and most intimate friend during the whole of the twenty years I had lived.'

'No one ever told me that grief felt so like fear,' wrote author C. S. Lewis after his wife died. It was acute, physical and unbearable. In the space of less than six months, Churchill had lost two of the most important people in his life. Even people who do not suffer any depression are often devastated by bereavement. These two deaths should have plunged Churchill into a deep depression; his mother was unable to comfort him as she herself was devastated by Kinsky having abandoned her. Yet Churchill did not sink into depression.

Some of the most detailed information on Churchill's moods was supplied by Brendan Bracken to Lord Moran. Bracken told Moran that 'this strain of melancholy, a Churchill inheritance, is balanced in Winston by the physical and mental robustness of the Jeromes ... The healthy bright-red American blood cast out the Churchill melancholy.' Moran accepted this observation as if it were scientific. Bracken added more usefully, 'At other times he goes off into a kind of trance. I have seen him sit silent for several hours, and when he is like that only a few people can make him talk.'

Drawing on what Churchill had told him, Bracken explained that Winston's youthful bluster covered his shyness. It need hardly be said that this was just what Attlee suffered from. Churchill had always been 'full of apprehension and had had to school himself to face anything'. He was well aware of his own anxieties and what provoked them; he hated going to hospitals and did not like to stand near the edge of a platform when an express train was hurtling by. To be safe, he usually placed a pillar between himself and the train. The sea also held dangers and he avoided looking down at the waves: one second, one move, could end everything. Bracken spoke of 'a few drops of desperation', but Churchill managed his despair, somehow, even at the bleakest of times. He told Bracken that he did not want 'to go out of the world at all in such moments', adding that when a black-dog period ended, 'it is such a relief' as 'all the colours come back into the picture'.

Despite his double bereavement, Churchill managed to bounce back. The contradiction is striking, Churchill wrote of that period that 'all the days seemed good', and that as soon as he had left Sandhurst, 'the world appeared like Aladdin's cave'; a world to explore and enjoy. These were extraordinary remarks given the deaths of his father and Mrs Everest.

Posthumous diagnosis is risky, but the contradiction – the grief and the gaiety – is understandable. To me it seems Churchill did not suffer from depression, but from a form of the far less common, manic-depressive psychosis. Writers have shied away from describing Churchill as suffering from the condition, perhaps because the term can conjure up images of florid lunacy. One of the few sources to suggest that Churchill's black dog was more than just depression is the partisan International Bipolar Foundation; bipolar is a term for manic-depressive psychosis that was first used in the 1960s.

Psychiatrists hardly knew of the condition when Churchill was young, partly because they chose to ignore history. The Greeks proved more observant, however; Aretaeus of Cappadocia, a physician and philosopher of the first century AD, was the first to suggest a relationship between mania and melancholy. He described some patients who played and danced both night and day. Their behaviour was hard to make sense of. At times, they seemed listless and sad, but sometimes they were lively and went to the market 'crowned', as if they had just triumphed in some contest. Dancing and depression were signs of one and the same disorder, Aretaeus claimed. But following his death, his ideas were forgotten.

In 2011, Dr Nassir Ghaemi of Tufts University agreed that bipolar disorder fitted Churchill's symptoms. In 'Winston Churchill and his "black dog" of greatness', Ghaemi wrote that 'Churchill was so paralysed by despair that he spent time in bed, had little energy, few interests, lost his appetite, couldn't concentrate.' He also quotes a letter written by Churchill in 1911, addressed to his wife Clementine, after hearing that a friend's wife had received help from a German doctor. Churchill told his wife: 'I think this man might be useful to me – if my black dog returns.' His sleeping patterns – going to sleep late after working and drinking hard, and then lying in bed till ten or later – reflect both depression and high, even manic, energy.

Churchill clearly needed to do something to help himself, and instinctively he knew this. After completing basic training in the Hussars, he persuaded his colonel to let him travel to Cuba, where the Spanish were trying to crush a local rebellion. He was there in two capacities – as a foreign army officer who wanted to observe the fighting at first hand, and also as a reporter who filed dispatches to the *Daily Graphic*. The fighting took place deep in the countryside and Churchill made his way there. The action proved sporadic, because both sides observed Latin rules of war; one simply did not fight during the siesta. Churchill himself discovered the value of the 'power nap', and also developed a taste for Havana cigars. He left Cuba with the Spanish Order of the

Military Medal of the First Class, which made his brother officers in England rather jealous. In Churchill's day there were no rules to stop soldiers from reporting on the wars in which they were also fighting. Churchill did and enjoyed both.

One of the tragedies of the 1880s from a British point of view was the defeat of General Gordon in the Sudan by the Mahdi, perhaps the first 'mad Mullah' to achieve worldwide notoriety. Thirteen years later, the Sudan was in turmoil again. In 1898, Lieutenant Churchill took to the field with gun, bayonet and notebook as the British prepared to attack the Mahdist forces and avenge Gordon's death at Khartoum. Soldier Churchill had to show respect to his superiors, but scribbler Churchill was not required to defer to his readers. Many people could not 'contemplate military operations for clear political objects', Churchill wrote, but had to convince themselves that the enemy 'are utterly and hopelessly vile. To this end the Dervishes, from the Mahdi and the Khalifa downwards, have been loaded with every variety of abuse and charged with all conceivable crimes.' He warned that, 'when an army in the field becomes imbued with the idea that the enemy are vermin who cumber the earth, instances of barbarity may easily be the outcome'.

When the British and Egyptian armies entered Omdurman, Churchill wrote, 'never were rescuers more unwelcome'. Lord (Herbert) Kitchener, who commanded the troops, commented on the defeat of the Dervishes: 'Well, we have given them a damn good dusting.' Victorious, Kitchener proved merciless. The Mahdi had died in 1885 (Dervish forces at the Battle of Omdurman were led by his successor), but this did not prevent Kitchener from having the Mahdi's head hacked from his dead body, his tomb blown up and his bones scattered to the four winds. Churchill was horrified. The victory had been 'disgraced by the inhuman slaughter of the wounded and ... Kitchener is responsible for this', he told his mother. Most of the wounded were Arabs and Africans. Churchill has been accused of racism, but certainly back then he saw no difference in the value of any human life.

His mother now arranged for Longmans to publish his first book, *The Story of the Malakand Field Force*. She was hopeless on details and the edition contained hundreds of misprints, which spoilt the author's pleasure, but it still proved something of a success. It had only just been published when the best news that Churchill could have hoped for arrived: tribesmen on the North-West Frontier in India were up in arms. Churchill sailed for the sub-continent immediately. During the voyage, Churchill cabled Sir Bindon Blood (has there ever been a better name for a general?), reminding him of his promise that if he ever had command of a force, he would allow Churchill to join it.

Churchill's journalism brims with bravura. He wrote, 'What Peter the Hermit was to the regular bishops and cardinals of the Church, the Mad Mullah was to the ordinary priesthood of the Afghan border. A wild enthusiast, convinced alike of his Divine mission and miraculous powers, preached a crusade, or *Jehad*, against the infidel.' Europeans did not see 'the force which fanaticism exercises among an ignorant, warlike and Oriental population'.

In victory Sir Bindon Blood, 'who watched the triumphant issue of his plans, must have experienced as fine an emotion as is given to man on earth'. The 11th Bengal Lancers 'began a merciless pursuit up the valley'. Churchill described the scene with the flare of an artist: 'Their bodies lay thickly strewn about the fields, spotting with black and green patches, the bright green of the rice crop.' For his readers, he listed the casualties. In all, thirty-three British troops were killed; sixteen of these were Sikhs.

The House of Commons cheered news of the action. Churchill never visited India again, which did not stop him from having very definite views on its future: the Raj should continue. Attlee, on the other hand, visited India a number of times and became perhaps the best-informed British politician on the issue of Indian independence. He moved in the 1920s to the view that the Raj had to end and that India had to become self-governing. Some of the fiercest quarrels between the two men would concern the future of India.

It was during his voyage to India that Churchill had started work on his only novel, *Savrola*, set in the fictional country, Laurania, five years after a civil war. Churchill told his brother in May 1898 that he had finished the book. The plot centres on Lucile, the young and beautiful wife of the Lauranian President, General Antonio Molara. When rebels plot against him, Molara asks Lucile to seduce the rebel leader, Savrola, in order to gain intelligence. Consciously or not, Lucile owes something to Churchill's mother. She abandons her husband for the dashing Savrola, who is 'vehement, high and daring', the sort of man who could 'know rest only in action, contentment only in danger, and in confusion find their only peace'.

Churchill sent a draft of the book to his grandmother, but although the Duchess of Marlborough liked the descriptions of fighting, she thought her grandson's portrait of Lucile betrayed his lack of experience with women. Churchill was offered £100 by *Macmillan's Magazine* to serialise the book. They wanted his words quickly; he wanted their money quickly. For all its faults, the book has remained in print for more than a century and offers some insights into Churchill as a young man.

'Ambition was the motive force,' Churchill wrote of Savrola; it was a force he could not resist himself. Writing from India in 1899, he told his mother: 'What an awful thing it will be if I don't come off. It will break my heart for I have nothing else but ambition to cling to.' He also tried to account for his 'suicidal daring' at the 1897 Battle of Malakand: 'Being in many ways a coward – particularly at school – there is no ambition I cherish so keenly as to gain a reputation of personal courage.'

In branding himself a coward, he was being hard on himself. In 1897, Churchill had travelled to Switzerland with his brother Jack and a tutor. While the brothers were out rowing on Lake Geneva, Jack decided that he was in the mood for a swim, and got into the water. He soon got into difficulties, though, and Lady Randolph's oldest boy had to dive in to save her youngest from drowning. But she never seems to have commented on the rescue. Strangely, when Churchill himself described the drama, he did not say that he had saved his brother. Some critics see this as evidence that Churchill wanted to airbrush his brother from history, but this seems to me to fly in the face of the facts. Churchill always displayed great affection for Jack.

Churchill may have coped outwardly with the death of his father, but it also triggered concerns about his lisp, which was similar to the speech impediment that Lord Randolph had suffered from. In 1897, Winston consulted Sir Felix Semen, a society doctor. There was no organic defect, Sir Felix told Churchill and explained that he could improve his speaking with practice. He suggested Churchill rehearse with phrases such as 'The Spanish ships I cannot see for they are not in sight.' Churchill heeded this advice.

The newspapers and magazines of the 1890s were packed with gossip and human interest items. Young Churchill, the son of a famous, if flawed, father, was becoming a celebrity, mainly because of his writing. He returned to England in October 1898 and began to address Conservative Party meetings and his interest in becoming a Tory MP grew. By 1899, Churchill had been nominated as a candidate for the Oldham by-election. The town had lost its two Tory MPs – one had passed away and the other had resigned due to ill-health.

The campaign started well and Churchill spoke to packed meetings. Before polling day, however, the Conservatives introduced the Clerical Tithes Bill, which proposed that the Church of England should be funded by local rates. Oldham was a non-conformist town, so most voters were reluctant to pay the wages of an Anglican priest. Churchill only denounced this 'stupid' Bill three days before the election, and it seems to have been too late. Oldham elected two Liberal candidates. He lost by 1,300 votes. As he put it in a letter to his mother, the defeat left him 'with those feelings of deflation which a bottle of champagne represents when it has been half-emptied and left uncorked for a night'. He needed some new fizz.

CHAPTER 3

AMBITION AND THE LACK
OF IT, 1896–1905

While Churchill had been at war, Attlee had been preparing to go to Oxford University, and started there in some style. A close friend at University College, Charles 'Char' Bailey, with whom he had studied at Haileybury, recalls often sending his scout (a member of staff assigned to students) to pinch Attlee's 'admirable silver' – first-class silverware is an indicator of the family's affluence. At Oxford, Attlee's father provided him with a yearly allowance of £200, which was generous, as the bill for his rooms, food and tuition only came to £100. Attlee 'breathed loving kindness', Bailey wrote, adding that he hoped Attlee 'may have learned from me to be a little less shy'. Attlee did not become confident enough to speak at the Union, though he often listened to the debates. Owen de Wesselow, another friend from Haileybury, was also at Oxford, studying medicine. He would go on to become a professor at St Thomas' Medical School.

As a student, Attlee became interested in the Renaissance. He was fascinated by the Italian princes of the era and read Machiavelli's *The Prince*, the ultimate cynical guide to power and politics. Studying the

endless rivalries between Italian royalty influenced his view of an incident involving his father. When Attlee Senior learned of a trade union
dispute involving Welsh miners who had been locked out by their
owners, he decided to donate towards a fund to help the men. Attlee
was shocked by his father's charity: 'I admired strong ruthless rulers. I
professed ultra-Tory opinions.'

Attlee had hoped to achieve a First in modern history, but he spent
much of his time reading material not on the syllabus so he was ultimately not unduly disappointed to get a second-class degree. 'If I could
have chosen to be anything in those days I'd have become a [univer-
isty] Fellow,' he later remarked. But a second-class degree was not good
enough to earn him a fellowship.

Returning home, Attlee had no specific ambitions. 'I rather thought
of some profession in which a living could be made while in my leisure
time I could continue my reading literature and history.' After a brief
stint at the Lincoln's Inn chambers of Sir Philip Gregory, a renowned
conveyancing counsel, Attlee joined his father's firm, Druces & Attlee.
However, after just four months at the company, Attlee decided that he
would rather read for the Bar. He passed the Bar exams with ease and
joined a firm where Sir Henry Fielding Dickens KC, son of Charles
Dickens, was practising. For three years, Attlee was a not particularly
happy junior barrister; he was not fond of one of the heads of the chambers, who Attlee found to be a hard task master that 'drove you to death'.
Appearing in court forced Attlee to practise speaking in public, though
he never wrote about that.

After his defeat at Oldham, Churchill went back to the life of a writing soldier, which led to the most dramatic adventure of his early life
– fighting the Boers in South Africa. In 1814, Britain had acquired the
Cape Colony and had encouraged Britons to settle, but these British

settlers were often at odds with the Dutch, who had already been there for 160 years.

In 1886, gold was discovered in fabulous quantities in Witwatersrand. But the Boers possessed neither the men nor the skills needed to develop the deposits. The independent Boer republic of Transvaal reluctantly agreed to let in thousands of English-speaking men. Soon there were more Brits than Boers. If these *uitlanders*, which translates literally as outlanders, were given full voting rights, the Boers would lose political control.

In September 1899, Joseph Chamberlain, Secretary of State for the Colonies, demanded full voting rights for *uitlanders* residing in Transvaal. The Boers rejected this demand and on 9 October, the President of the South African Republic, Paul Kruger, gave the British forty-eight hours to withdraw their troops from the borders of the Transvaal and the Orange Free State. Britain ruled an empire on which the sun never set; in Britain's eyes, the Boers were mere provincial farmers. Overconfident, the British thought they would resolve the conflict with ease.

After Kruger issued his ultimatum, Churchill went to see Oliver Borthwick, son of the owner of the *Morning Post*; Churchill persuaded Borthwick to pay him the huge salary of £250 a month to cover the story. Churchill sailed south on the same boat as General Sir Redvers Buller, the commander of the British forces. Churchill travelled in style, taking sixty bottles of claret, more than was usual for even the thirstiest of journalists.

As soon as he landed in South Africa, Churchill made his way to Estcourt, the most northerly position that the British controlled. It was a ragged collection of 300 houses situated on two broad streets – and a railway station. Captain Haldane, the officer in command, sent an armoured train to probe the Boer positions and asked Churchill and

J. B. Atkins of the *Manchester Guardian* to accompany him. After travelling about 14 miles, Boer horsemen appeared on the hills and proceeded to attack the train, which derailed while attempting to return to Estcourt.

Churchill found himself in a face-to-face confrontation with a Boer cavalryman, who was pointing a gun at him. Churchill fumbled for his pistol, but could not find it. 'I thought there was absolutely no chance of escape, if he fired he would surely hit me,' he wrote. Left with no other alternative, Churchill put up his hands and surrendered. He was taken to Pretoria, where the State Model School had been turned into a makeshift prisoner-of-war camp. A chapter of *My Early Life*, detailing Churchill's imprisonment, is titled 'In Durance Vile', neatly encapsulating his horrible confinement.

Churchill's first two escape attempts failed, but as always he remained determined. Finally deciding that he had reached a 'now or never' moment, he hauled himself up the wall surrounding the camp. His waistcoat became entangled in some metal at the top, but he managed to free himself and dropped down over the other side 'in sickly hesitation'. The guards were smoking. Churchill waited for a moment until they looked away and then, after ordering himself to '*toujours de l'audace*', 'always dare', he stole away into the darkness.

Churchill dusted himself and his waistcoat clean, and walked half a mile through Pretoria until he found a railway line. He hid on a train, which luckily started moving, and took him some 80 miles to a mining district at the end of the line. He had £75 with him. He hoped this would be enough to bribe someone to shelter him.

Hungry and desperate, Churchill knocked on a door at random and struck lucky; the man who opened it was an English manager of the Transvaal Collieries, John Howard. Churchill hid in Howard's cellar for a week while the Boers searched high and low for him and offered £25 for his capture. Howard then smuggled Churchill onto a freight train, hiding him under bales of wool. Churchill was accompanied on his journey by a local grocer, Charles Burnham, who used Churchill's £75 to pay small bribes whenever necessary. Finally, the train halted and Churchill caught sight of Portuguese uniforms. He had arrived in what is now Mozambique – he was safe.

The escape made headlines around the world, although these were not always favourable. 'Mr Churchill's escape is not regarded in military circles as either a brilliant or honourable exploit,' criticised the *Daily Nation*. The army was kinder and gave him a commission in the South African Light Horse. In his dispatches to the *Morning Post*, Churchill argued that a forgiving policy must be adopted with the Boers.

On 20 July 1900, Churchill arrived back in Southampton. Having made a name for himself, the Tories were delighted to adopt him again as a candidate for the Oldham constituency. Five years after his father's death, becoming a successful politician was now very much Winston's main ambition. The young hero entered the town in style, in a procession of ten landaus, and made his way to the Theatre Royal, where he described his daring escape to an eager audience. Walter Runciman, who had defeated Churchill two years earlier, was on this occasion pipped to the post, and lost by 222 votes.

Churchill made his maiden speech in the House on 18 February 1901. Wisely, he chose a subject with which he was familiar – the Boer War. Britain should make it 'easy and honourable for the Boers to surrender and painful and perilous for them to continue in the field'. He ended the speech by saying, 'I cannot sit down without saying how very grateful I am for the kindness and patience with which the House has heard me, and which have been extended to me, I well know, not on my own account, but because of a certain splendid memory which many honourable members still preserve.' It was the memory of his father.

In his book, *The Past Masters*, former Prime Minister Harold Macmillan describes how Prime Minister David Lloyd George invited him to his room after he had listened to Macmillan's rather stumbling maiden speech in 1924. Lloyd George told him: 'Never say more than one thing. Yours was an essay, a good essay but with many separate points. Just say one thing. When you are a minister, two things, and when you are a Prime Minister winding up a debate, perhaps three.' One point might be said 'forcefully, regretfully, even perhaps threateningly, but it is a single clear point. That begins to make your reputation.' Macmillan should learn 'to mix slow solemn phrases with witty passages'. Macmillan said he never forgot Lloyd George's wise advice.

Soon after making his maiden speech, Churchill met Lloyd George, who had been elected to Parliament eleven years earlier. It would have been out of character for Lloyd George not to offer Churchill advice, even though they came from very different backgrounds and belonged to different parties. Lloyd George's father, William George, had been a teacher who taught in London and Liverpool before returning home to Pembrokeshire, where he took up farming. William George died in 1864 when his son was just a year old.

Becoming an MP gave Churchill even more energy than usual. In the weeks after he took his seat, he gave twenty lectures and made some thirty speeches as well as nine in the House itself. He did not want to get into financial difficulties as his parents had done, so he arranged a speaking tour in Britain and the United States, which raised £10,000 (just over £1 million today). Churchill's attitude to money is not unusual in those who have a manic-depressive disposition, but are functional. Spend, spend, spend – but also use the manic energy to earn.

After Lady Randolph was replaced as the Prince of Wales's *maîtresse en titre* by Alice Keppel, she seduced George Cornwallis-West, a British officer with the Scots Guards who was believed to be the Prince's illegitimate son. In 1900, shortly after Keppel gave birth to her second daughter, Sonia (grandmother of Camilla, Duchess of Cornwall), Lady Randolph married Cornwallis-West. Her new husband was the same age as Churchill, but if Churchill disapproved of his mother's marriage, he never said so. Some years later, he helped Cornwallis-West by lending him £3,000. The money was not, in fact, Churchill's; it had been provided by banker and philanthropist Ernest Cassel. But Churchill made himself responsible for repaying the debt.

Watching his parents struggle financially may have encouraged Churchill to sympathise with people who battled to make ends meet. In December 1901, he bought a copy of what is now regarded as a classic, social reformer and industrialist Seebohm Rowntree's *Poverty: A Study of Town Life*. A month later, in Blackpool, Churchill told his audience that the book 'fairly made my hair stand on end'. A fifth of the people in York were living in dire poverty. The rich ate between half and three quarters more than the 'paupers in the York Union. That I call a terrible and shocking thing.'

In 1902, King Edward VII invited Churchill to Balmoral Castle, the royal family's private estate in Scotland, and treated him kindly. Churchill wrote to his mother, reminding her to 'gush' to the King about how much he had enjoyed the royal company. Few young parliamentary backbenchers ever received such invitations.

The King was meant to be impartial between the political parties. For nearly two centuries, Britain had operated a two-party system; usually Whigs succeeded Tories and Tories succeeded Whigs. For Churchill, the pressing social problems the country faced suggested this back and forth was no longer satisfactory and, on 10 October 1902, he wrote to the former Liberal Prime Minister, Lord Rosebery, suggesting a coalition. 'The government of the middle – the party shall be free at once from the sordid selfishness and callousness of Toryism on the one hand and the blind appetites of the Radical masses on the other.'

One great political controversy of the day was free trade. Joseph Chamberlain argued that Britain should impose tariffs on imports to boost the economy. Churchill, however, believed in free trade, a fundamental Liberal policy. In October 1903, he drafted a letter to Lord Hugh Cecil, Salisbury's son, writing, 'I am an English Liberal. I hate the Tory Party, their men, their words and their methods. I feel no sort of sympathy for them – except to my own people in Oldham.' Churchill never sent the letter, but the issue of free trade made it clear that he was not an entirely committed Tory. Churchill had realised an important truth about himself.

Despite bitter disagreements about policy, politicians would usually maintain at least a veneer of courtesy, as they had numerous social and family connections. On 29 March 1904, however, there was an extraordinary demonstration of discourtesy. Churchill rose in the Commons to speak on fiscal reform and explained that he was sorry to see that Prime Minister Arthur Balfour had left the House as he had wanted to ask him some questions. Many people were 'being placed in great difficulty with their constituents', because government policy was unclear. Churchill protested that Balfour had shown 'a lack of deference and respect' to the House, never mind respect to Lady Randolph. Could a gentleman play piano duets with the mother and walk out on her son? The Tory front bench now showed even less respect; it rose to a man and departed to the smoking room. Most Tory backbenchers followed, with the exception of a few diehard free traders, who remained in support of Churchill. One Tory, Sir John Gorst, called this walkout 'the most marked discourtesy which I think I have ever seen'. Apart from 'considerations of fair play, the young MP ought to have been better treated as a mark of respect for his late father,' Gorst said. The *Daily Mail* reported chilling and discourteous scenes in the Commons; the *Pall Mall Gazette* noted that young Churchill no longer looked 'the boy' but appeared harassed and tired.

With the Tories gone, Churchill was in no mood to compromise. For some months, he told the House, he had tried to work out what Balfour thought of Joseph Chamberlain's ideas on the imposition of tariffs. He had failed, but in the process he had become a declared opponent. He was quite prepared to resign on the issue, if that was what his constituents wanted.

After all, as President Harry Truman is believed to have said, if you can't stand the heat, get out of the kitchen. Politics is not for the faint-hearted.

Lord Moran reported that Churchill had told him that when he was young, 'for two or three years the light faded out of the picture'. His depression was not so extreme, however, that Churchill found it impossible to work. 'I sat in the House of Commons but black depression settled on me,' he wrote. His anxieties betrayed him on 22 April. He started to argue for the rights of trade unions, which led the *Daily Mail* to denounce his speech as 'radicalism of the reddest type'. Fear of lisping may well have contributed to what happened next. Having lost the thread of his argument, Churchill fumbled in his pockets for notes, which might have reminded him of what he had wanted to say. He sat down in some confusion, with rather lame thanks to 'honourable members for having listened to me'. Towards the end of his life, Churchill's father had also faltered and been unable to finish his speeches, so MPs might have been forgiven for wondering if the son was going to suffer a similar fate. The next day, Churchill started to research ways in which he could train his memory and, for the rest of his life, he usually learned speeches by heart.

By 31 May 1904, Churchill had made up his mind. He entered the Chamber, cast glances at both sides of the House, bowed to the Speaker, then went to sit on the Liberal benches. It must have been stage-managed, as he sat in the same seat that his father had occupied when in opposition. The general opinion was that Churchill had made a mistake. He was only at the start of his political career and would face competition from many able and loyal Liberals. These MPs would 'resent being set aside in favour of a late comer to the vineyard', wrote Henry Lucy, a veteran parliamentary commentator. The word vineyard seems a mild one to use to describe Westminster's political jungle.

The man who now offered Churchill help was Nathan Laski, the father of Harold, who would become a thorn in Attlee's side once Attlee became leader of the Labour Party. Nathan was a pillar of the Manchester Jewish community and, when Churchill needed a new seat, Nathan made sure he secured the nomination for Manchester North West. It was estimated that there were 740 Jewish voters Nathan could deliver, a useful number as it comprised about 8 per cent of the electorate. Lloyd George travelled to the city and made two speeches in support of Churchill.

Both Churchill and Attlee were men who changed their party allegiances in the early stages of their political careers. Leaving the Tories was a turning point for Churchill; Attlee, too, would face a similar situation.

In notes made in October 1905, Attlee described himself as still 'desperately shy'. He and his brother Laurence visited Haileybury House, a club that their old school had set up in London's East End to help working-class teenagers. The club was also affiliated to the Royal West Surrey Regiment and the boys wore uniforms, which they liked, but Attlee admitted that he did not know how to deal with them. He learned, though. The next year, having been made a second lieutenant, he attended his first camp with the boys at Deal. Military routine suited him and he was soon teaching the teenagers to drill. Though no one gave Attlee toy soldiers, he was fascinated by the military nearly as much as Churchill.

Attlee's reading at this time included works by the artist and novelist William Morris, who wrote *A Dream of John Ball*, where a nineteenth-century man imagines himself in Kent during the Peasants' Revolt of 1381. The book moved Attlee, and suited his slowly shifting political mood. He was already making changes to his lifestyle in sup- port of socialism. For example, he and his brother Tom used to get their clothes made 'very badly' by a cooperative. In his notes, Attlee said he was attracted by socialism, but put off by the bureaucratic at- titudes of social reformers and Fabian Society members Beatrice and Sidney Webb. They were too intellectual and too wedded to statistics, Attlee thought.

In October 1907, Attlee and Tom attended a meeting of the Fabian Society at Clement's Inn and attempted to join the group. 'Edward Pease, the secretary, regarded us as if we were two beetles who had crept under the floor.' Attlee recalled a group of men gathered on the platform, among whose number was the grand trio of Sidney Webb, H. G. Wells and George Bernard Shaw. Shaw made fun of pious bene- factors who spurned the 'undeserving poor', the phrase that a few years later, in *Pygmalion*, he put into the mouth of the verbally gifted rene- gade dustman Alfred Doolittle.

After listening to the discussion, Attlee travelled to Limehouse, one of London's poorest areas. It was a trip that changed his life. He was shocked to his core by the poverty. To Attlee's surprise, the poor 'were not poor because of their lack of fine qualities', and 'the slums were not filled with the dregs of society'. Attlee then took a radical step; he quit his comfortable home in Portinscale Road and moved to the East End, eventually taking four rooms in Narrow Street for 8/6 a week (around £115 today). Attlee's family had wanted him to join the civil service, but he yearned for freedom and jumped at the chance to acquire it. Leaving home was liberating.

Despite its good intentions, the Haileybury club could only do so much. At 6 p.m., it closed for the night, and the children were left on the often dangerous streets of east London, while Attlee returned to his comfortable lodgings to have a cup of cocoa, and to read. He studied *Riches and Poverty* by the Anglo-Italian economic theorist, Leo Chiozza Money. The aptly named Money found that, in Britain, less than one million people owned 89 per cent of all private property.

Inequality had psychological consequences. The poor grew bitter, while the charities set up for their benefit were often patronising, playing God in choosing who to help and who to refuse. One organisation proved especially unpleasant, as its policy was to serve burned porridge to poor boys, to prevent them from getting ideas above their station. One evening, a wharf keeper called Tommy Williams came to Haileybury House, brimming with 'burning indignation' over the uncharitable attitudes of the Charity Organisation Society. 'They believe in charity. I believe in socialism,' Williams said. It would turn out to be a telling sentence.

Biographers often look for the turning point – the conversion experience, the Road to Damascus moment – that provokes an irrevocable change. Perhaps it is a little bit of a cliché, but Tommy Williams's remark seems to have acted as a trigger, striking a nerve in Attlee. It came at a moment when one of the boys at Haileybury's club had been refused help for, as far as Attlee could judge, no good reason.

Author E. M. Forster once commented, 'How do I know what I think until I see what I say?' Speaking his words, Attlee had found himself: 'I am a socialist too,' the solicitor's son declared.

Tommy Williams told Attlee that, as a socialist, he should join the Independent Labour Party. Attlee wrote, and the language is telling, 'I knew at once this was the right show for me.' 'Right show' is, of course, the kind of phrase public school boys and officers used. Attlee just happened to be a very unusual one.

His family were unhappy with Attlee's decision. It was one thing to join the Fabian Society, quite another to leave home and hitch one's colours to the militants of the working class. The Independent Labour Party was seeking 'to rouse the populace slumbers and to hasten the end of capitalist domination'. Perhaps more realistically, it was also seeking links with trade unions. Attlee joined the National Union of Clerks. Everyone else in the Stepney branch worked full-time, so he soon became branch secretary.

Attlee had virtually no experience of talking to the working class, but he developed a surprising ability to engage with boys at Haileybury House's club. In his autobiography, he was surprised by the plain common sense that the boys possessed. They would often make blunt, but insightful, statements, such as: 'A pal is a bloke wot knows all about yer and yet loves yer.' A gentleman was 'a bloke wot does no work'.

One of the boys was forward-thinking enough to believe that women had a right to vote, as 'only a working woman knows what a working woman has to go through'.

The boys became more confident and eventually asked if they could hold a meeting of their own without the supervision of the ex-public school boys. They formed a league which took its name from Haileybury School's Latin motto, *Sursum Corda*, 'lift up your hearts'. Members pledged to lead 'a clean and manly life', not to swear and 'to help all fellow cadets when in trouble in rightful circumstances'. The cadets had to strive to be respectable.

Attlee soon began to demonstrate his gift for administration, conquering his shyness – and, it would also seem, his temper. He made his first speech on the corner of Salmon Lane, which possesses some relevant history. Across the road today stands a fine house which became the headquarters of the Sea Cadets. King George V inspected the cadets and watched them drill on the parade ground, which is now a garden shared by five very desirable residences. The local library on the Commercial Road was named after Attlee, and a statue of him stood outside it until both were removed in 2012, to make way for upmarket apartments.

Attlee had no permanent job when he joined the Independent Labour Party, so he often had to stand in for speakers who failed to turn up. The once timid young man had to get up on a soap box. 'It is not easy to speak to an empty street in order to attract passers-by,' he wrote. Once he even had to deputise for the Bishop of Wakefield, who had been due to give a talk called 'Problems of Birth and Infancy' to an expectant gathering of Liberal women in Bolton. As a bachelor, Attlee wrote that his acquaintance with these subjects was 'purely theoretical'.

He had to learn to deal with hostility too. At one meeting he told his booing audience: 'I gather that you Conservatives object strongly to these proposals.' The audience shouted 'yes', but Attlee was not to be deflected. He told them they had better take it up with their MP, Sir Gilbert Parker, who was in favour of the proposals.

Although Attlee's family was not fabulously wealthy, they were able to pay for a trip around Europe when he was still a teenager and, in September 1907, Attlee embarked on a much longer journey when he sailed across the Atlantic. His fellow passengers included the man credited as the inventor of radio, Guglielmo Marconi, as well as William Booth, the founder of the Salvation Army, who shouted out 'save your souls' when the ship docked in Quebec. Attlee had travelled to Montreal to escort his sister Mary home; she had gone out to help a cousin who had just given birth to her first child.

In 1908, Attlee's father died of a sudden heart attack while at his desk. He left his children £70,000 – a not inconsiderable sum. In unpublished notes, Attlee remarked that 'father's room was dark and very dusty'. Only his father's clerk could navigate a way through the papers. Attlee was methodical in grief; from his father's legal colleagues he collected three testimonials to Henry Attlee's character. 'This was a great loss to us,' one man said, adding that Henry 'had always been extremely kind and broadminded'. Another admitted that Henry's kindness had once brought him to tears – Attlee never went public with these memories. His father's death left him with £400. He would use the money generously.

Five years after first setting foot in Limehouse, Attlee was asked to become the secretary of Toynbee Hall, one of the first social and educational settlements in the East End. For the next four years, he lived rent-free and was paid a modest salary. He also became a member of a school care committee at Ben Jonson School in Tower Hamlets. He bought teaspoons and small forks for the younger children, who struggled with bigger cutlery, and he taught the older girls how to cut up meat for the younger ones. He also took children on occasional trips round London. Once, at the end of the day, a student asked Attlee where he was headed. He was going home to have tea, Attlee told her. 'I'm going home to see if there is any tea,' the girl responded. Her words made a deep impression on him.

Attlee was not the only middle-class presence at Toynbee Hall; William Beveridge, another young barrister, also worked there. Sidney and Beatrice Webb were both impressed by Beveridge and the regard was reciprocated – the Webbs' theories of social reform led Beveridge to study the causes of unemployment. It was a timely move. In 1805, Parliament had set up a Royal Commission to reconsider the Poor Laws, which were outdated and had not been changed since 1834. The Webbs now employed Attlee to organise propaganda for their ideas on how to reform the law. They believed the state, rather than local guardians, should be responsible for helping the poor. Attlee was also responsible for tracking down lecturers to address meetings. As ever, Beatrice Webb was not satisfied, carping in a letter to Attlee that a 'first rate organiser' needed 'rather more of the quality of "push" and the habit of a rapid transaction of business'.

Attlee was hardly idle, though. He stood at dock gates with a collection box during the Dublin lockout in 1913. 'I know what it is to carry a banner from Mile End Waste across Central London to Hyde Park,' he wrote. He worked for the suffragettes and heard Jean Jaurès, the French socialist leader, speak. He even saw the writer Anatole France kiss Bernard Shaw or, more likely, Shaw's beard.

It was during this period that Attlee started to investigate working conditions for those employed in tailoring in the East End; he was appalled by what he found. Women who were finishing trousers were paid a farthing a pair and had to buy their own thread. East End workers had many rival organisations, and Attlee was once asked to chair a meeting conducted almost entirely in Yiddish. Often several people spoke at once – it was chaos. Attlee biographer Francis Beckett wrote, 'One man in a top hat and a long black coat and a beard leapt on the platform, shouting and waving an umbrella.' Showing no trace of his shyness, Attlee 'shoved him off and carried on'. When the meeting finished, Attlee, who had not understood the Yiddish, of course, found 'somewhat to my surprise that it had been a complete success'. The four rival organisations had agreed on how to nominate workers as representatives for the board on tailoring. Attlee was becoming more self-confident or, as Beatrice Webb demanded, developing 'push'. He was also developing an ability that would serve him in politics: the ability to make people trust him.

Part of the reason the community was willing to trust Attlee was because he provided practical help. On one occasion, he went to court to speak on behalf of a half-starving boy accused of theft. When the local Independent Labour Party set up its headquarters in Galt Street, above an undertaker's business, Attlee paid some of the rent and provided furniture. But, according to Beckett, he never pushed for a leadership position.

Attlee would soon become interested in psychology. For his part, five years earlier, Churchill had begun to write a book that any psychologist would have warned him risked being fraught with danger – a biography of his father.

CHAPTER 4

WRITING THE FATHER,
1902–1914

By the time Lord Randolph died, his son had published only a few articles in the Harrow School magazine, so it was not surprising that Lord Randolph did not appoint him as his literary executor. In 1902, Churchill was negotiating to be allowed to write his father's biography, but, initially, Lord Randolph's literary executors wanted too much control over the content and style of the book. After much negotiation, they finally backed down, and so Churchill embarked on a project which he hoped would ensure that history remembered his father with honour.

Churchill threw himself into the research, tracking down letters and talking to men and women who had known his father; he was the model of a painstaking biographer. On 25 August 1904, he wrote to his mother that 'the difficulty of the task impresses me as I proceed'. He wrote the entire manuscript by hand.

The biography forced Churchill to examine his father's political career in detail, and he was often astute in his judgements. Lord Randolph's victories cost him dear, his son decided. He had 'overlooked the anger and jealousy that his sudden rise to power had excited'.

Churchill detailed the disputes in the Cabinet before his father's resignation. Lord Randolph and the Secretary of State for War, William Henry Smith, who was part of the famous family of newsagents and booksellers, exchanged letters in the late autumn of 1885. Ten days before Lord Randolph's resignation, Smith wrote to him to say there was no hope of reducing the War Office estimates down from £31 million, as Lord Randolph had demanded. The Prime Minister, Lord Salisbury, said the Cabinet would have to decide between the two men.

Churchill turned his father's resignation into fine drama. Lord Randolph was not confident of carrying his Budget. According to his son's biography, he confided in Lord Welby, a former Permanent Secretary to the Treasury, that 'the silence of his colleagues oppressed him'. He had the calculations checked repeatedly to make sure there were no mistakes in the estimates for the army and navy.

On 21 December, Lord Randolph was summoned to Windsor where Queen Victoria 'showed him most gracious favour, and kept him long in conversation'. After he said goodnight to the Queen, he went to his bedroom and drafted his letter of resignation. In an aside in his book, Churchill noted that no one enjoyed more 'the assurance of honours and the amenities of power' than his father. Yet Lord Randolph was willing to give everything up. In the morning, Lord Randolph read out his resignation letter to Lord George Hamilton, former First Lord of the Admiralty. The letter said that £31 million for the two services 'is very greatly in excess of what I can consent to'.

When Lord Randolph and Hamilton reached the train station in Windsor the next morning, they were keen to buy a newspaper, but neither man had any change. The bookstall keeper, recognising the two men, was duly deferential. 'Never mind, my lord – when you come back next time will do,' he said.

Lord Randolph smiled at Hamilton and said, 'He little knows I shall never come back.'

After arriving in London, Lord Randolph decided to visit the Master of the Mint near Tower Bridge. He travelled by Underground and, as he and the MP for Portsmouth, Sir Henry Drummond Wolff, paced the platform, Wolff asked Lord Randolph about Treasury policy.

'I don't know now whether I am Chancellor of the Exchequer or not,' Lord Randolph replied.

Churchill faced an issue common to many biographers, pinpointing the cause of significant events. His father had resigned because he could not compromise, but it was difficult to be sure why. His son's answers were not very revealing. Churchill simply wrote, 'But his gorge rose at it. It was almost impossible to him to defend courses of which he disapproved.' This did not amount to much more than saying that Lord Randolph had resigned on principle.

Churchill concluded that his father had been 'a great elemental force in British politics', but that his career had been 'broken irrevocably'. Lord Randolph 'was a proud, sincere, overstrained man'. Shrewdly, Churchill added that his father often won disputes in the Tory Party, but then lost the argument on matters of national importance. He concluded, 'Men are not really together bound together in a government until they have made mistakes in common and defended each other's failures.' Lord Randolph never gave his colleagues the chance to discuss any mistakes or defend his Budget.

As *Savrola* showed, Churchill's prose could be poetic. He ended the biography of his father with praise of what one could call the deepest England, akin to de Gaulle's vision of '*la France profonde*'. Churchill wrote, 'There is an England which stretches far beyond the well-drilled masses who are assembled by party machinery to salute with appropriate acclamation the utterances of their recognised fuglemen.' The now obsolete word 'fugleman' meant a soldier.

When the biography appeared, Lord Rosebery wrote to Churchill to tell him, 'I must congratulate you without qualification or reserve.' Joseph Chamberlain also offered congratulations. The book was warmly received by critics, with John Bailey writing in the *Times Literary Supplement* that 'It is a pleasure to be able to say that a life so well worth writing has been so admirably written.' In the midst of learned references to the young 'Achilles' who had 'done due honour to his Patroclus', the anonymous reviewer added that sons 'have not always proved the most judicious of biographers'. The review also reflected on Churchill's political reputation, noting that even his 'warmest admirers would not ask us to think him the most judicious of men'. The *Sunday Times* was struck by Churchill's 'maturity of judgment'.

The book sold 2,306 copies in the first week and, by the end of April, had added 3,521 more. According to Roy Jenkins, it remains a very readable biography. Churchill wrote in detail about Lord Randolph's declining health, though he did not specify the cause of his father's malady. Churchill described how his parents met, but said nothing of their marriage, and its tribulations, despite having been privy to many of them.

Soon after the biography appeared, Churchill got his first taste of office. The Liberals won the 1906 election by a landslide and the new Prime Minister, Henry Campbell-Bannerman, appointed Churchill Under-Secretary of State for the Colonies. Churchill proved himself to be a first-class administrator. As he was now responsible for the colonies, he decided that a visit would be appropriate, so in 1907, he followed in his father's footsteps and travelled to Africa, where he met the King of Buganda (now part of modern-day Uganda), who later sent him photographs of the two of them together.

Around the same time that Churchill published his biography, founder of psychoanalysis Sigmund Freud was devising his theory that would come to be known as the Oedipus complex. What follows is a crude simplification. Freud believed that, subconsciously, all little boys want to kill their fathers and sleep with their mothers. Boys who remained stuck in filial admiration would find it impossible as adults to develop relationships with women.

Churchill's relationship with his mother was a slightly romantic one, but that never stopped him from courting women. He fell in love with two rather glamorous society ladies, Pamela Plowden and Ethel Barrymore, but both women rejected him. It was not until Churchill met Clementine Hozier that he fell for a woman who could really love him. She shared with Churchill a childhood of emotional neglect; her elder sister had died of typhoid when Clementine was aged just fifteen. Her parents separated and her mother, like Lady Randolph, took a succession of lovers, though none as grand as the Prince of Wales. Financially, Clementine had problems too; her mother moved house several times to avoid creditors.

In 1908, Churchill invited Clementine to Blenheim and proposed to her. Although she was the granddaughter of an earl, her engagement triggered spiteful remarks because she made many of her own clothes. Still, the wedding was a grand affair. The guests included Lloyd George, then Chancellor of the Exchequer, and Churchill's cousin, the Duke of Marlborough; Winston chose Lord Hugh Cecil to be his best man.

The marriage captured the public's imagination, a sign of Churchill's growing celebrity. A crowd gathered outside the church, including Pearly Kings and Queens from London. King Edward VII gave the couple a gold-topped walking stick, while the Prime Minister, Herbert Asquith, presented them with the complete works of Jane Austen.

My Early Life ends with Churchill saying that he married Clementine and lived happily ever after. This was true, but partly because his wife was willing to put up with so much, often comforting him and coaxing him out of his depressions. The future Earl of Birkenhead, Frederick Edwin Smith, more commonly known as F. E. Smith, a brilliant barrister and the then MP for Walton, was another who helped ease Churchill out of his darker moods. Brendan Bracken explained, 'They both had tearing spirits – that is when Winston wasn't in the dumps – a kind of daring, a dislike of drab existence, a tremendous zest in life.' Clementine, however, disapproved of Smith because she thought he led Winston into 'strange ways'.

'Strange ways' inspires a perhaps strange comparison, for which I am indebted to Steve Ely, a poet as well as a biographer of Ted Hughes. When I interviewed him for a documentary, Ely argued that when Ted Hughes left Yorkshire for Cambridge at the age of nineteen, he was essentially formed as a poet. Hughes's wife, the poet Sylvia Plath, helped him but she did not change him. Ely's remarks suggest it is worth comparing Churchill and Attlee when they were a little older, aged twenty-five, and how formed they were then. Churchill showed the leadership qualities, the willingness to take risks, the energy and the depressions. Writing a biography of his father did not mean that he dealt with all the personal issues that had existed between them, as *The Dream* was to reveal years later, but it at least prevented Churchill from becoming emotionally crippled.

Attlee was not just shy; he had never even been a prefect at Haileybury. By the time he reached the age of twenty-five, he was still finding it hard to deal with the East End boys. Asserting his authority over the lower ranks was not something that yet came easy to him. No one could ever have imagined that Attlee would become a formidable politician, a man who respected Churchill but who was never subservient to him.

In the 1908 by-election, Churchill lost his Manchester seat. Some members of the London Stock Exchange were delighted at the news and joked: 'What is the use of a W.C. without a seat?' But Churchill was now a considerable figure and was quickly found a safer Liberal seat in Dundee. That year he invited Lloyd George to Blenheim and they enjoyed each other's company, as they would for many years to come. In Parliament, Churchill joined Lloyd George's movement for social reform.

As President of the Board of Trade in 1908, Churchill helped lay the foundations on which Attlee's government would build thirty-seven years later. Privately, Churchill was so radical that he wrote a paper on the abolition of the House of Lords, a paper that some of his colleagues felt was a little wild. Beatrice Webb then introduced him to William Beveridge, who joined the Board of Trade to work on unemployment insurance and other issues.

Meanwhile, Attlee was still working unhappily as a jobbing barrister, which perhaps encouraged him to write a number of poems that reflected his political views. A 1908 poem saw the Thames as a stream of misery.

> O London river rolling to the sea
> Your weight of weary waters sad and brown
> Upon your dusky bosom bearing down
> Light skiff and heavy laden argosy
> Devious and slow your journey seems to be.
> Threading the close packed reaches of the town
> By squalid tenements of ill renown.
> Where thousands dwell in want and misery.
> So in our age of poverty and grime

A sluggish winding stream our progress proves
So short the forward step, so weak our feet.
Yet list we to the watchers of the time,
Who weighing well advancement and retreat
Cry out with Galileo 'Yet it moves.'

Attlee's poetry was influenced by Emile Verhaeren, a Belgian poet who wrote darkly about the growth and poverty of cities, and by William Blake, who saw 'marks of woe' on the faces of the poor on London's streets. Attlee glimpsed these marks, too, in the squalid tenements of Stepney.

Attlee applied for a number of jobs, but without success. He blamed his failure on the fact that socialists were unpopular with employers. In the autumn of 1910, he and his brother Tom were employed by George Lansbury, who was trying to win Bow and Bromley for the Labour Party. Lansbury had failed to win the seat in January 1910, when the first of two general elections held that year took place, but he emerged triumphant in December. It has been said that during the campaign, Attlee wrote a song to the tune of 'All the Nice Girls Love a Sailor' to help win votes.

Attlee liked parody and wrote one of Kipling's 'Sussex'. The original was a rhapsody to the county's green, which Attlee turned into an attack on landlords' greed.

God gave all men our earth to use
But since our island's small
And landlords make what they choose
We own no land at all;
And as He watched Creation's birth

So they see well content
Our work create out of the earth
Their economic rent.
Some men live in Marylebone
Others in Rottingdean
One has a house in Leytonstone,
And one in Bethnal Green.
We have no choice; I'll not rejoice
The lot has fallen to me
In a vile place, a vile place
In Stepney London E.
No scent of fragrant pasture greets
No trees or fields elate
Our overcrowded stinking streets
But miles of brick or slate;
Main roads where chasing children play
And on each side there comes
Street beyond street, the ugly, grey
Dull foulness of the slums.

Poetry would not earn Attlee even a modest living. In March 1911, he gave ten lectures on trade unionism at Oxford's Ruskin College, which offered a university education for working-class people. He also wrote an article for the college magazine which imagined a conversation between a public school master and a Labour Party supporter. The master praised public schools for instilling a sense of responsibility and 'justice, good form and fair play' in their pupils. The Labour man complained that public schools 'carefully avoid teaching the boys anything of citizenship'. Citizenship would become an important issue for Attlee.

In the summer, Attlee finally got a job as an 'official explainer' for Lloyd George's National Insurance Act, which put into practice some of Beveridge's ideas on insurance against unemployment. So by 1911, Churchill, Beveridge and, in a very junior capacity, Attlee were all working for what Churchill regarded as reform and what Attlee viewed as socialism. The meetings Attlee addressed provided him with unexpected insight. He soon realised that the East End was utterly different from the Shires. Attlee was surprised by and admired the 'public spirit of the county notables'; they hated the Insurance Act, but were cooperative once it became law. Despite his respect for the country gentry, he found that they could still be shocked easily.

At one village meeting the local vicar denounced Attlee as a socialist because he wore a soft collar. On another occasion, Attlee stayed with a local magnate. The man's daughter said, 'I suppose you are a keen supporter of Lloyd George and the Liberals?'

'Good Lord, no,' Attlee replied.

'Then are you a Conservative?'

'Oh, no,' Attlee said.

'Then what are you?' she persisted.

'A socialist.' Following this revelation, Attlee recalls that 'there was a distinct sensation'. If Churchill had crossed the floor of the House, Attlee had crossed the boundary between the haves and have-nots; he wanted to change the lot of those living in less fortunate circumstances.

Both at the Board of Trade and at the Home Office, Churchill proved to be a reformer. He visited Germany, studied their system of labour exchanges and decided that he would set up something similar in England. As well as helping push through Lloyd George's National Insurance Act, he also got other significant Bills through Parliament, Bills which improved conditions for nearly two million workers. The callous coal industry was in his sights after two mining accidents – the May 1910 Wellington Pit disaster, which took the lives of 137 men and boys, and the December Pretoria Pit disaster in which 320 men were killed. Churchill was the driving force behind the 1911 Coal Mines Act, which raised the minimum age for miners to fifteen. The landmark Act also increased the number of inspectors and forced the mine owners to provide rescue services. Ramsay MacDonald, the future Labour Prime Minister, declared it 'a boon to our mining community'.

Other Acts Churchill introduced included a Labour and Shops Act, which pushed through Sunday closing, a meal break for assistants and one day early closing. Some historians believe that Churchill's time as a prisoner of the Boers made him particularly interested in prison reform. To keep petty offenders out of jail, he managed to persuade magistrates to imprison fewer drunks and debtors.

Churchill's ideas put him firmly on the left of political debates at the time. In 1909, he collected his ideas in a 140-page pamphlet, *The People's Rights*, which was influenced by the eighteenth-century American economist, Henry George. George had argued that people had the right to own what they produced, but that there was no such right to private ownership of basic elements – air, water, sunshine and land. The right to these was as strong as the right to life itself. It was no accident, then, that Churchill and Lloyd George pioneered the increasing intervention of the state; a shift in attitude that Attlee shared.

Perhaps the poem which best shows Attlee's intense hopes for change at the time is his 1912 work, 'Limehouse'.

> In Limehouse, in Limehouse, before the break of day,
> I hear the feet of many men who go upon their way,
> Who wander through the City,

The grey and cruel City,
Through streets that have no pity
The streets where men decay.

In Limehouse, in Limehouse, by night as well as day,
I hear the feet of children who go to work or play,
Of children born of sorrow,
The workers of tomorrow
How shall they work tomorrow
Who get no bread today?

In Limehouse, in Limehouse, today and every day
I see the weary mothers who sweat their souls away:
Poor, tired mothers, trying
To hush the feeble crying
Of little babies dying
For want of bread today.

In Limehouse, in Limehouse, I'm dreaming of the day
When evil time shall perish and be driven clean away,
When father, child and mother
Shall live and love each other,
And brother help his brother
In happy work and play.

Blake's influence is again evident, as is the fact that Attlee, who was usually reticent in person, was not so reticent in verse.

The first time that Attlee saw Churchill was in January 1911, during the 'Siege of Sidney Street' in the East End. Churchill, who was at the time Home Secretary, had rushed to Sidney Street to supervise the police and army. Attlee, aware of the commotion, walked from Toynbee Hall in nearby Commercial Street to find out what was happening. One newspaper claimed that the 'desperados', seeing no chance of escape, set fire to the building they were hiding in.

The police were defensive and told the press that, as the fire was started in the front room on the second floor, 'it is absurd to suppose that the volley fired by the soldiers caused the fire. Having started the fire, the desperados came down to the bottom floor.' Attlee watched; Churchill commanded. The two never spoke to each other.

In 1912, Attlee finally got a steady, if part-time, job. Beatrice Webb must have decided that he had acquired sufficient 'push', as she helped get him appointed as a junior lecturer at the London School of Economics.

Two years after Attlee had begun lecturing at the LSE, the First World War broke out. The experiences of the two men during the four-year conflict would prove to be very different. Churchill had been moved from the Home Office in October 1911 to become First Lord of the Admiralty, the political head of the Royal Navy, and in 1915 would be responsible for the disastrous Dardanelles campaign. Attlee never achieved a higher rank than major during the war. However, the two men were agreed on one important point – and this would prove to be something that really mattered when the world erupted into conflict again, twenty-five years later. Decisions had to be made swiftly, and carried out swiftly too.

CHAPTER 5

THE GREAT WAR: COMRADES-IN-ARMS – AT ARM'S LENGTH, 1914–1918

The death of King Edward VII in 1910 marked the end of a glittering social era. A beautiful document illustrates the playfulness of the fading Edwardian elite. Lady Randolph organised a ball to raise money for the 350th anniversary of Shakespeare's birth; she had the nice idea of getting members of high society to act out scenes from his plays. Jack Churchill's wife played Portia in an extract from *The Merchant of Venice*. Lady Randolph also persuaded George Bernard Shaw and G. K. Chesterton to write short stories for the extravaganza's programme. Tickets cost 30 shillings, which equates to around £400 today. The ball was a glorious success.

Lady Randolph's autobiography, *Reminiscences*, failed to mention one of her financial misdeeds. Early in 1914, Churchill and his brother, Jack, discovered she had been deceiving them about the money they stood to inherit from their father's will. The fairy princess had been funding her social life with expensive loans, while letting her sons believe that their father's estate had left the family with only a small trust fund, which would go first to his wife and upon her death to her sons. Lady Randolph had once complained that her husband could never be vindictive in politics, but in his will he displayed some spite. Only too aware of his wife's infidelities, he inserted a clause stating that if she ever remarried, her sons would immediately receive some of the money he had left her. Lady Randolph never informed Winston or Jack about this clause.

The deception was cruel. Jack, who had wanted to enlist in the army, had joined a City firm to make a living; ironically, it was while working in the City that he discovered the truth about the will. When Lady Randolph decided to divorce George Cornwallis-West, Jack had stepped in to help his mother sort out her finances, and this led him to finally read his father's will in detail. He was astonished to discover that he and his brother could have each claimed up to £600 a year (around £65,000 today) from the trust fund the moment when Lady Randolph had remarried. Jack let her know how pained he was at her dishonesty: 'We had always thought that Papa was very wrong in not making any provision for us during your life,' he wrote.

> It makes a considerable difference finding that Papa's will was not made – as we were always led to suppose – carelessly and without any consideration for us. It is quite clear that he never thought that while you were single you would be unable to pay us an allowance, and the clause in the will covered the situation – which did actually arise – of your remarriage.

Churchill may also have been upset, but there is no written record of him having chastised his mother for the deceit. He was forgiving to her, as always.

Although he was never wounded during the war, Churchill suffered disappointment, defeat and depression. Attlee, on the other hand, was injured in action, but his experiences boosted his self-confidence and did wonders for his shyness. The moment war broke out, Attlee volunteered; he 'thought it [his] duty to fight'. However, when he tried to enlist, he was initially told that at thirty-one he was too old. Nevertheless, he ultimately managed to obtain a commission and joined the 6th South Lancashire Regiment as a lieutenant. The war would teach him the pleasures of command; he wrote that 'this soldiering business is only tenable when one has a definite unit under one's command'. As an officer, he would be effective.

As First Lord of the Admiralty, Churchill threw himself into his work, often visiting France. He inspected units in Dunkirk and, as so often, what he saw spurred him into action. He ordered a fleet of Rolls-Royces to be armour-plated. It would not be such a leap from these armoured luxury cars to the primitive tanks that would appear later in the war. And these iron horses would prove far more deadly than Churchill's beloved cavalry.

Two months after war was declared, George Cornwallis-West, who had recently separated from Lady Randolph, went to Antwerp to command a battalion. His task was to prevent the Germans from taking the city, which controlled the mouth of the Scheldt. Cornwallis-West was faltering, so Churchill arrived to organise the city's defences more robustly. Lady Randolph's son replaced her lover and recent husband, a Freudian tangle. Churchill stayed in the best hotel and behaved with his usual unusual energy, fuelled by his customary cigars and cognac. After thirty-six hours, he was enjoying the situation so much that he telegraphed Prime Minister Asquith, offering to take a leave of absence from the Admiralty to command Allied operations in Antwerp.

Kitchener was ready to make him a lieutenant-general, as he was eager to remove Churchill from the centre of decision-making. But 'other voices prevailed', Churchill wrote, so he stayed at the Admiralty.

For his part, Attlee was promoted to captain, which put him in charge of seven officers and 250 men of the 6th South Lancashire Regiment. The men were 'excellent material', and reminded him of his boys at Haileybury House's club. As author John Bew notes, the men ranged 'from miners to errand boys – mostly from Wigan, Warrington and Liverpool'. Attlee and his company left Avonmouth on 13 June and stopped in Malta on their way to Egypt. At the end of June, having been briefed, the regiment left Alexandria and headed for the island of Lemnos in the Aegean, knowing they would soon be sent to Gallipoli.

Attlee and Churchill both learned from the failures of the Gallipoli Campaign. The evacuation from Dunkirk in the Second World War, twenty-five years later, would not have been so well executed had both men not experienced the evacuation from Gallipoli – Churchill from his desk at the Admiralty, Attlee on the beaches where he was the second-to-last man to leave. During preparations for D-Day, thirty years later, both men were haunted by the disastrous Gallipoli landings.

On paper, the Gallipoli strategy made sense. By attacking the Turks near Constantinople, the Allies would open up a second front and force the Germans to transfer troops from the Western Front in order to help the Turks. The Gallipoli peninsula lies at the European end of the Dardanelles Strait and is some 1,700 miles away from the German trenches on the Western Front. The strait is just under a mile wide at its narrowest point.

Eighteen British battleships bombarded the narrowest point of the strait on 18 March 1915, but failed to smash the Turkish batteries. That evening, afraid of suffering too many losses, the navy sounded the general recall. It was clear that an army would have to land, so forces were gathered from the empire. The contribution of Australian and New Zealand troops is well known, but the Gallipoli troops also included the exotically named Zion Mule Corps, 200 Jewish volunteers and 750 mules which transported ammunition and supplies. Their commander, Lieutenant-Colonel J. H. Patterson, author of *The Man-Eaters of Tsavo*, also wrote the less ferocious sounding *With the Zionists in Gallipoli*. Patterson's view of the donkeys leading the lions was dismissive: 'Responsible positions are unfortunately too often given to most unsuitable men with regrettable results.'

Patterson warned that the incompetence of the 'jobbites' would cost many lives. The Allies' misinformed view of the Turks allowed their forces to become too complacent. One Allied pamphlet warned soldiers that the Turks were so uncivilised that often they did not wave a proper white flag of surrender, but would use a greasy dish cloth instead. Sir Ian Hamilton, who commanded the Mediterranean Expeditionary Force, was intelligent, but indecisive and overly optimistic. He concentrated on the southern part of the peninsula at Cape Helles, where, he supposed, there would not be much opposition. To make matters worse, his orders were often unclear, so his commanders dithered about whether to advance or consolidate their positions.

The Turks, on the other hand, were led by Mustafa Kemal Atatürk, who became the founder of modern Turkey. British intelligence was poor, which gave him four weeks to prepare defences. Atatürk acted with Churchillian energy, making his men build roads and small boats to ferry troops and equipment across the strait, and ordering the mining of the Gallipoli beaches.

On 25 April, the Allies landed at Gallipoli, but some troops disembarked 2 kilometres from where they were supposed to be. Their maps were inaccurate, their orders unclear, while the enemy commander again acted in a rather Churchillian manner. Kemal Atatürk told his men, 'I do not order you to fight, I order you to die. In the time which passes until we die, other troops and commanders can come forward and take our places.' We shall never surrender, he might as well have added.

Two days later, Atatürk ordered six battalions to launch a counter-attack, which ended any chances of a swift Allied victory. Gallipoli became a battle of attrition. Three weeks later, 42,000 Turks tried to push 17,000 Australians and New Zealanders back into the sea – 3,000 Turks were killed. But Atatürk was willing to accept such heavy casualties; the Allies less so. The death of 160 Australians and New Zealanders produced dismay among the Allies.

Attlee and his men sailed from Lemnos to Gallipoli in two destroyers early in July. The conditions were dreadful; the companionship was good. While the flies and heat were savage, Attlee recalled 'many talks with men on the night watches', including one on trade unions with two of his sergeants, 'while Johnny Turk kept up a brisk fire'. A few days later, Attlee collapsed with dysentery. He was put on a ship bound for England, but when he woke up, he demanded to be let off in Malta, so he could return to his men as soon as possible. During his absence, the men had landed at Suvla Bay and suffered terrible casualties. Attlee's illness probably saved his life.

Many soldiers wrote memoirs of Gallipoli and Patterson was one of the most critical, complaining of nepotism and a fatal lack of drive. After the first landing, 'owing to lack of sufficient men to hold what they had made good, they were compelled to retire to the ridges overlooking the sea'. The Allies frustrated the Turks for eight months. 'One more division would have made the crucial difference,' Patterson believed.

Gallipoli was a complex fiasco and it greatly affected Churchill's mood; he admitted in *Painting as a Pastime* that it triggered a deep depression. Asquith yielded to pressure from the Tories and demoted Churchill from First Lord of the Admiralty to Chancellor of the Duchy of Lancaster. Churchill now commanded no ships, no men, no cannons, not even a canoe. 'I knew everything and could do nothing,' he wrote.

On 22 July, Hamilton landed reinforcements at Suvla Bay. His choice of local commander was straight out of a Gilbert and Sullivan comic opera, as Sir Frederick Stopford had commanded the Yeoman of the Guard at the Tower of London. He had fought at the Battle of Tell el Kebir in 1882, when British troops routed the Egyptians, but had no other experience of battle. When his troops landed and met little opposition, Stopford believed they had achieved a victory; it was a case of premature celebration. By the morning of 9 August, the Turks had taken back the heights of the ridge at Suvla. For three days Hamilton stubbornly continued to order fresh attacks, but every one of these failed. Stopford was sent home to London in disgrace, but Hamilton stayed on.

On 25 September, Kitchener transferred two British divisions and one French division from Gallipoli to Salonika in Greece; his decision marked the beginning of the end of the Gallipoli campaign. From Malta, now recovered, Attlee headed back to Gallipoli at the start of November. He was proud that he did not get seasick on the small Clyde steamer that ferried him back to his troops. He had fond memories of the voyage as he played bridge with Colonel Vigne, 'a very cheery old gunner'. Vigne described Attlee as a charming fellow who was, alas, 'a damned democratic socialistic tub-thumping rascal'.

Like so many soldiers in the battle, Attlee felt vulnerable. He wrote,

> From step and dug-out our huddled figures creep
> Yawning from their dreams of England; bayonets gleam...

And rat-tat-tat, machine guns usher in
Another day of heat, and dust, and flies.

Even in the Aegean, however, the East End was never far from his imagination. Nostalgically, he longed:

To see the busses throng by Mile End Gate
And smell the fried fish down Limehouse Way.

In the following weeks, Attlee's battalion encountered terrible weather: torrential rain, snow and blizzards. His men stood in water up to their knees. A heavy rainstorm at the end of November lasted for three days and there was yet another blizzard in early December. Some soldiers drowned; the water washed unburied corpses into the lines. 'A very disagreeable feature of trench life,' Patterson wrote, 'is the unpleasant odour of the dead'.

Attlee's company had few casualties because 'the captain bullied us', one of his privates said later. He bullied rather like a public school prefect would. He got his men to run about, instead of shivering under the trees, and chased them as if they were practising for a game of rugby. He knew foot rot was a threat and insisted on regular inspection to prevent it. He also learned how to command and to reward, and would congratulate those that did well with an extra tipple of rum. His politics, however, amused the officers' mess. His commanding officer would say, 'Let's have a good strafe, send for Attlee!' Attlee wrote, clearly relishing a strafe himself.

The Allies decided to evacuate a hopeless position in November. Attlee's men were ordered to hold the perimeter at the point from which the last Allied troops would leave. He was in charge of 250 men and six machine guns. He sent sixty men with two machine guns to hold the road to the sea and was the penultimate man to leave the beach. 'It was a tragic failure,' Attlee wrote. 'I always feel a sympathy with all old Gallipolitans.' He made them sound like the old boys of a public school.

For the Attlee family, 1916 provoked a crisis, as the Military Service Act introduced conscription. The government was willing to let Quakers avoid military service, but feared that many others would use religion as a reason not to serve their country. Tribunals would judge whether conscientious objectors were indeed conscientious. Lloyd George regarded the objectors as cowards and insisted on their harsh treatment. The philosopher Bertrand Russell, on the other hand, was vitriolic about the tribunals' decisions. 'The man who has been teaching physics must be made to hoe potatoes; the man who has been hoeing potatoes must be set to teach physics. Potatoes and physics both cease to be produced by this arrangement; but both men suffer, so all is well,' Russell observed.

Tom Attlee applied for exemption as a conscientious objector. His tribunal was held in Poplar and although he might have expected leniency due to his brother's local connections, this did not happen. When he refused to serve, even as a non-combatant, Tom was imprisoned. Wormwood Scrubs meant bread and water, and solitary confinement for a month. Tom was a talented architect, so he was made to sew mail sacks for the Post Office – as Russell might have predicted. Peggy Attlee, Tom's daughter-in-law, who wrote a loving biography of him, *With a Quiet Conscience*, quotes two letters that Tom received from his brother. It is unclear whether these were the only letters in Peggy's possession, or the only ones she chose to quote from; regardless, both indicate that Tom showed personal loyalty to his brother but was uncompromising in his political views. Attlee hoped that Tom would be released, but he also made clear his contempt for the faith that had prompted Tom not to fight, and indeed for all religion. In his autobiography, *As It Happened*, Attlee does not mention his brother's refusal to fight.

From Gallipoli, Attlee was sent to Persia. At El Hanna, on 5 April 1916, a bullet smashed into his thigh and a nose-cap lodged in his buttocks. He was evacuated to Basra, then sailed to Bombay and finally back to England. He was promoted to major on 1 March 1917, joining the 5th Battalion of the South Lancashire Regiment. Next, on 2 July, he took command of one of the newly formed Tank Corps at Bovington, in Dorset. The armoured Rolls-Royces had been utterly changed and the tank was a pet project of Churchill's.

In June 1918, Attlee was posted to France and remembered having a showdown in the trenches. A sergeant brought before him a man who stubbornly refused to return to the front line. Attlee adopted a method that had worked with disobedient boys in the East End. He took out his watch and said, 'You've got one minute to return to duty.' Attlee then proceeded to count each second. When he had reached forty-five, the man 'sloped arms and returned to the trench'. Normally, a soldier would have been put on a charge for his initial refusal to return, but Attlee let the matter drop and the soldier did not misbehave again.

The failure at Gallipoli seemed to mark the end of Churchill's political career and he resigned from his position as Chancellor of the Duchy of Lancaster. In November 1915, he wrote to Asquith, explaining that as he had been excluded from the War Cabinet – at the insistence of the Tories – he intended to resign. 'Even when decisions of principle are rightly taken, the speed and method of their execution are factors which determine the result,' he told Asquith. He added that time 'would vindicate his running of the Admiralty which had left Britain in command of the seas'.

Four days after he left office, Churchill delivered a well-received resignation speech in the House. Violet Asquith wrote to tell him that the speech had been 'flawless'. He did not attack Asquith or the Tories.

Andrew Bonar Law, the Tory leader who would later become Prime Minister, was full of praise for Churchill, commenting that 'in my judgement, in mental power and vital force, he is one of the foremost men in our country'. Bonar Law told Asquith that Churchill should go to East Africa as commander-in-chief – presumably of half a continent. There was to be no colonial consolation for Churchill, though. A week after he had resigned, he crossed the Channel to re-join his old regiment as a relatively humble major. But he would share the same rank as Attlee for only a few weeks, as he was soon promoted to lieutenant-colonel.

We know a good deal about Churchill at the front from his correspondence with Edward Marsh. One of his officers, Andrew Gibb, also wrote about the experience in *With Winston Churchill at the Front*. Gibb quoted Churchill saying 'war is a game to be played with a smiling face', and Churchill certainly got a laugh when he addressed his first parade. 'War has been declared,' he said, then paused dramatically, and added, 'on lice'. Gibb claims that it was in Churchill's unit that the term deloused was invented. He was also impressed by his commander's portable bathtub with a hot water heater, and by the way Churchill combined his British uniform with a light blue French Army helmet that a French general had given him. Even in the trenches, Churchill could be playful.

Churchill was a fearless leader, personally patrolling the front line and surviving several close calls with death or serious injury. He clearly inspired those who served under him. 'Our nights were spent in wondering what he'd do next, our days in doing it,' Gibb wrote. Roy Jenkins calculated that Churchill spent no more than eight weeks in the trenches. On 7 May 1916, Winston gave a fine farewell dinner for his officers before returning to England. He was the only man during the war to exchange a powerful position in the Cabinet for that of a minor military command, and then return to a powerful job in the government – all in the space of just over eighteen months. In July 1917, Lloyd George brought him back as Minister of Munitions. Despite his ongoing battle with depression, Churchill proved remarkably resilient and always seemed able to bounce back.

In office again, Churchill did not feel limited by the position he held. As usual, he saw no reason not to involve himself in the work of other departments. 'Red Churchill', as the *Daily Mail* called him, now advocated a dramatic policy that the Attlee government would adopt twenty-five years later – nationalisation of the railways.

Attlee was more elegiac than playful. In 1918, while on leave on Walney Island, he recalled that at Gallipoli, he had longed for the soft greys and greens of England and for Oxford. He loved his country deeply, a feeling that Churchill shared.

Attlee stayed in the army, fighting near Lille, and was wounded again. He underwent a minor operation and was taken back to England. He celebrated the Armistice in hospital, drinking champagne, but he was in a lot of pain from boils that refused to heal. Sick of lying in a hospital bed, Attlee crafted an exit pass, which would allow him to return home for Christmas, and persuaded a surgeon to sign it.

Both men were philosophical as the war ended. Churchill told his confidant and poetry editor Edward Marsh, 'I have fallen back reposefully into the arms of fate.' Fate made him hopeful. He professed to have an 'underlying instinct that all will be well and that my greatest work is at hand'. Attlee quoted the poet James Thomson, who praised 'the stir of fellowship in all-disastrous fight'. Echoing the views of Gallipoli veteran Lieutenant-Colonel J. H. Patterson, Attlee argued that the Allies had nearly achieved 'a great success which might have shortened the war and saved tens of thousands of lives'. But 'incredible blunders marred Churchill's fine strategic conception'. Attlee often wondered what the consequences would have been had decisions not been taken by 'elderly and hidebound generals', who were not the men 'to push through an adventure of this kind'. Both his and Churchill's experiences in the First World War would affect their decisions twenty-five years later, when it came to fighting Hitler.

CHAPTER 6

WHO'S IN, WHO'S OUT: THE CAROUSEL OF OFFICE, 1918–1929

In late January and early February 1918, the Allies were disappointed that the Germans, although facing inevitable defeat, stubbornly refused to accept this as reality. *The Times* reported that Germany's attitude stiffened the resolve of the Allies to fight on

> until such time as the pressure of that effort shall have brought about in the enemy Governments and peoples a change of temper which would justify the hope of the conclusion of peace on terms which would not involve the abandonment, in the face of an aggressive and unrepentant militarism, of all the principles of freedom, justice and the respect for the Law of Nations which the Allies are resolved to vindicate.

Nine months later, at 11 a.m. on 11 November 1918, Germany surrendered. The Allies then took an amazing decision, given that they professed to be committed to justice: the Germans would not be allowed to attend the peace conference in Versailles. They would simply sign any documents placed before them. No one seems to have considered this unwise or unfair.

As Prime Minister, Lloyd George led the British team to Versailles; he took Bonar Law, Balfour and economist John Maynard Keynes with him, but not Churchill. Churchill wrote later:

> War, stripped of every pretension of glamour or romance, had been brought home to the masses of the peoples and brought home in forms never before experienced except by the defeated. To stop another war was the supreme object and duty of the statesmen who met as friends and allies around the Peace Table.

The war had seen the introduction of new instruments of death – planes dropped bombs, machine guns fired more than 300 rounds per minute, poison gas sparked mass panic. Hitler himself developed hysterical blindness. Unlike many of the wounded, Hitler had been eager to return to the front, and he did so after being cured by Edmund Forster, a German psychiatrist who had been influenced by Freud.

It has often been argued that the harsh terms of the Treaty of Versailles 'caused' the Second World War. In Britain, there was a desire for vengeance. In the election of 1918, Lloyd George campaigned on slogans such as 'Hang the Kaiser' and 'Make them pay' – and his coalition won a landslide victory. After so much slaughter, the electorate's anger was understandable.

A peace conference after so much trauma required vision and maturity, but both were in short supply. US President Woodrow Wilson was cheered by thousands when he arrived in Paris to try to persuade the Allies to be more moderate and less vengeful, but French Prime

Minister Georges Clemenceau and Lloyd George proved too wily for him. John Maynard Keynes wrote that France wanted 'to set the clock back and to undo what, since 1870, the progress of Germany had accomplished'. If Clemenceau could take control of, 'even in part, what Germany was compelled to drop, the inequality of strength between the two rivals for European hegemony might be remedied for generations', Keynes argued. There was no limit 'to French vindictiveness and commercial jealousy', C. P. Snow commented. After the Second World War, Churchill famously recommended 'in victory magnanimity'; there was none at Versailles.

Lloyd George, who recognised that self-determination had become fashionable, could 'not conceive of any greater cause of war' than to surround Germany with small states, which had little history of stability, and where many Germans lived who wanted 'reunion with their native land'. The Poles wanted 'to place 2,100,000 Germans under the control of a people which is of a different religion and which has never proved its capacity for stable self-government'. Lloyd George was sure that this 'must, in my judgement, lead sooner or later to a new war in the East of Europe'.

Sigmund Freud's nephew, Edward Bernays, was one of President Wilson's aides, as was William Bullitt, who had been a patient of Freud. Bullitt co-wrote the last book that Freud published: a psychological analysis of Wilson. The authors claimed that the President had given in to Clemenceau and Lloyd George's bullying because Wilson's father had been domineering. Not having had the benefit of being psychoanalysed, Wilson had not worked through his conflicting emotions and was a mess of Oedipal conflicts. As a result, he let Lloyd George, Clemenceau and his unresolved feelings overwhelm his judgement. Clemenceau, who spoke English well, often flounced out of the proceedings at key moments, which upset Wilson greatly.

Seventeen hundred miles away from Versailles, Lenin was consolidating his power in Russia. For the next twenty-five years, Churchill and Attlee would be united in their hatred of communism, though for different reasons. For Churchill, the Bolsheviks triggered a raw emotional response: 'Bolshevism is not a policy; it is a disease,' he stated in the House of Commons on 29 May 1919. 'It not a creed; it is a pestilence,' he insisted. The Bolsheviks were a 'league of failures, the criminals, the morbid, the deranged and the distraught'. Churchill even went so far as to invoke Dracula; Bolshevism was 'the vampire which sucks the blood from his victims'.

Lloyd George commented that 'Churchill had no doubt a genuine distaste for Communism'. But it was more personal than this: 'His ducal blood revolted against the wholesale elimination of the grand dukes in Russia.'

For Attlee, lacking any ducal blood, communism was a blight because the comrades kept trying to infiltrate the Labour Party and take it over. Attlee sensed that the British would never take to Marxism. British socialism had to be less doctrinaire.

The war had changed the East End, too. Haileybury House, which had become a base for Attlee, had closed. Attlee decided to temporarily move back to Toynbee Hall, and returned to work at the LSE as a lecturer. He also began work on his first book, *The Social Worker*, which argued that the poor needed more professional help than charities could provide. He outlined a modern vision of social work that reflected his interest in psychology; social workers and their clients should have a reciprocal relationship. Attlee commented: 'It is not a movement concerned alone with the material, with housing and drains, clinics and feeding centres, gas and water, but is the expression of the desire for social justice, for freedom and beauty, and for the better appointment of all things that make up a good life.' Social service meant doing a 'personal service', whereas contributing just meant giving money to the charities involved. In social service, 'the labour of thinking out what is to be done, and doing the work, cannot be delegated; in charity it very frequently is'. Social services would be better organised, Attlee argued, if local authorities provided them, and if social workers regarded themselves 'less as philanthropists doing kindly acts than as citizens fulfilling their duties'. Help had to be professional.

After the 1919 local elections, Attlee took a flat off Commercial Road. His inheritance allowed him to lease the whole building, so he rented out the two other flats to Labour Party members. The building also became a club for the local Labour Party.

Like many others, Attlee had hoped that soldiers, airmen and seamen would return to a country that showed it valued the sacrifices they had made. But the promises that Lloyd George had made after the end of the war were broken; unemployment in Britain rose sharply. In the 1919 local elections, Attlee ran as the Labour Party's candidate for Limehouse, which was part of Stepney Borough Council. Attlee's Liberal Party rival defeated him in Limehouse by eighty votes, but forty-three of the sixty councillors returned in Stepney were Labour. Though he had not won a seat on the council, the councillors co-opted Attlee as Mayor of Stepney. It was a stunning piece of good luck and established him as a major politician in London. He was the unanimous choice, so there was no election.

Four times over the next fifteen years, in fact, Attlee would step from one office to another, more important role, without having to suffer the inconvenience of a contest. From Mayor of Stepney, he went on to become chair of the committee of London mayors, before being appointed deputy leader of the Labour Party – and also faced no opposition in one ballot for Labour leader. He walked into the council chamber to be greeted by loud cheers. He politely declined to wear the mayoral robes, but let the insignia of office be pinned on his three-piece suit, which was no longer made by a dysfunctional cooperative that was not overly skilled in the needlework department.

The new mayor encouraged people to come to him with their complaints, and immediately turned his attention to Stepney's dire housing situation. Housing plans were so often thwarted by government red tape that, on 12 April, Attlee wrote to *The Times*, asserting that 'either there is some influence at work, endeavouring to prevent local authorities from carrying out their work or that Messrs Dilly and Dally have not yet been demobilised'. London boroughs still had considerable powers, which allowed Attlee to push through measures to force landlords to repair their properties. He also funded centres where tenants could get advice about their many problems.

Attlee is sometimes portrayed as dour but, as his short verses and invoking Messrs Dilly and Dally show, he possessed a wry sense of humour. In 1920, he was proud of reducing the infant mortality rate. The councillor who delivered the vote of thanks at the end of Attlee's year as mayor said: 'During the year there has been a great increase in the birth rate mainly due, as we all know, to the personal efforts of the chairman.' The unintended joke touched a nerve, as the mayor was usually a married man. Attlee had no wife to accompany him to functions so his sister Margaret filled in sometimes, but she was living in Putney and had to spend much time with their sick mother. 'I was somewhat handicapped in my work as a Mayor by being unmarried,' Attlee wrote.

Attlee's mother died on 19 May 1920, and a month later his eldest sister, Dorothy, who was just forty-two, passed away, leaving seven children. Attlee recorded both deaths in *As It Happened*, but as had been the case with his father's passing, said nothing more about how the double bereavement had affected him. He busied himself with work and became vice-president of the Municipal Electricity Authorities. He also became chairman of the mayoral committee for all twenty-six London boroughs. He then arranged for a delegation of London mayors to meet Lloyd George, and made sure they were accompanied by a procession of the unemployed as they walked to Whitehall. He also arranged for journalists to be there to witness the proceedings.

When Attlee passed through the doors of 10 Downing Street, it was the first time he had set foot in the building. Since an earlier chapter is titled 'Ambition and the Lack of It', it is worth noting that Attlee was thirty-seven years old. Contrast that with the photograph of an eight-year-old Harold Wilson standing outside the famous door. The mayoral delegation made some powerful speeches – they had a powerful case – but Lloyd George did not offer much help. He was annoyed that he had had to cut short a holiday in the Scottish Highlands.

After the meeting, the mayors walked out into a near riot; the unemployed men, mainly from the East End, were pelting the police with stones. Attlee's men from Limehouse were about to start hurling stones, too, but the man who had been the penultimate British soldier to be evacuated from Suvla Bay did not feel awed. Storming to the head of the crowd, he ordered a 'Halt' and 'About turn'. Then he smartly marched his 'troops' back to Stepney – Major Attlee was never far beneath the surface of 'Civilian Attlee'.

After his two bereavements in 1895, Churchill had bounced back into action. He had needed time to recover from the loss and, as Churchill often did, decided to go abroad. Likewise, Attlee readily accepted an invitation to travel to Italy with Edric Millar, one of Tom Attlee's old college friends. Attlee was delighted; the Renaissance had always interested him when he was up at Oxford.

A few weeks before they were due to leave, Millar asked if Attlee would mind if his mother and youngest sister accompanied them. The group mainly stayed in Tuscany, where E. M. Forster had set his 1908 novel, *A Room with a View*. For Attlee, Tuscany also became a setting for romance. 'It seemed that I was more often the companion of Miss Violet Millar than of the other members of the party,' he wrote. The 24-year-old girl whom he now started to court was the daughter of a successful businessman and had worked for the Red Cross during the war.

As they travelled back by train, Violet woke up to find Attlee gazing at her. Later she told their daughter that this was the moment she realised that he was in love with her. 'Of course, I was already in love with him,' she added.

When they returned from Italy, Attlee asked Violet to accompany him to a football match, but the game was cancelled because the pitch was in a poor condition. The pair went instead to Richmond Park, where Attlee proposed and Violet accepted. He insisted, however, that she come to see him 'orating from a platform on Hampstead Heath' to understand what life with him might be like; then, he grew afraid that she might reject him. Seeing him speaking, however, did not put her off. Love transformed Attlee, his friend John Beckett said.

On 10 January 1922, the couple were married. The Attlees decided against living in Limehouse and moved instead to Woodford Green in Essex. One of Attlee's brothers, Laurence, who was already living in the area with his wife, found a semi-detached house that the newly married couple liked – they 'lost no time and secured it in three days'. They were to live in the area for nearly ten years.

Attlee's marriage was a happy one, though Violet suffered periodically from depression and, at times, could not cope with their children. Attlee protected her from the stresses of being the wife of a leading politician.

He and Churchill both had mothers whose behaviour impacted on their children – Ellen Attlee was something of a domestic tyrant, while Lady Randolph never seemed romantically or sexually satisfied; Clementine Churchill's mother also had a turbulent romantic and financial life. For Attlee, living with Violet's depression, and helping her cope, turned out to be good preparation for working with Churchill.

Only a year earlier, in 1921, Churchill and Clementine had suffered a crushing bereavement when their two-year-old daughter Marigold died from meningitis. Both parents were heartbroken and, sadly, more tragedy would soon follow; in April, Clementine's brother, Bill, committed suicide and, finally, in June, the Churchills received news of Lady Randolph's death.

Where Attlee was reticent about his mother's passing, Churchill romanticised his mother both in life and in death:

> I wish you could have seen her as she lay at rest – after all the sunshine and storm of life was over. Very beautiful and splendid she looked. Since this morning, with its pangs, thirty years had fallen from her brow. She recalled to me the countenance I had admired as a child when she was in her heyday and the old brilliant world of the '80s and '90s seemed to come back.

The tragedies affected Churchill's psyche and health. In 1922, doctors operated on him after he developed appendicitis, and he took a long time to recover despite only being in his mid-forties. So, for once, when the Conservatives withdrew their support from Lloyd George's Liberals in October, Churchill was not his usual energetic self. The Welsh Wizard, Lloyd George, resigned as Prime Minister and never held office again.

Attlee was chosen as the Labour candidate for the Limehouse seat in the 1922 general election. He was well known in the area and his war record inspired confidence – he knew how to use it too. During the campaign, he presided over a medal ceremony for war veterans of the war. His election address was uncompromising: 'I claim the right of every man, woman and child in the land to have the best life that can be provided,' he said, and then demanded that the wealth of the country should be used for all the people. He beat the sitting Liberal MP, William Pearce, by nearly 2,000 votes.

Churchill, however, lost his supposedly safe seat at Dundee. When he had resigned from the Cabinet, after the disaster of the Dardanelles, he had gone to fight in the trenches. Now he had no such immediate outlet for his frustrated energies. He turned instead to writing, which he loved nearly as much as politics and fighting. Writing had one advantage: it could be very lucrative. It also had one distinctive disadvantage: it mainly had to be done sitting down.

When Attlee became an MP, *The Times* commented caustically that he was 'a type that would construct a new heaven on earth on violently geometric principles'. The Speaker of the House of Commons, however, did not think Attlee such an extremist, and soon called him to make his maiden speech. He wanted to hear from a new Labour man who was probably more moderate than the 'Red Clydesiders', as the Labour members from Glasgow were known.

Attlee's speech was far from the conciliatory rhetoric that might have been expected, however. He called for an 'economy campaign', by which he meant 'economy in mankind, economy in flesh and blood, economy in the true wealth of the state and the community'. During the war, there had been full employment because 'the government controlled the purchasing power of the nation'. If Whitehall demanded guns, rifles, uniforms or saddles, they were bought and paid for from extra taxation.

Attlee agreed with future Prime Minister Bonar Law, who believed that one of the greatest reforms would be 'a better distribution of wealth'. While the few controlled purchasing power, Bonar Law believed 'there will be production of luxuries and not of necessaries'. During the war, even the Tories had accepted the central direction of the economy. It could also be made to happen in peacetime, Attlee insisted.

The *East London Recorder*, no lover of the Labour Party, predicted that Attlee would not stray from 'legislative rectitude'. Some newspapers might mock the fact that he looked a bit like Lenin, but Attlee was not going to arm the proletariat and then march on Buckingham Palace. Labour had to appeal to miners, casual workers in the docks and middle-class intellectuals, Attlee argued. For these very different groups, politics usually mattered without being an obsession. Political meetings had to fit in with supporting a football club, breeding rabbits and playing an instrument in a local band.

Ramsay MacDonald, now the Leader of the Opposition, appointed Attlee as one of his parliamentary private secretaries. Years later, Attlee stated that being in opposition had been an education for the new Labour MPs. He wrote,

> It's useful to have to sit in Opposition for your first few years, but it is particularly good for people to have to sit there unable to say very much while the ex-Ministers and the Privy Councillors are being called on all the time. Young chaps like me had to just sit there and keep quiet; but we could listen and watch points. Very important.

In fact, Attlee spoke quite often, especially on military matters. He felt strongly about taxing the pensions of widows who had lost their husbands in the war. Britain had needed the men back in 1914, but now the widows could 'go hang'. Attlee was beginning to make a name for himself, and became the subject of a profile in the Labour Party-supporting newspaper, the *Daily Herald*.

Stanley Baldwin, the key figure in persuading the Conservatives to ditch Lloyd George, became Chancellor of the Exchequer. When Bonar Law, who was dying of throat cancer, had to resign in May 1923, Baldwin took over as Prime Minister. He would occupy 10 Downing Street for more than seven of the next fourteen years. Baldwin clashed with both Churchill and Attlee, but, despite this, he was well disposed to the pair, especially to Attlee. Attlee once commented that Baldwin 'would prefer to have talks with one of his workmen sitting on a wheelbarrow than with the country notables'. Baldwin was Rudyard Kipling's cousin; Attlee knew and loved Kipling's poetry, a small bond, but a bond nonetheless.

Parliament was dissolved in October 1923 and the political carousel turned again. In the ensuing election, the Labour Party won 191 seats, the Tories 258 and the Liberals 158. The Liberals did not join the government, but agreed to back Ramsay MacDonald, who, as the first Labour Prime Minister, became a historic figure. MacDonald appointed Attlee Under-Secretary of State for War. Just as Churchill and Lord Randolph had done, Attlee now had to wrestle with the finances of the military. With Britain no longer at war, many political observers expected less money to be spent on the country's armed forces. Attlee, however, was not inclined to reduce military spending too much, for a number of reasons. The army must be well equipped, of course, but it could also help to educate working-class boys. Attlee insisted that boys should only enlist with the consent of their parents, and that the army should train young men not just to fight, but to take their places as citizens of the world.

Typically, his new job prompted Attlee to write poetry:

No more the old street corner
Where the busy traffic lies
No more the dear old platform
And the cause that never dies
I've got a government job now
Propaganda isn't wise.

The political carousel spun again when the Liberals abandoned MacDonald in the autumn of 1924. In the general election, Attlee increased his majority in Limehouse, but Labour lost forty seats and Baldwin became Prime Minister for the second time. The election also saw the fifty-year-old Churchill return to Parliament, as MP for Epping. Attlee dated their first meeting to when they both took their seats; in an undramatic way they liked each other. From the first, Attlee admired Churchill's courage.

Baldwin offered Churchill a very senior, but unexpected Cabinet role and, given his hatred of mathematics, one for which he was least suited: Chancellor of the Exchequer. Churchill was never going to refuse the office his father had held. According to his biographer Roy Jenkins, despite any mathematical deficiencies, Churchill took to the post 'as if he had the combined Exchequer experience of Gladstone, Disraeli, Lloyd George and Bonar Law'. But, perhaps because numbers remained something of a mystery to him, Churchill's self-confidence failed to win the argument on the key economic question of the day: should Britain return to the Gold Standard? Doing so would effectively mean revaluing the pound upwards so that it was worth $4.86.

Instinctively, Churchill thought that a return to the Gold Standard was a bad idea, but his eloquence could not win over sceptics when it came to economics. He lacked the skills needed to explain why it was a dangerous policy. Formidable opponents thought it necessary, including shadow Chancellor Philip Snowden and the Governor of the Bank of England, Montagu Norman. At the beginning of two months of intense, secret discussions, Churchill wrote, 'The Governor seems perfectly happy in Britain having the finest credit in the world while also having 1.25 million unemployed.' Unemployment was a human and financial tragedy: each person out of work cost the government £50 a year in dole payments. Unemployment was, of course, also a tragedy from Attlee's perspective.

In his speech introducing the necessary legislation, however, Churchill voiced no doubts and said, 'I will tell you what it [the return to the Gold Standard] will shackle us to … It will shackle us to reality.' This reality added some 10 per cent to costs to industry, according to the economist John Maynard Keynes.

Keynes then published a short pamphlet, *The Economic Consequences of Mr. Churchill*, in which he claimed that Churchill had no 'instinctive feel' to stop him making mistakes on the economy. Though he felt that Churchill had been misled by bankers and economists, Keynes was unforgiving of Churchill personally, believing that 'he who wills the means wills the end'. Churchill had willed the means, so he was responsible for the dismal end. Keynes believed that 'Mr Churchill's policy of improving the exchange rate by 10 per cent was, sooner or later, a policy of reducing everyone's wages by 2 shillings.' Wages did fall and the trade unions called a general strike in May 1926.

Churchill had often taken a moderate line with the unions, especially when he had been Home Secretary, but now he viewed them as enemies. I have already mentioned Sebastian Haffner's biography, which attributes two personalities to Churchill: the statesman and the generalissimo. Churchill now moved into generalissimo mode, a role which suited him better than that of the nation's chief accountant.

The general strike stopped work in the docks. Churchill wanted tanks to escort convoys of food into London, and for the BBC to act as a government information agency. Baldwin had the clever idea of asking Churchill to edit an official daily paper, the *British Gazette*, which first appeared on 5 May and condemned the strikers. Churchill made it both effective propaganda and hugely popular – the paper's circulation rose from 200,000 copies to more than 2 million for the eighth and last edition, which was dominated by articles on the collapse of the strike.

Surprisingly, Attlee also opposed the general strike; he felt that a strike should not be used as a political weapon. Practical as ever, as chairman of the Stepney Borough Electricity Committee, Attlee negotiated a deal with the Electrical Trade Union so that power would continue to be supplied to local hospitals, but not to factories. One firm, Scammell and Nephew Ltd, took out a civil action against Attlee and the other Labour members of the committee. Attlee and his fellow committee members were ordered to pay £300 in damages. Curiously, given his relative prosperity, Attlee said that the financial problems caused by this episode almost forced him out of politics. The threat of bankruptcy depressed him and it depressed his vulnerable wife even more.

Two months after the strike, in a retrospective debate, Churchill wound up for the government. 'I have no wish to make threats which would disturb the House and cause bad blood,' he said, and then paused dramatically. 'But this I must say, make your minds perfectly clear that if you ever let loose upon us another general strike, we will let loose upon you' – and again he paused – 'another *British Gazette*.' Both sides of the House burst into laughter. Churchill had defused what might have been an explosive debate.

Adolf Hitler had been sentenced to five years in prison for his part in the failed Munich coup of 1923. He was afforded many privileges while in jail, which allowed him to write his hate-filled autobiography, *Mein Kampf*. The book did not appear in English until 1933, so it is unlikely that either Attlee or Churchill read it before then. *Mein Kampf* demanded revenge for the harsh terms of the Versailles Treaty, but Germany was not yet in any state to contemplate starting a new war. That did not stop equable men like Baldwin from worrying, though. He wrote, 'Who in Europe does not know that one more war in the west and the civilisation of the ages will fall with as great a shock as the end of Rome.' The lure of pacifism in the 1930s is not hard to understand.

Hugh Dalton was one of many Labour MPs who later thought themselves more fitted to lead than Attlee. Like Baldwin, he feared a new war. Dalton was an Old Etonian and offers a good illustration of the continuity in the politics of the time. His father had tutored the future King George V and his wayward brother Albert, who had risked bringing the monarchy into disrepute through a string of homosexual liaisons; although cruel, it could be said that Albert did the Crown a favour by dying young.

Dalton had some very public school notions of how to achieve peace; he believed that if the Germans would only learn to play cricket – a sport which had enthused King George II's German-born son, Frederick, almost 200 years earlier – there would be no war. Enthralled by his sporting theory, Dalton also pointed out that in 1927, when France beat Germany 30–5 in rugby, the French had cheered the sole German try. To avoid war, Europe merely had to bat and scrum. Playfully, Dalton coined the term 'bellifist' – *bellum* being the Latin word for war – to contrast with pacifist.

Dalton had studied economics, so numbers never became an issue for him. Churchill and Attlee's governess, Miss Hutchinson, however, seems to have failed both her charges in this department, as neither man operated at his best when discussing details of economic policy.

Despite his relative failure as Chancellor, however, Churchill still hoped one day to achieve his ambition of becoming Prime Minister. It seems improbable that Attlee ever considered himself a candidate to be Prime Minister. Ambition grew slowly for Attlee – and it was never as personal as it was for Churchill.

Attlee was now offered an opportunity to stretch his wings out in the East. The 1919 Government of India Act had given the vote to a small number of wealthy Indians and established a national Parliament. In the summer of 1927, Ramsay MacDonald appointed Attlee to the Simon Commission that would review the status of India and recommend changes to its constitution. Attlee loved Kipling's works, many of which were set in India, so the mission excited him. When he served on the Commission, he often talked with Churchill's friend, F. E. Smith, who had now become Lord Birkenhead, the Secretary of State for India, who 'showed [him] every kindness'.

The Commission's first aim was to study the administrations of Madras and the Punjab; Attlee was in his element examining local government procedures. Despite the Westminster delegation's best intentions, Congress, Jawaharlal Nehru and Gandhi's party, boycotted the Commission. The disregard and contempt for the British government was evident almost immediately upon their arrival in India – Attlee and his colleagues were targeted by a would-be killer. Attlee remarked that 'a bomb had been prepared for us'. It was a stroke of luck that their assailant proved clumsy and dropped his device 'from the rack of a railway carriage with unfortunate results for himself'. The would-be assassin dead, and Madras and the Punjab dissected, Attlee returned to London. When the Commission travelled back to India in the autumn of 1928, he took his wife with him, leaving their three young children to be cared for by close friends.

The Commission went to Burma as well as to the remoter parts of Assam. 'Very few Europeans and, for that matter, only a few Indians had studied conditions in all parts of India,' Attlee commented, unusually boastful for once. Lord Randolph's decision to seize Burma in November 1885 had been a mistake, the Commission found. Although the Commission comprised politicians from different parties, Attlee found that it was 'harmonious'. He became one of the first politicians to understand how complex and difficult an issue India was. Following his visit, he remained quite conservative on the British Empire as a whole and about India in particular. Attlee was criticised by those on the left of the Labour Party for not going far enough with regards to India, and by Churchill for having gone too far. Churchill's views on India were both romantic and reactionary. In his opinion, the sub-continent was Britain's to rule.

Baldwin was not the only politician to worry about how to avoid a new war. US President Calvin Coolidge's Secretary of State, Frank Kellogg, a former farm boy who had then practised as a lawyer before entering the Senate in 1916, shared those anxieties. He co-authored the idealistic Kellogg–Briand Pact, whose signatories promised not to use force to resolve disputes. Parties who resorted to war 'should be denied of the benefits furnished by [the] treaty'. Quite what these benefits were was slightly vague. Kellogg and Briand shared the Nobel Peace Prize in 1929. They were not the first, nor would they be the last, to discover that it was easier to be recognised for their ideals than have those ideals put into practice.

In the spring of 1929, Attlee returned from India to learn that Baldwin had called a general election. Attlee immediately rushed to Limehouse, anxious that he might lose his seat, and his concern proved well founded: detractors were accusing him of abandoning the East End. Attlee's response was firm: 'I am not prepared to take my orders from any superman, or from people I do not know, or people from abroad – Russia, Europe, France, or Italy.' Yet he was an internationalist and an advocate of the League of Nations.

Churchill spent the night of the election in No. 10 with Baldwin. Tom Jones, the Deputy Secretary to the Cabinet, wrote that Churchill 'became more and more flushed with anger' as news of more and more Labour gains came in on the ticker-tape machine. He looked as if he were going to smash the machine. Ramsay MacDonald's Labour Party captured 287 seats, while the Tories took 260. The Liberals won fifty-nine seats and thus held the balance of power. MacDonald returned to Downing Street, but his would be a forlorn triumph if the Labour Party could not deal with the worsening global economic situation. Chronic unemployment and hyperinflation had triggered an economic crisis in Germany, and as a result, Hitler was becoming a major political figure.

America was not immune from economic woes. By 1929, Wall Street had become the greatest bubble in stock market history, with radio stocks leading the way. The economist John Kenneth Galbraith blamed the bubble on the practice of buying on the margin. Investors only had to pay 10 per cent of the cost of a share, which they could then sell at the full price when it rose in value, and pocket the profit. Banks loaned investors the remaining 90 per cent. When stocks rose, margin-buying was good news for investors, but when share prices fell, the practice proved ruinous. Banks called in the loans, but investors could not repay them, and the market plunged further. In the space of just two days, in October 1929, shares shed a quarter of their value.

Dozens of bankrupt speculators were jumping off skyscrapers in New York, newspapers claimed. This was actually a myth, Galbraith discovered; very few people plunged to their deaths. But Galbraith made much of the 'psychic wealth' that had been lost. Churchill himself took a hit in the crash; he told friends his stock losses amounted to $50,000. American financier Bernard Baruch felt somewhat responsible; he had encouraged Churchill to invest in the stock market, even introducing him to his own brokers. In a gesture of both pity and guilt, he transferred $7,200 to Churchill's account: petty cash for Baruch; life-saving for Churchill.

After the election, MacDonald appointed Attlee as Under-Secretary of State for War, a position Attlee enjoyed and excelled at. A year later, after Oswald Mosley resigned, MacDonald promoted Attlee to be Chancellor of the Duchy of Lancaster, his first Cabinet post, and the office Churchill had been demoted to after the Gallipoli fiasco. Mosley was surprisingly complimentary about Attlee – they had played tennis together once – and judged that he had 'a clear, incisive and honest mind' before delivering a familiar uppercut: 'within the limits of his range'. In 1931, limited Attlee became Postmaster General, which made him responsible for the telephone service, and he did much to make it cheaper and more accessible. He felt that the telephone should not just be an instrument for the privileged.

The crash on Wall Street contributed to a worldwide depression. August 1931 saw financial panic and a run on the pound. MacDonald and his Chancellor, Philip Snowden, were prepared to implement the May Report, which had recommended heavy cuts in unemployment benefits. But most of the Cabinet rejected the idea, so MacDonald sprang a surprise on 24 August. Attlee and other Labour MPs were summoned to No. 10, where MacDonald announced that he intended to form a National Government with the Conservatives and Liberals. The economic crisis demanded a coalition, MacDonald insisted. He persuaded three senior Labour politicians – Chancellor Philip Snowden, Secretary of State for the Dominions Jimmy Thomas, and Lord Chancellor John Sankey – to join him.

For Attlee, joining the National Government would have been a betrayal of the Labour movement. He was offended by the proposal and commented, after making sure that MacDonald was within earshot, on how 'Esau sold his inheritance for a few pieces of silver.' Attlee then appealed to MPs who had fought in the war; they knew that 'there [was] only one occasion when a soldier [was] justified in disobeying orders. That [was] when his senior officer goes over to the enemy.' MacDonald was a deluded snob who

> had for some time been more and more attracted by the social environment of the well-to-do classes. He had got more and more out of touch with the rank and file of the party, while the adulation which is almost inseparable from the necessary publicity given to the leader of a great movement had gone to his head and increased his natural vanity.

On 28 August, Arthur Henderson replaced MacDonald as leader of the Labour Party. Attlee wrote to his brother Tom, telling him that 'things are pretty damnable – I fear we are in for a regime of fake economy and a general attack on the workers' standard of life'.

Churchill found the moment damnable, too. Though Churchill had been Home Secretary and Chancellor, MacDonald did not offer him a post in the new National Government. This was the first of many disappointments and rejections that Churchill suffered in the 1930s.

Attlee described the 1931 election that followed MacDonald's decision as the most 'unscrupulous' he could remember. The Liberals and Tories claimed that Britain risked economic chaos like Germany. They even claimed that the Labour government had raided the Post Office

Savings Bank, which Attlee was responsible for as Postmaster General, to pay money into the unemployment fund. When he saw that Labour had been defeated in the working-class stronghold of St Helens, Attlee grew worried and, when he went to his count, he 'was very doubtful as to the result'. He was right to harbour doubts. He scraped in by a mere 551 votes, by far his lowest ever majority in Limehouse.

Attlee was just one of fifty-two Labour members in the new parliament. Apart from him, only two other Labour men who had held ministerial office survived – the pacifist George Lansbury and Stafford Cripps. The three men reflected Britain's class divisions – Lansbury was working class, Attlee middle class and Cripps was the son of Lord Parmoor. One other survivor was the young Aneurin Bevan, later to become famous as the architect of the National Health Service, who held his seat at Ebbw Vale.

Though he had had lost his seat, Arthur Henderson remained leader of the Labour Party. He now told Attlee that Lansbury would become leader of the parliamentary party and Attlee would serve as his deputy. Their nominations were not opposed. When Parliament reconvened, Churchill confided to Attlee that he had 'seldom been so nervous about the state of British democracy'. They would both grow even more nervous during the 1930s, the poet W. H. Auden's 'low dishonest decade'. Even Baldwin was concerned by the immense majority the National Government had won. It captured 90 per cent of the vote and a total of 554 seats, with 470 of these seats won by Baldwin's Conservative Party.

Decimated in numbers, Labour needed a good operator in the House to enable the party to make any impact. Attlee described Lansbury as 'by nature an evangelist rather than a parliamentary tactician'. That gave Attlee the sort of opportunity to shine that he had never had before, and he seized it with both hands. He worked long hours, speaking on many different topics and, as Deputy Leader of the Parliamentary Labour Party, he joined the Privy Council. He made forty-six speeches in 1933, seventy-eight the year after and ninety in 1935: a phenomenal work rate.

Attlee needed all his calm, and much resilience. His friend Jack Lawson said that when he was standing at the dispatch box, Attlee 'must have felt submerged' as he had to speak on so many issues, 'but he showed no signs of it'. He spoke on foreign affairs and defence, but it was the economy that concerned him most. When he attacked the new National Government, he stressed the need to fight unemployment, a topic on which the government stayed silent. Attlee told his brother Tom that he thought Labour had 'put up a fair show on the address'. Attlee also had to cope with domestic problems. Violet had become depressed again, so he was under great pressure both at home and at work.

The contrast between Attlee and Churchill's fortunes is striking. Though Labour had lost badly, 1931 was the year when Attlee had the opportunity to develop the skills that made him such a formidable politician; 'the firmest of the lot', as Attlee's friend Lord Taylor put it in his memoirs. For Churchill, it was the year when his exile in the political wilderness began in earnest. As so often when he seemed to have reached a dead end politically, Churchill turned to writing, and his writing in turn demanded that he travel. In August and September 1932, he was in southern Germany, visiting the battlefield at Blenheim as part of his research for a biography of the 1st Duke of Marlborough. It nearly led to a meeting which might have been historic.

After Blenheim, Churchill went to Munich and met a man who knew Hitler quite well, Ernst 'Putzi' Hanfstaengl. The two politicians should meet, Hanfstaengl suggested. Churchill agreed, commenting later that he had 'no national prejudices against Hitler at that time. I knew little of

Hitler or his doctrine or record and nothing of his character.' Churchill asked about Hitler's attitude to Jews: 'What is the sense of being against a man simply because of his birth?' Hanfstaengl reported these remarks to Hitler, who then decided not to meet Churchill.

When Churchill returned to London, he wrote articles for the *Daily Mail*, pointing out the dangers of aerial bombardment by the rapidly expanding German air force, the Luftwaffe; Churchill wanted Britain's Royal Air Force to match the Luftwaffe's growth. Air power would be an issue for him for the rest of the decade.

In October 1932, Arthur Henderson resigned as Labour's leader and Lansbury succeeded him. Attlee now became the deputy leader of the party, again with no election. When he paid tribute after Attlee's death in 1967, Harold Macmillan recalled how Churchill had once told him that politics was not like a race on the flat, but more like a steeplechase. 'You never know at what fence a horse may stumble or a jockey fall. This is of course what makes [politics] so fascinating.' Attlee was the horse who had somehow survived Labour's catastrophic defeat and had even achieved promotion because of it.

On 23 November 1932, Churchill spoke on the loyal address, the debate after the speech in which the monarch outlines the government's policies for a new session of Parliament; he made no mention of the economic problems Attlee concentrated on. Churchill argued that the hopes once invested in the League of Nations were illusory, and warned that 'sturdy Teutonic youths marching with the light in their eyes of desire to suffer for their Fatherland' were not looking for status, a fine-fangled socio-logical concept, but 'looking for weapons'. Once they were armed they would 'ask for the restoration of lost territories', Churchill warned. One legacy bequeathed by the Versailles Treaty was fear; 'Britain's period of weakness is Europe's period of danger,' Churchill said. He recalled a grim statistic. In the First World War, it had required 'two to three Allied lives to take one German life'. Having previously ridiculed Mac-Donald as a sheep in sheep's clothing, Churchill now went further by mocking the Labour leader: 'I will go tiger hunting with you, my friend, on the one condition that you leave your rifle at home.' The defenceless hunters would probably end up as lunch – for the tiger.

When Attlee rose to speak, two days later, he again stressed the economic problems more than the Nazi threat. He was by now a sharp debater. When a Tory MP claimed that Attlee and the socialists thought they were the only people to sympathise with the downtrodden, Attlee snapped, 'I said nothing of the sort.' It was a phrase he would use a number of times over the next few years.

The apparently unstoppable rise of Hitler inspired two classic satires: Bertolt Brecht's *The Resistible Rise of Arturo Ui* and Charlie Chaplin's *The Great Dictator*. Both assumed that Hitler was a pawn of German industrialists and the army. Berlin journalist Rudolf Olden even wrote a book titled *Hitler the Pawn*. An American journalist, Dorothy Thompson, interviewed the new Chancellor. 'When I walked into Adolf Hitler's salon, I was convinced that I was meeting the future dictator of Germany,' she commented. Yet Hitler seemed so 'inconsequent ... and insecure', she went on, before weaving in Nietzsche's 'he is the very prototype of the Little Man.' But great dictators tend to resent being called little men. When Thompson returned to Germany, a few months later, Hitler had her thrown out of the country.

Hitler made clever use of people's memories of the horrors of the First World War. Those memories made pacifism not just respectable, but popular all over Europe. Attlee's attitude to pacifism was not a simple one. Unlike the appeasers, he never played down the dangers of Nazism, an ideology he loathed for much the same reasons as Churchill.

Attlee hoped, though, that there would be a saner way of dealing with conflict, through the League of Nations.

MacDonald had not offered any office to either Lloyd George or Churchill. Attlee wrote that the government might falter and 'as we get deeper into the mire' the two men might join the National Government. But Churchill had no such immediate hopes of a Cabinet post. In December 1931, he went to America on a lecture tour, which became peppered with incidents. He took a cab to Bernard Baruch's house on New York City's Upper East Side, assuming that his financier friend was so famous that any driver would know where he lived. This particular cabbie did not. Annoyed, Churchill climbed out of the cab, stalked across 5th Avenue and was very nearly 'squashed like a gooseberry'. If the military alter ego always lurked in Attlee, then the journalist alter ego was never far from Churchill. He turned his close encounter with death into copy for the *Daily Mail*.

In England we frequently cross roads along which fast traffic is moving in both directions. I did not think the task I set myself now either difficult or rash. But at this moment habit played me a deadly trick. I no sooner got out of the cab somewhere about the middle of the road and told the driver to wait than I instinctively turned my eyes to the left. About 200 yards away were the yellow headlights of an approaching car. I thought I had just time to cross the road before it arrived; and I started to do so in the prepossession – wholly unwarranted – that my only dangers were from the left.

Churchill was taken to Lenox Hill Hospital, where he identified himself as 'Winston Churchill, a British Statesman'. He had a deep gash to the head, a fractured nose, fractured ribs, and was suffering from severe shock. A further shock was Prohibition. Lenox Hill's admitting physician took pity on him, and just as Attlee had persuaded his surgeon in 1918 to sign a letter of discharge, Churchill now persuaded his doctor to issue the following declaration:

> This is to certify that the post-accident convalescence of the Hon. Winston S. Churchill necessitates the use of alcoholic spirits especially at meal times. The quantity is naturally indefinite but the minimum requirements would be 250 cubic centimetres.

When he was well enough to leave, Churchill and his family went to the Bahamas for a holiday. Being a British colony, Bahamas had not inflicted Prohibition on its residents. The accident had forced Churchill to cancel lecture dates, which he could ill afford to do. As so often, though, he bounced back. Six weeks after nearly being squashed like a gooseberry, he was lecturing again.

For the next eight years, both Attlee and Churchill were out of office and on different sides on many crucial issues. It took a long time for Attlee, who had joined the No More War movement, to accept that Britain needed to rearm and prepare for another war. The likelihood of the two men working well together would have seemed remote indeed.

CHAPTER 7

NO PEACE IN OUR TIME, 1931–1939

The dynamics that make for good collaboration have been studied in personal relationships and in business – mainly. Shared history, shared values and shared purposes make it easier to work together well. Churchill and Attlee shared few of these things in 1932. Over the next eight years, they would find themselves on opposite sides on many issues, including the Spanish Civil War, the abdication crisis and the future of India.

On one subject, however, Attlee's views changed, if only gradually. As the Nazi threat became harder to ignore, and as it became obvious that the League of Nations was ineffectual, Major Attlee ironed his uniform again, as it were. He was helped into it by the trade unions and by two union leaders in particular: Walter Citrine and Ernest Bevin. Citrine had worked as an electrician after leaving school at the age of twelve, while Bevin worked as a labourer before becoming a lorry driver in Bristol, where he joined the Bristol Socialist Society. Intelligent and energetic, by the time he was thirty Bevin had become secretary of the local branch of the Dock, Wharf, Riverside and General Labourers Union. In 1914, he became a national organiser for the union.

Bevin and Citrine both thought that Lansbury gloried too much in his image of himself as a Christian socialist, but he was not so out of touch with public opinion. As much as did the left of British society, the right did not want to fight either. The appeasers included many members of the House of Lords, numerous ministers, a small group of Labour MPs and three Prime Ministers: MacDonald, Baldwin and Lloyd George, the hero of the Great War.

Attlee continued to hope that the League of Nations would make war an obscenity of the past. In 1932, it commissioned Einstein and Freud to collaborate on a long paper, *Why War?*, and hoped that the great physicist and the eminent psychologist might solve the problem. In the previous fifty years, human beings had learned to fly, laid telephone cables across oceans, invented the automobile and radio, made films, reached the South Pole, revolutionised physics, improved medicine, and manufactured new weapons to kill each other more efficiently. Surely such a creative species might also learn to live in peace? Freud was not encouraging, however. Violence came naturally to human beings. To become less aggressive, they would need to change their basic natures; if there were one truly peaceable people living on the Earth, Freud would like their address.

The fact that humans could not master their aggressive instincts did not, however, stop them longing for peace; no one more so than George Lansbury, one of the most lovable men ever to have entered Parliament, according to the historian A. J. P. Taylor. Lansbury was lovable, but otherworldly too; for him virtue was more important than victory. Under his influence, the Labour Party's 1933 conference passed resolutions calling for the 'total disarmament of all nations'. If other nations did not follow the example, it made no difference. Labour would never fight. On 9 February 1933, the Oxford Union voted by 275 to 153 in favour of the motion that it would 'in no circumstances fight for its King and Country'. Six months later, a Labour pacifist won the Fulham East by-election. In an interview for *The Star*, Lansbury sent a triumphant message to the constituency: 'I would close every recruiting station, disband the army and disarm the air force. I would abolish the whole dreadful equipment of war and say to the world: "Do your worst."' A week later, Churchill, addressing the Anti-Socialist and Anti-Communist Union, denounced this 'abject, squalid, shameless avowal'. Churchill still had a reputation as being a war lover, though, which made it easier for people to dismiss his warnings as exaggerated.

Lansbury has been unfairly treated, according to the late Bob Holman, a professor at the University of Bath as well as a Christian socialist. Holman, who wrote a fine biography of Lansbury, *Good Old George*, told me that although he believed Lansbury was a wise man, he also viewed him as having been impossibly idealistic. Attlee did not think that such idealism made Lansbury ineffective, however. Attlee's biographer, John Bew, argues that 'the work of Attlee and Lansbury is more important to the course of 1930s British history than is recognised'. For Attlee, Hitler's success showed that if capitalism did not reform, Western civilisation would crumble 'before the irresistible rush of the discontented'.

In 1933, Hitler played the role of discontented victim to perfection. Versailles had ruined Germany, he ranted to rapturous applause. The country would be justified in rearming. Churchill's intuition told him that Hitler was a manipulator and loved being a manipulator: the jackboot was Hitler's joy, violence his drug of choice. But few others realised this at the time. Roy Jenkins called Churchill 'an early alarm clock'.

Hitler did not wait long to show his hand. The burning of the Reichstag on 27 February 1933, with communist agitators blamed for the arson, was a mere prelude. It was followed, on 6 May, by an attack on Magnus

Hirschfeld's *Institute of Sex Research*. This was not an unthinking act of aggression. The Nazi hierarchy suspected that some of their colleagues had homosexual tendencies, so they were eager to destroy files which might contain damaging information. The Nazis denounced psychotherapy as a Jewish perversion, but many of them actually had personal experience of it. Hermann Göring's cousin, Matthias, was a competent psychoanalyst, although he refused to treat Jews because he claimed they were so different. He also objected to his patients lying on the couch, as he believed that healer and patient should face each other like men, as it were. Göring himself had had psychiatric treatment. Edmund Forster, the psychiatrist, who helped Hitler return to the front in 1918, was murdered not long after the Nazis seized power. Forster's death was made to look like suicide and all his papers were destroyed. No hint that the Führer had ever needed therapy could be allowed to survive.

On 10 May, Nazi students, the 'Teutonic youths' Churchill had warned of a few months earlier, burned 25,000 'un-German' books outside the State Opera in Berlin. Nazi propaganda minister Joseph Goebbels told the crowd: 'No to decadence and moral corruption! Yes to decency and morality in family and state!' Then he flung books by Stefan Zweig, Erich Kästner, Freud and many others into the flames. 'And thus you do well in this midnight hour to commit to the flames the evil spirit of the past,' Goebbels shouted.

The book-burning made headlines all over the world, but many influential Britons shrugged it off, just as they had the fire at the Reichstag. If the Nazis loved a good bonfire, let them have as many as they liked. In August 1933, the influential General Sir Maurice Hankey visited Germany on an informal fact-finding mission. He returned with a riddle:

Are we still dealing with the Hitler of *Mein Kampf*, lulling his opponents to sleep with fair words to gain time to arm his people, and looking always to the day when he can throw off the mask and attack Poland? Or is it a new Hitler, who discovered the burden of responsible office, and wants to extricate himself, like many an earlier tyrant from the commitments of his irresponsible days? That is the riddle that has to be solved.

Hankey was not too much bothered by the arrests, imprisonments without trial and murders committed at Hitler's behest. Churchill did not believe there was any riddle, however. Hitler was a tyrant who would stop at nothing.

Attlee used the book-burning to attack MacDonald as much as Hitler, and said,

> There has been a deliberate attempt made to suggest that after all there are no real political differences in this country, and everybody is really in agreement. The increasing danger of the international situation affords an opportunity for pressing this point. The speeches of Mr Ramsay MacDonald are full of fascist ideas and even fascist phraseology. The essentials of the corporate state without any coloured shirts might be introduced in this country in a period of international tension.

Writing poetry was not the only surprising aspect of Attlee's character. In 1933, he wrote a satire on the upwardly mobile Bullions, who were the MacDonalds in very thin disguise. The Bullions rise from the street of Scarcity to Abundance Avenue, where their selfishness causes problems, both intentionally and unintentionally. The head of the family, Ramsay Bullion, prides himself on being a 'cultured Christian gentleman' and always starts meetings by preaching moral fervour. Austerity is his lifeblood. The children, who represent the people, must not be spoilt, so Ramsay is adamant they only need two shillings a week to survive. His wife comes from the Neville Tories, a dig at Neville Chamberlain, and is even meaner. The children only get pocket money after they have been means tested.

The Bullions are plagued by poor relatives who want a handout. Mrs Bullion realises that her family is the only one that can afford to buy from the butcher, and tells him to increase his prices, so that his shop can survive. Believing herself to be a decent woman, she also offers to buy more meat than she and her family need. Different classes deserve different cuts of meat. The rich chomp on the choicest cuts, while the poor must settle for gristle.

The Bullions' neighbours are a problem since there has been a fire in their house, a reference to the Reichstag blaze, and many people think a Mr Göring is to blame. But he escapes prosecution. Attlee also has fun with the Bullions' policy on the unlikely subject of plums. They offer to stop growing plums that are more than three inches in diameter, in order not to upset the neighbours. Foreigners are a continual problem as they are irrational and violent; they are also acrobatic. A Mr Yen, presumably Japanese, stabs a Mr Tael, presumably Chinese, while picking his pockets.

The Bullions have two cars and a chauffeur called Monty Norman, a less than subtle dig at Montagu Norman, still the Governor of the Bank of England. One day the car, a model called Bank Charter, will not start until it is greased with the oil of Private Profit. When they run out of Private Profit, the Bullions resort to a donkey called Barter for Transport. Barter, much like Boxer in Orwell's *Animal Farm*, represents the loyal working class, who are always willing to bear the load. Attlee's last line is pessimistic: 'The result of the game was the same. All the players lost.' Attlee did not publish this engaging work during his lifetime.

The depression was ravaging the United States, leading Hitler to think that there was a possibility of winning support there. His deputy, Rudolph Hess, gave Heinz Spanknöbel the authority to form the Friends of New Germany, which was known by the ridiculous name of the FONG. But the FONG had few fangs, even though its members trained in camps and wore uniforms: a white shirt and black trousers, and a black hat festooned with a red symbol. P. G. Wodehouse satirised British Union of Fascists leader Oswald Mosley, turning him into the bullying buffoon Roderick Spode, and branding his supporters 'black shorts' rather than blackshirts. Spode is eventually ruined when Jeeves discovers he owns a shop selling lingerie, not a good side-line for any would-be dictator. Though he was living in America, Wodehouse ignored the FONG's considerable comic potential; the group even claimed that the long-dead President George Washington was apparently 'the first fascist'.

Churchill was far-sighted about the Nazis and, for the next six years, he kept a keen eye on the way Hitler was building up the German air force and navy. Admiral Erich Raeder, head of the German Navy, provided Hitler with a shopping list for the future: by 1948, Germany would need three aircraft carriers, eighteen cruisers, eight heavily armed cruisers, forty-eight destroyers and seventy-four U-boats. Hitler finally settled for a navy with a third of the tonnage of Britain's Royal Navy. He would be more ambitious when it came to aircraft.

Churchill paid great attention to the relative strengths of the British and German air forces. Air power was not simple to define, however. It was not clear if it was just a matter of numbers. How did one calculate the worth of a bomber against a fighter plane, a model with the latest technology against one that was five years old?

Churchill could be specific about German military developments because he was being briefed by Ralph Wigram, the head of the Central Department in the Foreign Office. Wigram was also far-sighted. In a memo of November 1934, he warned that Germany would absorb Austria and dominate central Europe. MacDonald ignored the warnings and Chamberlain told the Cabinet that such alarmist reports were exaggerated. He himself was rather vague, though. When comparing air forces, he suggested that one could ignore the numbers of planes each country had and focus instead on 'air power', a term which he never defined precisely and which, as suggested, it was hard to be specific about.

While Churchill had become an outsider, Attlee was becoming an insider. As deputy leader of the Labour Party, he sat on the Committee of Privileges, 'a very elder statesman position,' he told his brother Tom. He would soon find himself almost sitting in judgment on Churchill in a row about evidence given to the Joint Select Committee on India, a country that Attlee knew well, though his views on the British Empire were far less rose-tinted than Churchill's. 'The history of colonial expansion is a terrible record of cruelty to, and exploitation of, backward peoples by the advanced races. Great Britain must take her full share of blame,' Attlee wrote.

On 16 April, Churchill accused Samuel Hoare, the Secretary for India, of putting pressure on the Manchester Chamber of Commerce to modify their evidence to the committee. Manchester was a centre of the textile business, and could suffer if a change in the status of India allowed Indian politicians to impose tariffs on cotton. The Chamber, however, did not insist on protecting Manchester. Churchill wanted the question of whether Hoare had bullied the Chamber referred to the Committee of Privileges. Attlee saw Churchill at his worst as Winston bombarded members of the committee with claims that Hoare had behaved improperly. Unanimously, though, the committee ruled that there had been no breach of any privileges.

'Winston was a complete failure,' Attlee reported, and told him so to his face. He also wrote to his brother Tom, telling him that 'Winston made an awful bloomer. He was severely castigated in the House by Lloyd George. He takes things very badly. I thought one moment that he was going to burst into tears. His stock is much down just now.'

A month later, however, Churchill was more effective when he compared London to a fat, valuable cow which offered the greatest target in the world. 'The flying peril is not a peril from which one can flee,' he argued. There was no point in planning to move people or factories because German aircraft had a long range. In November, Churchill made a similar speech and sat down to almost an ovation. Critically, Churchill got the government to undertake not to let the strength of the RAF fall below that of the Luftwaffe. But Labour still voted against any increase in its strength, and Baldwin hesitated to honour the pledge.

June 1934 saw two ominous developments, which nudged Attlee towards a less pacifist position. Oswald Mosley had resigned from the Labour Party and founded the British Union of Fascists. His blackshirts held several meetings at the Albert Hall, and then one at Olympia on 14 June, which ended in a riot. In the parliamentary debate that followed, Attlee referred to the riots of 1884 in Birmingham, which had been partly provoked by a speech Churchill's father had made.

Churchill approved of Attlee's speech, it seems. 'People who have studied Sir Oswald Mosley's career know that there is a certain megalomania about him,' Attlee said. 'I think there is a streak of cruelty in his character, and I doubt whether he is mentally entirely stable.' Mosley was 'backed by big money power', Attlee added, revealing that he had been threatened himself, 'because I have protested against the treatment of Jews in Germany'.

Hitler was not just targeting the Jews. Two weeks after the Olympia riots in Britain, he ordered the murders of hundreds of Nazis who had once been some of his fiercest supporters, but who Hitler now feared might become his political enemies. The victims, on what became known as the Night of the Long Knives, included the leader of the Nazi brownshirts, Ernst Röhm, Hitler's loyal ally since 1923. Once again, though, the reaction in Britain was muted.

On 28 November 1934, Churchill told the House of Commons that Germany had an air force that was already larger than Britain's, and that the Luftwaffe would be nearly double the size of the RAF by 1937. Baldwin realised how well briefed Churchill was and pledged to keep up with Germany in terms of military spending. Five months later, a Defence White Paper outlined plans to spend an extra £10 million on the RAF in the coming year. Hitler did not approve and cancelled a planned visit to Germany by Britain's Foreign Secretary, Sir John Simon.

Attlee was still not willing to take up arms, however. On 11 March 1935, he attacked the proposed £10 million increase in defence spending as 'nationalist and imperialist'. Yet again he called for a new world policy and 'the abolition of national armaments'. The next day, Hitler introduced compulsory military service in Germany. Churchill wrote to his wife, telling her that 'all the frightened nations were at last beginning to huddle together … There is safety in numbers.' If war broke out again, it would be 'the end of the world. How I hope and pray we may be spared such senseless horrors.'

On 5 April, the Air Ministry gave precise numbers – Britain had 453 frontline aircraft compared to a German minimum of 690. Four days later, the precise numbers turned out to have been imprecise. The British ambassador to Germany, Sir Eric Phipps, reported to the Foreign Office that Germany could muster 800 to 850 frontline planes. By passing such confidential information to Churchill, Ralph Wigram was risking his career and possibly his own safety. On 16 April, he wrote to Churchill to say that he could no longer visit him at Chartwell.

Armed with knowledge of the Foreign Office figures, Churchill sent a memorandum to Baldwin. It was not enough to promise parity with Germany in the future. More planes must be built immediately, Churchill insisted. 'Never must we despair, never must we give in, but we must face facts and draw true conclusions from them.'

MacDonald fell ill and his speeches in the House became incoherent. One observer noted how 'things … got to the stage where nobody knew what the Prime Minister was going to say in the House of Commons, and, when he did say it, nobody understood it'. Then Lansbury fractured his thigh, so Attlee became the acting leader of the Labour Party – once again without the inconvenience of a contest.

Churchill and Attlee were not totally obsessed with politics, which may have helped both of them to stay healthy. Not content with writing and painting, Churchill also learned the skill of bricklaying, something he found repetitive and calming; he even insisted on joining the union of bricklayers. If the idea of Churchill as a brickie Rembrandt seems improbable, that of Attlee as a British Cecil B. DeMille seems an even more unlikely one. In October 1934, Attlee drafted an idea for a film. His outline read, 'War fomented by rival armaments who own the Press of two governments.' The script was melodramatic: the son of one arms dealer sees his wife and children killed; his father repents and reveals details of the conspiracy to the *Daily Herald*, just in time to swing the general election. The 'good guys' win and create something that Attlee had long dreamed of – an international utopia. It was not an original dream, of course; author H. G. Wells had dreamed about it long before.

After George Lansbury's thigh had healed, he resumed his role as

Labour's leader and continued to preach the virtues of total disarmament. Walter Citrine, General Secretary of the Trades Union Congress, commented how Lansbury 'thinks the country should be without defence of any kind ... it certainly isn't our policy'. Ernest Bevin, who had amalgamated many smaller unions to form the huge Transport and General Workers Union, had no time for pacifism either. Hugh Dalton, who had become Labour's spokesman on foreign affairs, was also willing to consider rearmament. These were persuasive voices, but Attlee had always argued that the Labour leadership should listen to the rank and file, which was far from ready to fight. He wrote,

> I am not prepared to arrogate to myself a superiority to the rest of the movement. I am prepared to submit to their will, even if I disagree. I shall do all I can to get my views accepted, but, unless acquiescence in the views of the majority conflicts with my conscience, I shall fall into line, for I have faith in the wisdom of the rank and file.

The important thing to note here is that, although Attlee said he was prepared to accept the opinion of the rank and file, he would only do so if this did not conflict with his conscience. Walter Citrine and Ernest Bevin, key leaders of the rank and file, began to argue that Britain must be realistic and rearm. Their support, and that of Dalton, made it easier for Attlee to voice his doubts about appeasement with growing confidence, a development that Churchill noticed.

In May 1935, Hitler offered to outlaw all bombing from the air if other European powers would do the same. Both Foreign Affairs Minister Anthony Eden and Attlee welcomed the proposal. On 31 May, however, Churchill warned the House of Commons: 'Do not close your eyes to the fact that we are entering a corridor of deepening and darkening danger.' Furthermore, Britain would have to pass through that corridor for months and possibly for years to come.

A week later, on 7 June, with MacDonald too ill to continue in his post, Stanley Baldwin became Prime Minister. Churchill hoped to be recalled to the government, but Baldwin did not offer him anything, throwing Churchill into a depression.

Labour's 1935 annual conference took place as the Italian dictator, Benito Mussolini, was preparing to launch an invasion of Abyssinia. Bevin attacked Lansbury for putting his private beliefs before party policy, and accused him of 'hawking your conscience round from body to body asking to be told what to do with it'. It was clear that a Christian pacifist could no longer lead the party; Lansbury resigned a few days later.

When Mussolini ordered 400,000 troops into Abyssinia in October, the League of Nations condemned Italy's aggression and imposed economic sanctions. But these proved to be no more effective than they have been ever since, and for much the same reasons; countries were happy to go along with the sanctions only if they did not harm their own trade. For all of the League's fine words, oil and petrol were still bought and sold; Italian ships could still use the Suez Canal.

Attlee commented wryly on Churchill's views about Abyssinia: 'As an old imperialist, I don't think Churchill much objected to a backward country being taken over by Italy.' Attlee added that 'the battle of Abyssinia had been lost on the playing fields of Harrow.' It was a witty twist on the claim that the Battle of Waterloo was won on the playing fields of Eton.

The 1935 general election saw a revival in Labour's fortunes as they won 154 seats. Churchill got a telegram of congratulations from Baldwin, but no offer of any office. Three times now, a government had been formed in which he had no place. He left for the Riviera to paint, recover and, perhaps, to sulk a little in the sun.

Lansbury had resigned, so the Labour Party needed to choose a new leader. This time Attlee did have to endure the indignity of a contest. He stood against Herbert Morrison and Arthur Greenwood. Greenwood came third in the first ballot and dropped out. In the second ballot, Attlee won by eighty-eight votes to Morrison's forty-four. Morrison huffily rejected the role of deputy leader; he claimed that the Freemasons in Labour's ranks, who had initially supported Greenwood, had then switched their votes to Attlee.

The editor of *The Times* again was not impressed by Attlee's triumph, commenting that 'he is worthy but limited.' Limited Clem again. In his biography of Hugh Dalton, Ben Pimlott claims that Attlee was little more than a figurehead, a leader often in danger of being deposed. But the figurehead would remain leader of the Labour Party for the next twenty years. Attlee may not have been considered a starter, but he was a sticker.

In his first speech after Parliament had reconvened, Attlee again urged the government to support the League of Nations as a way of dealing with Mussolini's aggression. Labour continued to press for total disarmament because 'we recognise that war no longer is, if it ever was, the sport of kings,' Attlee said. Nevertheless, he did something that Lansbury would never have done and organised a defence committee. He also arranged meetings with senior military men to keep his MPs briefed on developments in the armed forces.

One of the oddly influential events of the mid-1930s was the Peace Ballot, possibly the only major development in world politics to start in Ilford, where the League of Nations Union had a local branch. The Union was not the same as the League of Nations, which was an international forum. The Union had been formed in 1918 to support human rights cases and the peaceful resolution of conflicts. In 1934, the Ilford branch joined forces with the local newspaper, the *Ilford Recorder*, to organise a local referendum, asking for people's views about the League and disarmament. The turnout for the referendum was higher than that in local elections, and people voted overwhelmingly in favour of the League. The leaders of the League of Nations Union thought it would be worth holding a national ballot on similar lines. They received the enthusiastic backing of many politicians and clergy. One of the organisers was Lord Robert Cecil, a reform-minded Tory who had been a minister in various governments. He was also one of the advocates of the original League of Nations. He recalled in his autobiography,

> The most common criticism of the whole enterprise was that those who voted did so without thinking. I can only say that my small personal experience in canvassing was quite inconsistent with this view. Those I asked were usually much interested. They read the questions carefully and gave their answers in writing. In a certain number of cases, qualifications were added to a negative or affirmative answer.

The organisers had hoped for a turnout of some five million. In the event, more than 11.5 million people voted. Astonishingly, it was then believed that voters could handle five questions, rather than a basic Yes or No.

> The first question was: Should Great Britain remain a Member of the League of Nations? The results were emphatic – Yes: 11,090,387. No: 355,883.

> The second question was: Are you in favour of all-round reduction of armaments by international agreement? Yes: 10,470,489. No: 862,775.

The third question was: Are you in favour of an all-round abolition of national military and naval aircraft by international agreement? Yes: 9,533,558. No: 1,689,786.

The fourth question was: Should the manufacture and sale of armaments for private profit be prohibited by international agreement? Yes: 10,417,329. No: 775,415.

The last question was: Do you consider that, if a nation insists on attacking another, the other nations should combine to compel it to stop by economic and non-military measures? Yes: 10,027,608. No: 635,074. (b) if necessary, military measures? Yes: 6,784,368. No: 2,351,981

The ballot had not asked, however, whether Britain should fight alone in any circumstances, a serious omission. Lord Robert Cecil said that Baldwin told him the ballot had been 'of very great value'. Cecil was sure that it influenced the government's policy, 'but not permanently or, from my point of view, sufficiently'.

Baldwin could not ignore the fact that eleven million voters wanted peace. His local and favourite newspaper, the *Birmingham Post*, pointed out that 'the answers given to questions 5a and 5b are most significant. Peace-loving as this nation is, it still believes in a need to resort to arms.' But the Peace Ballot had only asked if Britain would resort to taking up arms with other countries; it had not asked if Britain should rearm urgently so that it could fight the Nazis alone if necessary. Ten million voters had supported economic sanctions, but that would mean blockading German ports. Baldwin was not prepared to do that until he knew what American policy was likely to be. The ballot confirmed Baldwin in his foreign policy, which was cautious, but not totally supine.

Baldwin encouraged official and unofficial emissaries to explore avenues which might defuse the risks of war. On 13 February 1936, Ralph Wigram, the head of the Central Department at the Foreign Office, met Prince Bismarck at the German embassy in London. The British government, Wigram said, wanted to agree the air pact that would outlaw bombing. In return, Britain would consider revising the Treaty of Versailles and giving Hitler some concessions.

Churchill's sense of 'feel', that quality Keynes said he never had while at the Treasury, was proved right when it came to Hitler. Three weeks after Wigram had made emollient noises, Hitler ordered troops into the Rhineland in breach of both the Treaty of Versailles and the 1925 Treaty of Locarno. Hitler could have been stopped, Churchill wrote later. The French had far more troops, but did nothing. The uncontested takeover of the Rhineland had a psychological effect on the German military. The Little Corporal had shown that he possessed daring, vision, and that all-important quality that Napoleon wanted in his generals: luck.

On 12 March, five days after Hitler's troops had marched into the Rhineland, Baldwin announced, not a new Minister of Defence or Supply, which Churchill had been urging, but a Minister for the Coordination of Defence. Baldwin gave the job to his Attorney General, Thomas Inskip, who knew nothing about the military. Inskip's appointment was a rebuff to Churchill and had an electrifying effect. Churchill had carefully been avoiding criticising the government because he hoped to be recalled to office. He said later that Baldwin 'thought no doubt that he had dealt me a politically fatal stroke, and I felt he might well be right'. The day after Baldwin had ignored him by appointing Inskip, Churchill began a series of fortnightly articles for the *Evening Standard*. These were not wholly belligerent, however. In the first article, Churchill renewed his call for League of Nations action, which Attlee had also always urged.

MacDonald said that he was glad the Rhineland had been remilitarised, and more surprisingly, Lloyd George travelled to Germany to meet Hitler. Ivan Maisky, the Russian ambassador to London since 1932, tried to dissuade Lloyd George, but failed. 'Germany', Lloyd George said, 'does not want war, but she is afraid of an attack by Russia, and is suspicious of the Franco-Russian Pact. I have never seen a happier people than the Germans, and Hitler is one of the greatest of the many great men I have met.' He was not too bothered that the attitude of many Germans to Hitler

> amounts almost to worship. I have never seen anything like it. Some men I met, who are not Nazis, told me that they did not know what the country would have done without him. They are inclined to blame Hitler's supporters for some of the things which they do not approve, but there is no whisper of criticism of Hitler. It is just like our motto, 'The King can do no wrong.'

Yes, Jews were persecuted, but they had also been persecuted in many other countries. The Germans were not unhappy about restrictions imposed by the Nazis because they were 'a highly disciplined people'.

Germany wanted to 'remain on terms of closest friendship with Great Britain', Lloyd George said. 'I found that among everyone I met, from Hitler down to the working men with whom I spoke. Everywhere Britain is held in deepest respect, and there is a profound desire that the tragic circumstances of 1914 should never be repeated.'

It would be wrong to suggest that Lloyd George was uniquely stupid. Author George Orwell understood Hitler's emotional appeal. 'I should like to put it on record,' Orwell wrote, 'that I have never been able to dislike Hitler ... I have reflected that I would certainly kill him if I could get within reach of him, but that I could feel no personal animosity. The fact is that there is something deeply appealing about him.' Hitler was a figure of the 'pathetic, dog-like face, the face of a man suffering under intolerable wrongs', the wrongs of Versailles.

The year 1936 also saw the British monarchy faced with a crisis that found Churchill and Attlee on opposing sides. When George V died on 20 January, his eldest son, David, became King, but did not take the name George VI, because the relationship with his disapproving father had been so fraught. Instead, he chose the name Edward VIII. His assistant private secretary, Alan Lascelles, took the adage that no man is a hero to his valet to extremes, telling Baldwin, 'I can't help thinking that the best thing that could happen to him, and to the country, would be for him to break his neck.'

The new King wanted to marry the American socialite Wallis Simpson, who was divorcing her second husband. But Lascelles warned Edward that the British public would not tolerate a Queen who was 'a shop soiled American with two living husbands'.

As the King was the Supreme Head of the Church of England, which did not allow divorcees to remarry in church, his proposed marriage would trigger a constitutional crisis. In the 1530s, Henry VIII had had unsatisfactory wives executed, or in the case of Anne of Cleves, sent off to a luxury nunnery. In 1936, the King did not have those options.

Churchill had been friendly with the new King for decades, and his childhood had taught him that romantic passion could be overwhelming. Baldwin and Attlee, however, both disapproved of Edward, and regarded him as too flashy. For a year, the worried Prime Minister managed to keep the story of Edward and Wallis Simpson out of the British newspapers.

On 15 June, Baldwin lunched with King Carol II of Romania and his Foreign Minister Nicolae Titulescu. King Carol boasted that a true King had the freedom to do whatever he liked, just as he did in Romania. A few days later, Titulescu, when discussing the lunch with Hugh Dalton, explained he 'had seen a frightened look come into Baldwin's eyes. [Baldwin] had a sudden vision of what Edward might turn into when he was a few years older. Carol was rather like Edward. It was at my luncheon that Baldwin decided to get rid of Edward.'

Baldwin consulted Attlee who told him that the Labour Party, especially in the provinces, would never stand either for a divorced woman being Queen or for a morganatic marriage, where her children would not inherit the throne. Edward had 'no balance' and 'would not last the course', both men agreed. Baldwin also consulted the Prime Ministers of Australia, New Zealand and Canada, who were all hostile. Edward was given an ultimatum. He had to choose – his crown or his marriage.

Churchill supported the King and became slightly obsessed with the issue. On 3 December, he addressed a rearmaments meeting at the Albert Hall, which was chaired by the TUC's Walter Citrine. Churchill told Citrine that they needed to have a word about the King.

'What's that got to with this meeting?' Citrine asked.

'People will expect a statement from me,' Churchill replied.

'I don't see that at all,' Citrine said, closing the discussion. Churchill deferred to him and then addressed the meeting in 'the most masterly fashion', Citrine wrote. Churchill did manage one allusion to the royal scandal, however. He told the audience that when it came to the national anthem, 'I shall sing it with more heartfelt fervour than I have ever sung it in my life.'

On 4 December, Churchill dined alone with the King. A few days later, he sent him a jaunty letter, which promised 'no pistol to be held at the King's Head'. His Majesty should read George Bernard Shaw in the

Evening Standard, which had published a short play Shaw had dashed off. In *The Kingdom of the Half-Mad*, a King confronts the church and politicians in order to marry his twice-divorced American mistress. In Shaw's longer play, *The Apple Cart*, King Magnus faces opposition from his Prime Minister when he wants to marry his mistress. Magnus abdicates in favour of his son, but says he intends to run for election. The Prime Minister then agrees to the marriage because he recognises how popular the King is with the public.

When the crisis was finally reported in the British papers, Evelyn Waugh wrote that it 'delighted everyone' and improved the health of many old people as it gave them luscious tittle-tattle. Alice Keppel, Edward VII's mistress of nearly forty years earlier, wrote that her friend Lady Hamilton objected to Wallis Simpson's lack of class. Churchill may have had some sympathy for Mrs Simpson as well as for the King. She was American, as his own mother had been, and was also seductive.

Churchill was far from a lone voice in supporting the King. Many letters urged him to back Edward, including one which read, 'Vox Populi Vox Dei – and rub it in'; the voice of the King was the voice of the people. But on 8 December, when Churchill spoke in favour of the King in the House of Commons, MPs howled their disapproval. He was 'completely staggered by the unanimous hostility of the House', wrote his old Harrovian friend Leo Amery. In just a few minutes, any last hopes that Churchill had had of government office were dashed.

On 11 December, Edward VIII abdicated. His brother became King and had no difficulty in taking the name George VI. The abdication was a blessing as, once he had secured the throne, Edward VIII would probably have pressed his governments to please and appease Hitler.

Despite their differences over the abdication crisis, Attlee and Churchill both became involved in a pressure group. The Focus Group began as a cross-party luncheon club where key political issues of the day could be discussed. The Liberal Archibald Sinclair and Labour men Hugh Dalton, Philip Noel-Baker and Walter Citrine attended some of these lunches. The Focus Group decided to produce a manifesto for the League of Nations. Churchill wrote much of the manifesto and Attlee was persuaded to sign it. It was the first document on which they collaborated.

While Britain agonised over Edward, Europe faced turmoil in Spain. Attlee said, 'I regarded the Spanish Civil War as a very crucial test. Quite obviously Musso and Hitler were trying it out.' Republican sympathisers saw the war as a struggle between tyranny and freedom; Nationalists viewed it as a conflict between 'red hordes' versus 'Christian civilization'. Hitler agreed to help the Nationalists; Stalin offered military assistance to the Republicans.

Churchill had reservations about Franco, but tended to support him, while Attlee sided wholeheartedly with the Republicans. Later Attlee wrote of Churchill, 'I don't think he judged the Spanish show rightly.' Attlee's behaviour showed that his attitude was changing; events were making it difficult to remain a pacifist. The anti-fascist fight in Spain showed that, if Attlee was not ready to support rearmament, he was ready to take up arms again – and not just symbolically. He travelled to Spain to visit British volunteers who made up No. 1 Company, which came to be called Major Attlee's company. Few of those who allow army units to be named after them are irrevocably pacifist.

Hindsight can be blinding. In 1940, Churchill 'saved the world', which made it easy to forget that the many intrigues of 1937–39 could have led to Edward VIII remaining King and appointing a Prime Minister who was in favour of appeasement. Two diaries offer fine accounts packed with gossip of the plots, counter plots and rumours; the diaries of Hugh Dalton and Leo Amery.

Dalton helped to shift the Labour Party away from appeasement. He did not have a high regard for Attlee, but he was even more critical of Herbert Morrison, who suffered from 'persecution mania' after he lost the 1935 leadership election. Stafford Cripps ruled himself out as a potential leader, for Dalton, as he leaned too far to the left. The situation as Dalton saw it was this: Attlee was inadequate, Morrison paranoid, Cripps too left-wing. The only possible choice was Dalton himself. As it happened, he never stood for the leadership.

In the Commons on 12 November 1936, Churchill attacked the government on rearmament for being 'decided only to be undecided, resolved to be irresolute, adamant for drift, solid for fluidity, all-powerful to be impotent'.

Baldwin rebutted with a vigorous defence:

My position as a leader of a great party was not altogether a comfortable one. I asked myself what chance was there … within the next year or two of that feeling being so changed that the country would give a mandate for rearmament? Supposing I had gone to the country and said that Germany was rearming and we must rearm; does anybody think that this pacific democracy would have rallied to that cry at that moment? I cannot think of anything that would have made the loss of the election from my point of view more certain.

Churchill wrote to a friend: 'I have never heard such a squalid confession from a public man as Baldwin offered us yesterday.' On 16 March 1937, Churchill told fellow MP Harold Nicolson that he might refuse the Tory whip and take some fifty members with him. Churchill's old idea of a party of the middle still attracted him. That same year, Attlee published *The Labour Party in Perspective*. The book sold 50,000 copies and bolstered Attlee's position. One point underlines some of the similarities between him and Churchill. Attlee saw the Labour Party as the successor of the Liberals, who, he said,

> sought to free the individual from the power of the state. They believed that economic liberty meant political freedom. Realising that British liberty was essentially the liberty of the man of property, they thought that under free competition, and with a wide distribution of individual property, this could be achieved.

One of Attlee's strengths was his ability to understand those who were not obsessed by politics and ideology. The Labour Party was, like the country itself, practical and 'has always comprised people of very various outlooks ... The natural British tendency to heresy and dissent has prevented the formation of a code of rigid Socialist orthodoxy. Those who have sought to impose one have always failed to make real headway and have remained sects rather than political parties. As in religion, so in politics, the Briton claims the right to think for himself.' Revolution, however, was not the British way and Britons were 'unlikely to accept Communism and Fascism. Both systems appear to the politically immature. Both are distasteful to peoples like the British and French, who have had years of experience of personal freedom and political democracy.'

Baldwin resigned in May 1937 and was succeeded as Prime Minister by Neville Chamberlain. He had been both a successful businessman and Chancellor, but he was also vain and insecure, and masked his insecurities with arrogance. The roots of those insecurities remain a little unclear. He was the son of Joseph Chamberlain's second wife, and after Neville's mother died, his father remarried for a third time. He sent Neville to the West Indies, to save a family business in sisal, only for the young man to fail dismally and lose the family some £50,000. Over the next forty years, however, Neville had proceeded to enjoy a glittering career. But, as we shall see, this success had not managed to rid him of his insecurities. Attlee found Chamberlain to be very aloof. 'He always treated us like dirt,' Attlee complained. Aneurin Bevan, quoted by Michael Foot in his biography of the architect of the NHS, dissected Chamberlain. Bevan sniped that he

> has the lucidity which is a by-product of a fundamentally sterile mind … He does not have to struggle, as Churchill has for example, with the crowded pulsations of a fecund imagination. On the contrary, he is almost devoid of imagination … Listening to a speech by Chamberlain is like paying a visit to Woolworth's: everything in its place and nothing above sixpence.

Initially, Chamberlain hoped to conclude an alliance with Mussolini in order to restrain Hitler. In February 1938, Anthony Eden resigned as Foreign Secretary, because Mussolini was already violating an agreement by sending troops to Spain. Eden thought that Mussolini should honour the first agreement before any new negotiations started. He said later, 'I was trying to fight a delaying action for Britain, and I could not go along with Chamberlain's policy.'

Attlee regretted Eden's decision to resign. Lord Halifax, who replaced Eden, had two unflattering nicknames: the Holy Fox and the Trimmer. Churchill felt it was 'derogatory' to have a peer leading the Foreign Office. Their views were also diametrically opposed. Halifax had met Hitler in 1937 and had appointed the passionate appeaser, Rab Butler, as his deputy. Butler had spent time in Germany in the 1920s, spoke the language fluently and felt that Versailles was unfair. He was also close to Lord Brocket, an admirer of Hitler and, inevitably, a fervent anti-Semite.

Lloyd George called Butler 'the Artful Dodger', as he never gave straight answers about the government's views on Spain, where General Franco's victory was now clearly imminent. Artful Dodger may have been too polite a nickname. Halifax's biographer, Andrew Roberts, is scathing: 'It is hard to see Butler as a sympathetic figure in the 1930s. He took to appeasement with an unholy glee not shared after the Anschluss by anyone else in the Foreign Office ... a thoroughly unattractive figure.'

Disappointment at being denied office did not rob Churchill of his humour. On 21 December, he made fun of Mussolini in the House. Amery noted that MPs laughed with him, and that if Mussolini had witnessed the scene, 'it would have led to an immediate bombardment of [the British colony of] Malta.'

It was a tense, uncertain time. Attlee was exploring various cross-party avenues, as well as attempting to strengthen links with other countries. He dined with Maisky, the Russian ambassador, on several occasions. On 11 January 1938, he met Subhas Chandra Bose, a young Indian politician and friend of Nehru's. The following week, Attlee and Leo Amery dined together; Amery hoped that Attlee would get a debate going on the structure of the government. By March, Attlee was trying to find a way for Britain to rearm and exchanged letters with Lord Robert Cecil to try to establish a rearmament programme in the name of the League of Nations. The Cecil family had relevant history. One of Lord Robert's ancestors was Queen Elizabeth I's minister who had helped her defeat Philip II and his Spanish Armada way back in 1588.

On 20 March, Attlee pointed out in the House that, while German ambassador Joachim von Ribbentrop had been in London to negotiate peace, Fascist planes were bombing Republican Spain. The government did not 'take a stand on a moral basis', and ignored 'the greatest reality of all, the international situation' as well as 'the mentality of the dictators'. This last was another of Attlee's references to psychology. During the debate, Attlee waved a copy of the *Morning Post*, in which Chamberlain had boasted he would deploy the practicalities of 'realpolitik' to deal with Mussolini. Attlee knew the origins of realpolitik well, as he had studied Machiavelli at Oxford, and now countered that Machiavelli was the natural 'teacher of Signor Mussolini'. Il Duce would make a deal with Hitler the moment it suited him.

On 7 April, Dalton noted in his diary that Chamberlain was becoming more dictatorial. US President Franklin D. Roosevelt had proposed an international peace conference, which the new Prime Minister rejected without consulting anyone, although Chamberlain himself claimed that he had discussed the plan with at least three members of his Cabinet. Dalton also described a conversation about Attlee that he had with TUC leader Walter Citrine, which implied that the Labour leader was not manly enough.

'Does he swear?' Dalton asked about Attlee.

'Not very efficiently,' Citrine replied.

That Attlee was a second-rate cusser was yet another of his deficiencies. On 15 June, Dalton wrote that 'little [Harold] Laski has been suggesting Attlee's leadership was intolerable.' There were four obvious candidates, but the party could not agree on any one of them. One of Attlee's strengths was that he did not seem too concerned about the risks of being toppled. He prided himself on being able to take things in his stride. The question is, however, whether Attlee really was so naturally sanguine, or whether he had learned how to hide his feelings as an adult, just as he had learned how to repress some of them as a child. The latter seems more likely. It helped that he loved many things outside politics. The day after Dalton's diary entry, for example, Attlee attended a non-political dinner that he enjoyed; the great Australian batsman, Donald Bradman, was guest of honour.

Attlee was becoming concerned about an issue Churchill had often raised, that of air power. There were many links between British and German aircraft manufacturers and this led to some astonishing engineering history. Aircraft manufacturers resented the government's efforts to control their industry and especially their exports. Rolls-Royce worked throughout the 1930s on improving engines for Kestrel planes and developed a new pressurised cooling system; Messerschmitt had to buy one of their engines in 1935 as Germany lagged behind. In 1936, another German manufacturer, Junkers, needed an engine, which was kindly sold by Rolls-Royce again – and then installed in the first prototype of the infamous Junkers Ju 87 dive bomber. The Reich Air Ministry then bought four of the latest Kestrel VI engines. Rolls-Royce got a Heinkel He 70 Blitz mail plane to use in testing.

A week or so after his talk with Citrine, Dalton discussed air production with Attlee. Both knew that planes incorporating the most recent technology had been exported to Finland, while Britain's RAF was still awaiting delivery of the latest models. The exchange between the two men seems to suggest they were not aware of the Kestrel exports. Cripps had even more bizarre news. In Bristol, he had seen swastikas being painted on fighter planes which were being exported to Germany. Dalton did not doubt this was true.

A rather technical dispute then found Attlee and Churchill on the same side. Air power was again involved. On 18 September 1938,

Churchill's son-in-law Duncan Sandys came to see Dalton. Sandys was fearful about the dire state of the RAF, and also raised the subject of possible cooperation between Tory rebels and the Labour Party. When Sandys then asked a question in Parliament about London's anti-aircraft defences, he was threatened with military discipline as he was a serving officer. Sandys had raised the issue in the House because to threaten him seemed to be a breach of parliamentary privilege. There was a lengthy report and Attlee, as well as Liberal leader Archibald Sinclair and Churchill, sided with Sandys. In the end, Sandys was not disciplined.

In the political wilderness, Churchill felt some need to blow his horn – and his horn was often his pen. Churchill's writing helped keep him in the public eye, and he published *Step by Step*, a collection of his newspaper writings, which included articles on the poor state of the navy, the Spanish Civil War, the influence of the Soviet Union and the alliance between Hitler and Mussolini. He also included a tribute to the Turkish leader Atatürk, who had bested the Allies at Gallipoli.

> The tears which men and women of all classes shed upon his bier were a fitting tribute to the life work of a man at once the hero, the champion, and the father of modern Turkey. During his long dictatorship a policy of admirable restraint and goodwill created, for the first time in history, most friendly relations with Greece.

Churchill did not send Chamberlain or Baldwin a copy of *Step by Step*, but he sent one to Attlee. Attlee responded with a warm 'My Dear Winston' letter of thanks.

Three events in 1938 should have made the British government realise there was no hope of peace with Hitler. On 9 March, the Austrian

Chancellor, Kurt von Schuschnigg, announced a plebiscite to decide whether Austria would remain independent or merge with Germany. A furious Hitler reacted swiftly because the Austrians seemed likely to vote against a merger. On 11 March, Schuschnigg and the President of Austria, Wilhelm Miklas, were forced to resign. That day Chamberlain gave a farewell lunch for von Ribbentrop, the German ambassador, who was returning to Berlin to become Hitler's Foreign Minister. Surprisingly, Churchill was invited to the lunch. It shows how well his informal channels worked that, during the meal, he received a message that German troops were massing on the border ready to invade Austria. Luck again was on Hitler's side. No one resisted. The next day Hitler entered his home town of Linz and was cheered by jubilant crowds.

The Little Corporal now trained his guns on Czechoslovakia. In August, Chamberlain sent the Liberal politician Lord Runciman to Prague. On 30 August, the Cabinet refused to issue a formal warning to Hitler that Britain would intervene if he attacked Czechoslovakia.

That weekend in Wales, an unlikely picnic acted as an opportunity for politicians of different parties to put feelers out to each other. Attlee and his family visited Lloyd George and they took their hampers to Snowdonia where the Welsh wizard, now not such a fan of Hitler, predicted that the Nazi dictator would gobble up Czechoslovakia. Hitler became the passionate champion of some three million Sudeten Germans, who lived in the border areas of Czechoslovakia and did not have any rights of self-determination, which the Führer suddenly claimed to cherish.

Hitler assumed his most reasonable persona at the National Socialist Congress.

I am asking neither that Germany be allowed to oppress three and a half million Frenchmen, nor am I asking that three and a half million

Englishmen be placed at our mercy. Rather I am simply demanding that the oppression of three and a half million Germans in Czechoslovakia cease and that the inalienable right to self-determination take its place.

Chamberlain soft-soaped that the Sudeten grievances were justified, claiming Hitler would make no further demands if he were allowed to take over the Sudenetenland. It could be argued that Chamberlain was simply reflecting the results of the Peace Ballot. But Lady Gwendolen Cecil, a woman steeped in snobbery, held a different view. She blamed Lord Halifax for encouraging appeasement, but he at least had some ancestry, even if his family had only been ennobled in the nineteenth century. Chamberlain, on the other hand, was 'a poor old middle-class monster [who] could not be expected to know any better'. He had learned nothing during his distinguished political career. For Lady Gwendolen, only persons of long breeding could manage the diplomatic arts.

Britain and France told Czechoslovakia to concede the Sudeten-land, but the Czech leader Edvard Beneš resisted. A familiar pattern followed. The Nazis presented impossible demands and the Sudeten Germans broke off negotiations on 13 September. Violence ensued, giving the pro-Nazi Sudeten leader Konrad Henlein an excuse to demand that Germany invade.

Chamberlain behaved like a supplicant over the next three weeks. He flew to meet Hitler at the Nazi leader's retreat at Berchtesgaden on 15 September. Chamberlain had stood up to Lloyd George during the First World War, so the question of why he let Hitler bully him is not an easy one to answer. Hitler was not an aristocrat who would trigger the social inferiority in Chamberlain that Lady Gwendolen Cecil had detected. On a social scale, the Little Corporal actually ranked below Lady Cecil's 'middle-class monster'.

On 8 September, Dalton journeyed to Attlee's home in Stanmore to meet the Czech minister Jaromír Nečas, who told them his people would rather die than become 'Hitler's slaves'. The next day Attlee issued a statement of solidarity with the Czechs. Churchill phoned him. 'Your declaration does honour to the British people,' he said.

'I am glad you think so,' Attlee replied.

A few days later, Churchill received a phone call from the Czech ambassador, Jan Masaryk, confirming that Hitler had demanded the Czechs pull out of the Sudetenland. The next person on the phone to Churchill was Attlee. If Churchill broke with the government, Attlee said, Labour would support him. Churchill knew that at most he could count on the support of fifty dissident Tories, so he did not commit himself. He merely said that if Chamberlain 'ran away again', he would side with Labour. Both Attlee and Churchill then visited Chamberlain in a desperate effort to convince him that Hitler could not be trusted. They did not get far. Chamberlain still hoped to dissuade Hitler from war.

Chamberlain flew to see Hitler again, at Bad Godesberg on 22 September, but the Nazi dictator proved unyielding. Five days later, Chamberlain made a broadcast that began in a very insular way.

> How horrible, fantastic, incredible it is that we should be digging trenches and trying on gas masks here because of a quarrel in a far-away country between people of whom we know nothing ... However much we may sympathise with a small nation confronted by a big and powerful neighbour, we cannot in all circumstances undertake to involve the whole British Empire in war simply on her account. If we have to fight, it must be on larger issues than that. I am myself a man of peace to the depths of my soul; armed conflict between nations is a nightmare to me.

The next day, Chamberlain asked Hitler for yet another conference. Chamberlain then flew to Munich to meet with Hitler, Mussolini and French Prime Minister Édouard Daladier. The Nazis made sure that cheering crowds lined the road from the aerodrome. According to a journalist whom Dalton refers to as 'Pertinax', Daladier drank too much and so missed many of the 'crucial moments'. No one bothered to consult the Czechs whose fate was to be decided. The Munich Agreement was signed early on 30 September.

After signing, Chamberlain requested a private conference with Hitler and pressed him not to bomb Prague if the Czechs resisted. When the two men were alone, Chamberlain pulled a paper headed 'Anglo–German Agreement' from his pocket. It said that the two nations considered the Munich Agreement 'symbolic of the desire of our two peoples never to go to war again'. According to Chamberlain, Hitler said, 'Ja! Ja!' ('Yes! Yes!'). The two men signed the paper then and there and Chamberlain replaced it in his pocket. Later that day, Ribbentrop told Hitler he should not have signed it. The Führer made fun of him: 'Oh, don't take it so seriously. That piece of paper is of no further significance whatever.'

Chamberlain, on the other hand, thought that he had achieved a triumph, and so did much of Britain. The King wrote a letter that was handed to Chamberlain when he returned. George VI assured his Prime Minister of the country's gratitude and asked him to come to Buckingham Palace to report on the meeting. The streets were packed with cheering crowds and it took Chamberlain ninety minutes to drive the 9 miles to the palace. Chamberlain and his wife appeared on the palace's balcony with the King and Queen. Later, when he went to Downing Street, someone in the crowd shouted: 'Neville, go up to the window and say "peace for our time".'

'No, I don't do that sort of thing,' Chamberlain responded.

But the temptation ultimately proved too much. He went to the first-floor window, remembered his history, and repeated some of the words Disraeli had spoken after returning from the Congress of Berlin sixty years earlier.

'My good friends, this is the second time there has come back from Germany to Downing Street peace with honour. I believe it is peace for our time. We thank you from the bottom of our hearts. Now I recommend you go home, and sleep quietly in your beds.'

In Paris, Daladier was expecting a hostile crowd, but he was acclaimed as Chamberlain had been. Daladier said to an aide: '*Ah, les cons!*' ('Ah, the morons!') Daladier was right. The peace would not last even for one year. For the Czechs, 'peace for our time' meant accepting that their country would be divided.

The Focus Group had met at the Savoy Hotel while Chamberlain was in Munich. The purpose was to get Churchill, Attlee, Eden, Sinclair and Lloyd George to send a telegram to Chamberlain begging him not to betray the Czechs. But Eden refused to sign the telegram, saying it would be seen as a vendetta against the Prime Minister. Attlee said he needed the approval of his party. The evening ended gloomily. According to Violet Bonham Carter, 'When we parted there were tears in his eyes.' The tears were Churchill's, of course, but they did not stop him from seeing the danger clearly.

On 3 October, Attlee and Leo Amery lunched together just before the Munich debate in Parliament. In his speech, Attlee recalled Gallipoli. When he had heard of Munich he remembered the sorrow he had felt at Suvla Bay.

Every one of us has been passing through days of anxiety; we cannot, however, feel that peace has been established, but that we have nothing but an armistice in a state of war. We have been unable to go in for carefree rejoicing. We have felt that we are in the midst of a tragedy. We have felt humiliation. This has not been a victory for reason and humanity. It has been a victory for brute force.

There was relief after the Munich Agreement as 'war had been averted, at all events for the time being; on the other hand, there was a sense of humiliation and foreboding for the future,' Attlee told the House. He compared Chamberlain to the reckless captain of a ship who had steered it into danger, 'but then made frantic efforts to try to save something from the shipwreck.' People cheered that, but there had to be 'an inquiry, an inquest, on the victims, and the question will be asked how the vessel got so far off its course, how and why it was so hazarded'. Hitler had fooled Chamberlain into believing he cared about the Sudeten Germans when, in fact, he 'had decided that the time was ripe for another step forward in his design to dominate Europe'. Attlee finished by declaring: 'The Prime Minister has been the dupe of the dictators, and I say that today we are in a dangerous position.'

Samuel Hoare, now Home Secretary, remarked that Attlee had miscalculated. In describing the Prime Minister as the captain of a sinking ship, Attlee had been 'picturesque', an adjective rarely aimed at him. Chamberlain had the pulse of nation, Hoare insisted, adding: 'I believe that the criticisms to which we have listened in the House today very little represent the great body of feeling. I believe the great body of our fellow citizens, not only in this country but in the Dominions and in the whole empire, are grateful to the Prime Minister for the efforts that he has made.'

Even though Churchill was out of power and out of favour, the Speaker recognised his right to a key position in the debate, so he was the penultimate speaker on 5 October. Hitler was a dinner guest, who 'instead of snatching his victuals from the table, has been content to have them served to him course by course', Churchill told MPs. He then varied the metaphor. '£1 was demanded at the pistol's point. When it was given, £2 were demanded at the pistol's point. Finally, the dictator consented to take £1 17s. 6d. and the rest in promises of good will for the future.' The Czechs could have negotiated better terms on their own, Churchill insisted, lamenting that 'all is over. Silent, mournful, abandoned, broken, Czechoslovakia recedes into the darkness.'

Churchill then turned Chamberlain's own words against him. 'We are talking about countries which are a long way off and of which, as the Prime Minister might say, we know nothing.' Viscountess Astor interrupted to say this was 'rude'. Churchill delivered a tart reply. 'She must very recently have been receiving her finishing course in manners. What will be the position, I want to know, of France and England this year and the year afterwards?'

In closing, Churchill said he feared that was 'only the first sip, the first foretaste of a bitter cup which will be proffered to us year by year unless by a supreme recovery of moral health and martial vigour, we arise again and take our stand for freedom as in the olden time'.

Chamberlain did not rise to Attlee's jibe that he had been duped; instead, the Prime Minister harped on his hatred of war. He did not accept 'that the assurances which have been given to me personally are worthless, that they have sinister designs and that they are bent upon the domination of Europe and the gradual destruction of democracies'. He despaired that if he had been duped, then there was no hope 'for civilisation or for any of the things that make life worth living'. Chamberlain questioned whether 'the experience of the Great War and of the years that followed it give us reasonable hope that if some new war started that would end war any more than the last one did'. The answer to this question was 'no', he declared. And then, in a contradiction which he did not admit to, he insisted that 'people hated war'. Yet history showed they found it easy to kill each other, especially for what they imagined was a good cause. Freud and Einstein had noticed this fact, too, in *Why War?*

Chamberlain ended with platitudes. His policies had ushered in 'something like a new spiritual revival, and I know that everywhere there is a strong desire among the people to record their readiness to serve their country'. He concluded, 'I must frankly say that at this moment I do not myself clearly see my way to any particular scheme [how people might help]'. It was a feeble way to end a speech. Nevertheless, he won the vote which followed by 369 to 150.

Hitler took the Munich Agreement as proof that he could now unleash his furies with no fear of retribution. On 9 November 1938, in what became known as Kristallnacht (the Night of Broken Glass), Nazi thugs burned some 1,000 synagogues as well as Jewish-owned businesses and homes. At least ninety Jews were killed and around 30,000 Jewish men sent to concentration camps. Even *The Times*, which backed appeasement, found Hitler's attacks on Jews 'wholly intolerable'. A week later, Churchill warned the country that it should see this as 'the deep repeated strokes of an alarm bell', which demanded action if Britain were to stay a great power. Attlee, who had seen Churchill cry over the India Bill in 1934, said he also once saw Churchill weeping as people described the suffering of the Jews.

Chamberlain was devious as well as insecure. He did nothing to stop Tory loyalists from trying to get Churchill deselected in his Epping constituency. These efforts would rumble on for months, but would ultimately fail. Churchill voted with Labour on 17 November 1938 on the setting up of a Ministry of Supply. He was so exasperated with Chamberlain that he told Harold Nicolson that at the next election, 'I shall speak on every socialist platform in the country.' Chamberlain retaliated, telling the House that he recalled a Dominions' statesman saying that the most valuable quality a statesman should possess was judgement. Chamberlain coated his dagger with honey. Churchill had many strengths, but, 'If I were asked whether judgement is the first of my right honourable friend's many qualities, I should have to ask the House of Commons not to press me too far.'

A month later, at a meeting in his constituency, Churchill barbed that Chamberlain 'had said tension in Europe had greatly relaxed; a few weeks later Nazi Germany seized Austria'. For his part, Attlee noted that Chamberlain was simply the wrong man in these circumstances. The Prime Minister knew nothing about foreign policy or defence. Early in 1939, Attlee met Chamberlain to hear what he had to say after visiting Mussolini. Chamberlain betrayed his vanity and told Attlee that he had been impressed by the large crowds that turned out to greet him.

Hitler kept the pressure up. On 15 March, he summoned Czech President Emil Hácha to Berlin and bullied him again. Hácha suffered a heart attack, but Hitler's doctor revived him and, half-alive, Hácha accepted the surrender terms. When German troops entered Bohemia and Moravia, they met practically no resistance.

The relationship between Churchill and Attlee at this time has been described as a 'mating dance' by John Bew in his 2016 biography, *Citizen Clem*, but Bew's image is a little too intense perhaps. In France, the wedding ring is called *l'alliance*. There was much shimmying forward and then scurrying back, but neither man had yet singled out the other as the key ally; neither Churchill nor Attlee was in government, after all. Attlee had offered to support Churchill if he broke with the Tories, but Churchill had remained ambivalent about doing so. Now Churchill circulated a letter of protest about the treatment of the Czechs and asked Attlee to sign. But the Labour leader refused.

Attlee was well aware the country did not want a war which he, like Churchill, thought was increasingly inevitable. Some members of the Labour Party pressed for a popular front even if it meant a delay in introducing socialist policies. In response, Attlee penned another of his short lyrics which were to be sung to the tune of 'The Red Flag'.

> The people's flag is palest pink
> It's not red blood but only ink

It went on:

> Then raise our pallid standard high
> Wash out all trace of scarlet dye
> Let Liberals and Tories too
> And socialists of every hue
> With heads uncovered swear we all
> To have no principles at all.
> If everyone will turn his coat
> We'll get the British people's vote.

The so-called sheep could bite. Attlee often kept his adult aggression bolted in, just as he had learned to keep his fury under control as a child. His lyrics let some of his aggression out.

The left was also sensing that war might lead to profound social changes. Orwell wrote,

Lord Halifax, and all his tribe, believe that when the war is over things will be exactly as they were before. Back to the crazy pavement of Versailles, back to 'democracy', i.e. capitalism, back to dole queues and the Rolls-Royce cars, back to the grey top hats and the sponge-bag trousers, *in saecula saeculorum*. It is, of course, obvious that nothing of the kind is going to happen. A feeble imitation of it might just possibly happen in the case of a negotiated peace, but only for a short while. *Laissez-faire* capitalism is dead. The choice lies between the kind of collective society that Hitler will set up and the kind that can arise if he is defeated.

In March 1939, Churchill wrote to Chamberlain for the first time since their exchanges the previous November. Chamberlain felt harassed because Attlee and the Liberals were pressing for a recall of Parliament. 'Winston is the worst of the lot, telephoning almost every hour of the day. I suppose he has prepared a terrific oration he wants to let off,' Chamberlain wrote to his sister. Churchill then invited David Margesson, the Tory Chief Whip, to dinner, and said that he could work amicably under Chamberlain.

On 27 March, Chamberlain warned his Cabinet that an attack on Poland was imminent. Finally showing some resolve, he offered a commitment to attack Hitler if the Nazis made any military move against Poland. At the end of the month, Hitler renounced his own non-aggression pact with Poland and the naval treaty with Britain, which limited the size of the German Navy to just over a third the size of the Royal Navy.

Attlee and Dalton met Chamberlain on 13 April and pressed him to announce a guarantee to Romania. The Poles and Romanians did not want to risk the Russians coming to defend them, Chamberlain said, as once in they might never leave. In the House that afternoon, Labour members demanded answers on the question of working with Stalin. Chamberlain was furious, feeling that Attlee should have controlled his MPs, since he had already explained the situation regarding the Soviet Union to him.

After the debate, Chamberlain wrote to his sister again. 'Attlee behaved like the cowardly cur he is.' No wonder, Attlee felt he 'always treated us like dirt'. Chamberlain had hoped, however, 'for a better speech from Winston', who had apparently promised to make 'a not unhelpful one'. At the end of the debate, the mood on the Tory benches was subdued, while the Labour benches cheered Churchill.

In May, Dalton met Churchill in the corridors of the House. Churchill complained that the Czechs were gallant while many of Poland's actions were highly questionable. Chamberlain now, however, had no option but to back Poland. But it was clear to Churchill that the Cabinet had no plan. Dalton reported all this to Attlee. On 19 May, Attlee and Eden both raised in the House the possibility of an alliance with Stalin. Churchill agreed. 'If you are ready to be an ally of Russia in a time of war ... why should you shrink from being an ally now?' he said.

Later in the day, Attlee was on his way to the Labour Party conference in Southport and fell ill on the train, embarrassingly so. He had a chill on the bladder and suffered much pain, as he coyly put it, in the J. T. or John Thomas, slang for his penis. Attlee had to spend two weeks convalescing and missed the meeting of the Labour Party's National Executive Committee.

Germany imagined that the appeasers were still likely to succeed, so the Nazis probed the soft underbelly of England, to use Churchill's phrase. Hitler sent emissaries who offered reassurances: if Britain would leave Europe to him, he would make no move against the British Empire. Indeed, he would even help protect it from the Japanese. Hitler was issuing threats from a position of strength. With Czechoslovakia safely out of the way, he could now attack Poland.

On 7 August, Herman Göring and a very senior team of Germans secretly met a group of British businessmen on the island of Sylt in the Baltic. The British team insisted the country would stand by the government's promises to Poland, but they were willing to recommend a second conference to solve outstanding European problems. The British businessmen were bad judges of character; Göring impressed them as being 'surprisingly honest and straight'.

Sir Neville Henderson, the British ambassador to Germany, handed Hitler a letter from Chamberlain on 23 August, which stated that war between England and Germany 'would be the greatest calamity that could occur'. Hitler was undiplomatic, even aggressive, and denounced the 'blank cheque' Britain had given Poland, raging that the British were bent on destroying Germany. Hitler's tirades, according to the historian Ian Kershaw, were often theatrical. 'Chamberlain won't survive this discussion. His Cabinet will fall this evening,' the Führer predicted, wrongly as it turned out. Britain now finally turned the pledge it had made to support Poland in March into a treaty, which committed it to give military assistance to the Poles.

Only three days later, Henderson saw Hitler again and reiterated the British position. Germany and Poland needed to settle their differences first, and then Britain would work towards a long-term deal with Germany. Hitler's response was to order the plans to attack Poland to be put into action. The failure of all his peace hopes should have made Chamberlain consider resigning, but he refused to do so. Unlike his father Joseph and his half-brother Austen, Neville Chamberlain had actually become Prime Minister. He would not give up the keys to 10 Downing Street easily. The next months would see him try to compromise in many ways to keep control.

The first compromise came on the afternoon of 1 September;

Chamberlain summoned Churchill and offered him a place in the War Cabinet and the office of First Lord of the Admiralty. Churchill was delighted to be back in charge of the navy. The navy was delighted by his return too.

There were plots and counter-plots. The following day, Eden, the flamboyant Robert Boothby and other MPs met in Churchill's flat and discussed how to bring about the fall of Chamberlain. But the Prime Minister himself was not staying idle. Leo Amery noted that Chamberlain had begun to plot bringing the Labour Party into the government. Chamberlain convened a meeting which Halifax, Churchill, Tory Chief Whip David Margesson, Attlee and Arthur Greenwood attended. Chamberlain offered Labour three Cabinet seats, but Greenwood rejected the offer, and Attlee then added that Labour's National Executive Committee would never accept Chamberlain. Churchill started to protest but, according to Amery, Greenwood cut him short, saying this was not a moment for oratory. 'The truth is that there is no one on our side who trusts the Prime Minister,' Greenwood finished.

Chamberlain implied that he would not be declaring war on Germany immediately even if it had invaded Poland. Amery was furious and, like many others, felt Chamberlain was out of touch with the national mood. With Attlee absent from Parliament because he was still convalescing, Greenwood stood up in his place and announced that he was speaking for Labour. That would not be enough, Amery called out to him across the floor: 'Speak for England, Arthur.' Greenwood made a considered speech, insisting that the situation allowed no time for delays.

Dalton thought Greenwood did so well that he should replace Attlee as leader, but Greenwood put on an exaggerated Yorkshire accent and declined. 'Nay, it wouldn't be fair to Clem,' he said. Fairness was not the only issue. Greenwood knew that many people were aware he had a serious drinking problem.

Chamberlain finally steeled himself and made his historic broadcast.

This morning the British ambassador in Berlin handed the German Government a final note stating that, unless we heard from them by 11 o'clock that they were prepared at once to withdraw their troops from Poland, a state of war would exist between us. I have to tell you now that no such undertaking has been received, and that consequently this country is at war with Germany.

He added, 'You can imagine what a bitter blow it is to me that all my long struggle to win peace has failed. Yet I cannot believe that there is anything more or anything different that I could have done and that would have been more successful.'

Chamberlain did not admit he had misjudged Hitler or the situation. He simply said that the German leader 'had evidently made up his mind to attack Poland whatever happened'. The Nazis claimed to have 'put forward reasonable proposals which were rejected by the Poles, [but] that is not a true statement'. Hitler paid no attention and ordered his troops into Poland. Chamberlain finally conceded that 'there is no chance of expecting that this man will ever give up his practice of using force to gain his will. He can only be stopped by force.'

The declaration of war made Attlee a key figure. As Leader of the Opposition, he made a powerful broadcast supporting the government, stating that 'where there is Nazism, there is cruelty, tyranny and the rule of the secret police.' The views of Churchill precisely.

The early days of the land war were known as the 'Phoney War' but, at sea, it was a different matter. Dalton saw Churchill at the Admiralty on 13 September and was encouraged by his account of naval operations. The main problem was how to counter the threat of German U-boats. On 26 September, Attlee welcomed the 'robust, vigorous' statement Churchill made on the naval situation. It was optimistic, 'but not wildly optimistic'. Attlee called for more information and said he was disturbed that the Cabinet had ignored the importance of the economic aspects of the war.

On 3 October, Attlee told the Commons, 'The Prime Minister is right, in my view, to say we must examine carefully every kind of proposal for peace, but we must deal with the realities.' Hostilities had begun long before any formal declaration of war. He also praised Churchill for providing more information than the Ministry of Information had about the Battle of the Atlantic, which was not going well for Britain.

Firepower alone would not win the war, Attlee argued. Britain needed to realise that the Germans had a different mentality and Attlee was keen to know how the Ministry was 'getting on to study the psychology of the German'. It was a prelude to a very political point. 'Far too many people think you can get back to the past,' Attlee said, and then forecast that the social structure of the country would have changed by the end of the war, a hope never far from his mind.

In November, Attlee issued a pamphlet which stated the British had 'no desire to humiliate, crush or divide the German nation'. Dalton now offered another unflattering animal analogy and referred to this document as the Rabbit's Peace Aims. Dalton then found out how dire the different strengths of the air forces were. The situation had actually deteriorated since 1937. The Germans now had 1,750 bombers, while the RAF possessed only 270. On 15 November, the mouse-rabbit Attlee should have faced a challenge for his leadership, but his three rivals all withdrew, timidly.

The end of 1939 and the start of 1940 saw continuing intrigue as Tory rebels and Labour politicians pondered the possibility of getting rid of Chamberlain and forming a coalition. Chamberlain had no gift for enthusing the people, Attlee wrote, which was a serious failing. Attlee himself felt it was important to keep in contact with the military. On 8 January, he visited the headquarters of the British Expeditionary Force.

The war was not phoney in the shops. Rationing was introduced at the start of 1940. Lemons and bananas became impossible to obtain, and only children and pregnant women who had special ration books were allowed oranges. Greengrocers often sold just one apple to each of their customers. When questioned about bananas, many children did not believe they even existed.

In March 1940, Hugh Gaitskell, the future Labour leader, wrote that the idea of a coalition seemed excellent, but not 'under these old gentlemen with their optimistic twaddle'. On 9 April, the Parliamentary Labour Party discussed the possibility. That day, Hitler invaded Denmark and Norway. Dalton thought Churchill was 'our great white hope in the black flock'.

Churchill was the driving force behind Britain's decision to send troops to Norway to deny the Nazis a base from which to attack Britain. But he had been too optimistic, Attlee complained. 'I have heard stories of boys sent there [to Norway] quite young and with little training.' Attlee again referred to the disaster of the Dardanelles in the First World War, where 'we have experience of having young boys sent out. They did not last long.' The British newsreels did not tell the truth about the Norwegian campaign; one showed a Scottish sergeant piping a reel while British troops performed a victory dance. Disinformation ruled, but only for a short time.

On 13 April, Attlee told the House of Commons that trying to make peace with Hitler was like 'proposing to make an agreement with a criminal lunatic'. Ten days later it was obvious the British were failing in Norway. The order to occupy the port of Trondheim had been given four times and rescinded four times. No one had trained British soldiers to ski and, anyway, they had few skis. So the troops were forced to stick to the roads when they advanced, making them easy targets.

Trying to get some consensus, Chamberlain asked Attlee and Greenwood whether they thought Norwegian waters should be mined. They were allowed to veto the government's plans, so the navy did not mine the waters until late March. Jock Colville said that, nevertheless, the First Lord of the Admiralty had 'made a good case for the navy's achievements during the last few days'. It had destroyed three cruisers and ten destroyers, a useful dent in the German fleet.

On 4 April, speaking at Central Hall, Westminster, Chamberlain told a Tory meeting that he was confident of victory, and that the government had now made good its initial weaknesses and lack of preparation. He added a phrase which would be long remembered: Hitler 'had missed the bus'. Like 'peace for our time', the remark about the bus would also haunt Chamberlain till he died.

During the 13 April parliamentary debate, Attlee noted that Chamberlain

struck a rather different note; there was a good deal more of a note of excuse and explanation. No one of us wishes to give any handle to the enemy, but we have a service and a duty to the nation to perform in examining into the events that have occurred. We have to face facts. We are not afraid of facing facts. This is a reverse, and, let it be re-membered, high hopes were raised, raised partly in the speeches of ministers, but very much so in the press and over the wireless.

Attlee argued that 'it was extraordinarily ill-advised that the people of this country should have had their spirits raised by accounts' which suggested that a military fiasco was something of a victory.

One of the achievements of Westminster was that war did not stop it dealing with routine business. On 21 April, in a debate on customs and excise, Attlee showed his interest in psychology again. The topic was the touchy subject of increasing duties on beer, tobacco and matches. Attlee had no problem with taxing these luxuries, as he called them. He then moved to the price of postage and said:

> I doubt whether it is wise, when you are calling up for service, and when there is evacuation, with the result that people want to keep in touch with each other, that you should tax the simplest method of communication. I think that will require a great deal of consideration as to whether it is worthwhile. We have always to consider the psychology of the people in these things. Nothing irritates people more than having to fork out 1½d. instead of 1d. There is nothing sacrosanct about a penny post, but the additional halfpenny is irritating and the 2½d. will be even more irritating.

Attlee wanted the idea to be re-examined. The impact of the proposed Budget on the means test also worried him. This had been introduced so the unemployed could have some help. Some bankers, however, had told him that the means test was a psychological barrier to people saving, as once they had over £375, they did not qualify for any assistance when they became unemployed.

Attlee then returned to the war. He backed Churchill, who had been insisting on the need for more air power since 1932. British forces should have seized an airbase in Norway so the RAF could support the troops,

Attlee said. He then contrasted Chamberlain with Churchill, who had 'great abilities'.

On 2 May, Chamberlain reported on the Norway campaign to the House, but hid behind the need not to reveal much military detail. He admitted, however, that the German Army had been effective, and said British troops had failed to secure the ports of either Narvik or Trondheim. Chamberlain blamed Hitler's cunning for the military set-backs and went on to describe deceptions that seemed a bit like scenes in an Ealing comedy; many German sailors in Norway had disguised themselves as merchant seamen and had slept in doss houses. Unwise-ly, Chamberlain also invoked Sir John Moore's retreat to Corunna in Spain in 1809, claiming it was seen as something of a success in the long run. Chamberlain's speech 'was a very obvious flop', Amery wrote. Attlee felt differently, though, describing the speech as 'pretty good'. He asked for a full debate to be held the following week, something that Chamberlain had to concede.

This debate would be the prelude to one of the most successful collab-orations in British politics.

Psychologists should have studied why they collaborate well when they do, because the discipline has had a long history of feuds where they failed to do so. My first book, *Psychologists on Psychology*, interviewed thirteen of the world's great psychologists and examined their often bitter quarrels. Excess ego was a common problem. Sigmund Freud and Carl Jung fell out, for instance, after Freud refused to tell Jung his dreams. Freud did not want his authority challenged by revealing too much of his own inner life.

Sometimes feuds were even more personal. Melitta Schmideberg, the daughter of Melanie Klein, one of the first female psychoanalysts, never forgave her mother for the death of her brother. Klein's daughter became an analyst herself. She did not speak to her mother for twenty years. She even wore red shoes to celebrate on the day of her funeral. Melanie Klein had many loyal followers but also many enemies. She and Anna Freud feuded for years.

We know, however, a good deal about one successful collaboration between two groundbreaking psychologists. Two years after the Six-Day War between Israel and the surrounding Arab nations of Egypt, Syria and Jordan, Daniel Kahneman invited Amos Tversky to speak at his seminar in Tel Aviv. Tversky had been an Israeli fighter pilot during the war. When he became an academic, he devised experiments that claimed to show people made decisions less rationally than psychology assumed. Kahneman told him, 'Brilliant talk, but I don't believe a word of it.' They started off rather like Beatrice and Benedict in *Much Ado About Nothing*, arguing about everything – something which Churchill and Attlee did not do.

Kahneman and Tversky worked intensely together and excluded all other colleagues. Graduate students 'wondered how two so radically different personalities could find common ground, much less become soul mates,' according to Michael Lewis, who wrote an account of their friendship. One reason why the two men thought the way they did, according to Lewis, was because 'Danny was always sure he was wrong. Amos was always sure he was right.' But Tversky proved uncharacteristically receptive to Kahneman's ideas. Kahneman was surprised that he found Tversky's arrogance liberating: 'It was extremely rewarding to feel like Amos, smarter than almost everyone.' They also laughed together a lot, just as the Irish politicians Paisley and McGuinness had done. As Kahneman said, 'Amos was always very funny, and in his presence

I became funny as well, so we spent hours of solid work in continuous amusement.' Between 1971 and 1979, they published the work that would eventually win Kahneman the Nobel Prize in Economics. (The prize would certainly have been shared with Tversky had he still been alive. Nobel Prizes are not awarded posthumously.) In an interview on YouTube, Kahneman was very warm about their collaboration. A new science – behavioural economics – grew out of their collaboration.

In Britain, as Members of Parliament prepared to debate the failure in Norway, no one knew what would happen next, let alone that the Norway debate would change history

CHAPTER 8

COALITIONS ARE MADE OF THIS, 1940–1941

In 1939, a German journalist, Heinz Medefind, predicted what would happen next. The British were always harking back to the Battle of Waterloo. In *England Seen From the Inside*, he mocked the country for being so besotted with old glories and traditions – 'the tested methods', as he called them. He was especially virulent about Churchill. He wrote: 'What was the first thing Neville Chamberlain did after declaring war on Germany? He brought the men into his Cabinet that he knew had a sick hatred for Germany.' Medefind added, 'Churchill was a man who over his entire career had made one serious mistake after another – but at least he knew the "tested methods." Churchill immediately declared a blockade. He began to incite the world against Germany by using the most outrageous lies. It was the same method that seemed to work the last time.' The Nazis approved of the book.

The tested methods also dismayed the veteran politician Lord Lloyd, who had served as High Commissioner to Egypt and who had warned of the dangers the Nazis posed even before Churchill. On 6 May, Lloyd wrote to his son about 'the terrible complacency of Neville, Simon and

Sam Hoare'. That night Leo Amery decided to look up Oliver Cromwell's speech to the Rump Parliament in 1653, which ended dramatically,
with Cromwell telling MPs, 'In the name of God go.' Three centuries
later, Amery sensed the House was set for an emotional debate, but he
had not decided how far he would go in his criticism of the government.
Chamberlain still seemed secure, and Attlee believed that if the Prime
Minister rallied his supporters, 'the present political crisis may blow over'.

The Commons has age-old traditions. When the House met at
2.45 p.m. on 7 May 1940, it started as ever with prayers. The most important parliamentary debate of the twentieth century was technically held
on the motion that the House 'do now adjourn' – and was moved by the
Tory Chief Whip, David Margesson.

At 3.48 p.m., Chamberlain opened with a timid speech, but was interrupted by shouts of 'missed the bus' and had to break off until the
Speaker restored order. The Prime Minister then admitted that the
army, navy and air force had not worked together well in Norway. To
mollify critics, he announced that Churchill had been authorised to
roam beyond his Admiralty role and had the power to give direction
to the Chiefs of Staff committee. Maisky, the Russian ambassador, felt
the speech 'was simply rot'. It was all too ambivalent, Attlee thought,
and from a military point of view it made little sense as it gave Churchill
two roles. 'It is like a man commanding an army in the field and also a
battalion,' Attlee said.

Attlee then unleashed a devastating critique. 'It is not Norway alone.
Norway comes as the culmination of many other discontents,' he said.
The war was being badly run. The government's refrain was always that
it was too late. It was not Hitler but Chamberlain who had missed the
bus time and again. No Conservative interrupted or heckled. To win
what was a life and death struggle, Attlee concluded, 'We want different

people at the helm from those who have led us [into the war].' Whether he sensed that he would be one of those at the helm is not clear.

After speeches by Liberal leader Sinclair, Brigadier-General Sir Henry Croft and Colonel Wedgwood, Lewis Jones, a Chamberlain supporter, was clearly aware of the rumours of plots.

'I am amazed and shocked that the political opponents of the Prime Minister have directed their attention, in the main, to political and personal attacks,' he said. Lewis Jones stressed the need for national unity, but

at no time has so much lip service been paid to the ideal of national unity, with such unreality. We on all sides of the House, belonging to all political parties, have pledged ourselves that Hitler must go, and I am surprised to find that the concern of many members in this House appears to be that the Prime Minister should go. They are apparently more concerned about the Prime Minister's downfall than about the defeat of Hitler.

Jones criticised Lloyd George for committing the blunder of visiting Hitler.

He blazoned it forth to Europe that Hitler was the George Washington of Germany. The right honourable gentleman, whose articles have greatly disturbed the people of this country, has had in his time some strong political hates, but he never had a bigger hate than that which he has at the present time towards the Prime Minister. But if we are, as we believe we are, up against the biggest task of our lives in this war, I would appeal to him and to all members of the opposition to heed the words of the Prime Minister today when he asked that we should all play for the country and not for ourselves.

Labour's Captain Frederick Bellenger followed. He was a journalist and army officer who held the Bassetlaw seat. Bellenger spoke forcefully.

> If we believe that the times are so critical, we should say openly – if we believe it, and many of us do – that the government should make place for one of a different character and a different nature. I believe, at any rate I hope, because the times are so critical, that if there were a possibility of forming that government – and it rests mainly with honourable members on the other side of the House – we should play our part, as we so often say, 'in the public interest'.

Admiral of the Fleet Sir Roger Keyes turned up for the debate in full naval uniform, medals sparkling on his chest. He intended to cut a dramatic figure, as he wished to speak for officers and men of 'the seagoing navy' who were deeply unhappy about the conduct of the war. Trondheim should have been seized – and could have been seized, Keyes claimed. 'The iron of Gallipoli had entered his soul', and he sniped that wars could not 'be run by a committee'. Keyes urged the House to put Churchill in charge. He then quoted Nelson who had once said, 'I am of the opinion that the boldest measures are the safest – and that still holds today.' Keyes sat down at 7.30 p.m. Churchill, who was scheduled to wind up for the government, was heard to say that 'this is making it damned difficult for me.'

Leo Amery rose at 8.30 p.m. The House was fairly empty when he began speaking but members 'steamed in pretty rapidly'. Amery said that 'there was not one sentence in the Prime Minister's speech this afternoon which suggested that the government either foresaw what Germany would do or came to a clear decision.' He begged the Labour Party to play a constructive part:

The whole of Parliament has a grave responsibility at this moment; for, after all, it is Parliament itself that is on trial in this war. If we lose this war, it is not this or that ephemeral government but Parliament as an institution that will be condemned, for good and all.

'I fully realise that this is not an easy debate,' Amery said, adding that, 'we cannot go on as we are. There must be a change.' War demanded different politics and different politicians.

Facility in debate, ability to state a case, caution in advancing an unpopular view, compromise and procrastination are the natural qualities – I might almost say, virtues – of a political leader in time of peace. They are fatal qualities in war. Vision, daring, swiftness and consistency of decision are the very essence of victory.

The government must include 'men who can match our enemies in fighting spirit, in daring, in resolution and in thirst for victory'. It was time to summon the spirit of Oliver Cromwell. Amery first harked back to parliamentarian John Hampden, who had been a thorn in the flesh of Charles I three centuries earlier. Cromwell had blasted Hampden after one battle, saying, 'Your troops are most of them old, decayed, serving men, tapsters and such kind of fellows. You must get men of spirit.' Tapsters is now archaic; they were seventeenth-century barmen who were reckoned to drink too much. The troops might have been decayed in 1640, but 300 years on, it was their leaders who were not up to standard. Then Amery slashed with the sabre and addressed Cromwell's barb directly to Chamberlain: 'You have sat too long for any good you have been doing. Depart, I say, and let us have done with you. In the name of God go.'

Hansard records what MPs say, not the looks on their faces: a pity, as Chamberlain was worried enough to contact Amery after the debate and offer him a choice of either the Exchequer or the Foreign Office if he pledged to support him.

The House adjourned before midnight.

When Attlee arrived at the House the next morning, he was met by Captain Martin Lindsay, who had just returned from Norway. Attlee was astonished to see him; Lindsay had been a prospective Tory candidate for Brigg, which Labour held by just 203 votes in 1935. His battle-stained uniform making him look even more dramatic than Keyes, Lindsay handed Attlee a memorandum he had written based on his experiences in Norway, and told the Labour leader that he was quite convinced 'we should lose the war if we went on like that'.

After reading the memorandum, Attlee decided Labour must put down a motion of censure, so there would be a division at the end of the debate. Labour MPs met at around 10.30 a.m., but Dalton argued against the move, as he believed that no more than fifteen Conservatives would rebel. Attlee, now not remotely rabbit-like, overruled Dalton.

Sometime before the debate resumed, Lloyd George told Attlee that he thought Chamberlain should resign. Over lunch, Attlee pressed Lindsay for more details. These were disturbing and all too reminiscent of Gallipoli: units had arrived in Norway without the proper military equipment. Lindsay came close to accusing Chamberlain of misleading the House. Far from having limited objectives as the government claimed, British troops in Norway were always meant to capture Oslo, but that ambition had been quickly forgotten amid all the chaos.

Attlee gave Hebert Morrison the notes he had made from Lindsay's memorandum. The second day's debate started at 4.03 p.m. Morrison behaved shrewdly. He waited until he was well into his speech before announcing that Labour would be demanding a vote of censure. Chamberlain rose to interrupt and Morrison gave way as courtesy demanded. Chamberlain spoke for only a minute. 'I do not seek to evade criticism but I say this to my friends in the House – and I have friends in the House – I accept the challenge,' he said. Chamberlain had a majority of over 200, so it should not have been much of a challenge. But there was a sense among MPs that instead of dealing with the gravity of the situation, the Prime Minister had let his vanity get the better of his judgement.

Lloyd George had been reluctant to speak and had left the Chamber early in the debate. His daughter, Megan, found him in his room with his feet up and told the Welsh wizard – in Welsh – that he could not dodge this historic moment. Boothby also sent him a note, telling him that forty Tories might vote against the government. So Lloyd George came back, and being a former Prime Minister, the Speaker called him quickly. Lloyd George first said that he wished to see the proper use of sea power, adding that he did 'not think that the First Lord [Churchill] was entirely responsible for all the things that happened there [in Norway]'.

Churchill interrupted, 'I take complete responsibility for everything that has been done by the Admiralty, and I take my full share of the burden.'

Lloyd George told his friend of thirty years,

The right honourable gentleman must not allow himself to be converted into an air raid shelter to keep the splinters from hitting his colleagues. But that is the position, and we must face it. I agree with the Prime Minister that we must face it as a people and not as a party, nor as a personal issue. The Prime Minister is not in a position to make his personality in this respect inseparable from the interests of the country.

A tetchy Chamberlain retorted, 'What is the meaning of that observation? I have never represented that my personality—'

A number of MPs shouted, 'You did!' It was not Hansard but the Russian ambassador, Maisky, who usefully noted that Chamberlain looked as 'white as chalk'.

'On the contrary,' Chamberlain insisted, 'I took pains to say that personalities ought to have no place in these matters.'

Lloyd George was not going to allow that.

The Prime Minister has said: 'I have got my friends.' It is not a question of who are the Prime Minister's friends. It is a far bigger issue. The Prime Minister must remember that he has met this formidable foe of ours in peace and in war. He has always been worsted. He is not in a position to appeal on the grounds of friendship. He has appealed for sacrifice. The nation is prepared for every sacrifice so long as it has leadership, so long as the government show clearly what they are aiming at and so long as the nation is confident that those who are leading it are doing their best.

Lloyd George now wielded the knife with all the authority of the Prime Minister who had led the country to victory in the Great War. 'I say solemnly that the Prime Minister should give an example of sacrifice, because there is nothing which can contribute more to victory in this war than that he should sacrifice the seals of office.'

It was left to Arthur Greenwood to close for Labour. He pointed out that the House was troubled and offered an image of total German efficiency: 'I see Hitler sitting before an enormous file and pressing buttons A, B, C, D, E, F as his temperament determines.' Once Hitler pressed a button, the plan was implemented. Chamberlain could never match that.

At 10.11 p.m., Churchill gave the closing speech for the government. He called Lloyd George 'my right honourable friend', which was the wrong form of parliamentary address since they belonged to different parties, but explained that it was an old habit which reflected his affection for his former mentor. Churchill even managed a joke: Hitler had condemned most of Scandinavia to enter 'the Nazi empire of Hungryland' – hungry being a pun on Hungary. Then he turned to strategy. Norway might seem like a reverse, but Hitler had 'committed an act of self-blockade'. Churchill ended with a plea for unity: 'Let pre-war feuds, let personal quarrels be forgotten.' The speech was 'a very loyal effort to turn the tide', Attlee noted.

When it came to the vote on 8 May, the figures were strange. Remarkably, in the light of what was at stake, only 486 of 615 members passed through the lobbies. Some 129 MPs abstained or did not vote. Forty-three Conservatives voted with Labour and seventy Tories abstained. The government's majority was more than halved to eighty-one. Dalton wrote that many youngish Conservatives in uniform, such as Harold Macmillan, voted in the No lobby. When the result was declared, members shouted, 'Go, Go, Go.' The reduced majority demonstrated the weakness of Chamberlain's position, but he remained determined to cling on.

The next day, the House adjourned until 15 May. But Tory Chief Whip David Margesson promised that it would be recalled if events demanded this.

In his 2017 book, *Anatomy of a Campaign: The British Fiasco in Norway,*

1940, General Sir John Kiszely, a former assistant chief of the defence staff, questions whether the Allied campaign in Norway was a complete failure. He argues that, while the campaign was poorly executed, it nevertheless drained German resources. Eventually Hitler had to commit 400,000 troops to defend the 1,650-mile-long Norwegian coastline, and his navy lost numerous warships, making an invasion of Britain more difficult. Norway might have been a failure but, unlike Gallipoli, it was not a total failure.

Around midnight, Churchill told Chamberlain that 'this has been a damaging debate', but his advice was that the government should carry on until their majority deserted them. Chamberlain's family motto was *Je tiens ferme*; he told his sister he had 'often steadied myself by repeating that motto'. But repeating it now did not help him. He went to bed that night shaken and had decided to resign. When he woke up, though, he felt differently and fought like 'a tiger to keep power', according to Lord Dunglass, Chamberlain's Parliamentary Private Secretary, who became Prime Minister twenty-five years later as Alec Douglas Home.

I suggested earlier that MPs can display the characteristics of a crowd and pointed out that crowds can behave very emotionally. Emotions ran high that night and the next morning. A young John Profumo, Conservative MP for Kettering, was summoned to see the Chief Whip and branded 'a contemptible little shit' for betraying everything he had been elected to uphold.

Piecing together the events of 9 and 10 May is like piecing together a jigsaw, some of whose pieces do not fit. Divide and rule is one of the oldest political maxims, which Chamberlain now tried to follow. He summoned the two candidates who were the favourites to succeed him to a meeting at 10 Downing Street.

The classic Japanese film *Rashomon* tells the story of a rape and murder

from four different perspectives, but that is a simple jigsaw by comparison with the plots, counter-plots, real plots and imagined plots to replace
Chamberlain. There are disputes about when meetings took place and
who was present at which meeting. For example, Roy Jenkins argues
that when Attlee and Greenwood met the Prime Minister, Halifax and
Churchill were the only people in the room. Halifax's biographer Andrew
Roberts claims the Tory Chief Whip, David Margesson, was also present.

Chamberlain still hoped to persuade Attlee to join a coalition. Dalton
wrote that Chamberlain 'seems determined to stick on like a dirty old
piece of chewing gum on the leg of chair'. The Prime Minister was on
the phone from 8 a.m. and offered to sacrifice Hoare and Simon in a bid
to stay in 10 Downing Street.

At 9.30 a.m., Eden came to see Churchill; he was followed by Lord
Beaverbrook, the Canadian who had turned the *Daily Express* into a
mass-circulation paper, and who had won a seat in the House of Commons in 1910 before being made a peer. Clementine disliked him and
told her husband, 'Try ridding yourself of this microbe which some
people fear is in your blood.' One should add microbes to the insults
of mouse, rabbit and rogue elephants. Churchill informed Beaverbrook
that he would serve under any minister capable of prosecuting the war.
Brendan Bracken arrived next and managed to persuade Churchill not
to say too much at any meeting about who could become Prime Minister. It was good advice.

Shortly after noon, Chamberlain arrived late for a meeting of the
War Cabinet. He looked shaken and harrowed. At the same time,
the forty-three Tories who had voted against him met, with Leo Amery
in the chair. They agreed not to support any government in which
Labour and the Liberals did not take part.

When the Cabinet met at 11.45 a.m., 'the air was full of rumours of impending resignations', wrote Alexander Cadogan, the Permanent Under-Secretary for Foreign Affairs. In typical civil service style, he moaned that they had to wait while the House was 'wrangling and intriguing'. Despite the crisis, everyone of any importance managed to take a break for lunch at either the House, the Beefsteak Club or The Travellers.

At 4.30 p.m., Halifax, Chamberlain, Churchill, Butler and the Tory Chief Whip, David Margesson, met. Churchill told Butler, 'There is no place for you here. Your turn will come later.' Butler left. In his 2017 book, *Six Minutes in May: How Churchill Unexpectedly Became Prime Minister*, author Nicholas Shakespeare offers a summary of what we know and don't know about the meetings that followed. The key questions to consider are:

Did Chamberlain urge Halifax to replace him, as Cadogan says?

Did Chamberlain suggest Churchill would not get Labour support?

Did Margesson say that the House was in favour of Halifax, as Beaverbrook and Cadogan stated – or did he say nothing, as Halifax himself claimed?

Was Churchill's famous and uncharacteristic silence long or short, or was there no silence at all, as Halifax and Cadogan claimed?

Did the crucial part of the conversation as to who should succeed take place before Attlee and Greenwood arrived at No. 10?

At 6.15 p.m., Chamberlain waited for Attlee and Greenwood. Some versions of the event have him waiting in the garden of Downing Street; others insist that he sent Churchill and Halifax to take tea in the garden, knowing full well that tea was hardly Churchill's favourite drink. Everyone agrees, however, that six men finally sat around the Cabinet table: Chamberlain, Halifax, Churchill, Margesson, Attlee and Greenwood. Chamberlain urged Attlee and Greenwood yet again to join a coalition government under him, but their response was blunt. 'Our party won't have you, and I think I am right in saying the country won't have you either,' Attlee said. He was 'very rude', he admitted. Greenwood spoke even more sharply. He told Chamberlain the Labour Party did not just dislike him, but saw him as 'something evil'. Churchill, however, wrote later that the conversation was 'very polite'. The most polite exchange others recorded was when Greenwood accepted that Halifax was a 'God-fearing gentleman', but would not now make a good Prime Minister, as 'he's no bloody good for war'. The Labour men then left.

Churchill assured Chamberlain afterwards that he would not communicate with either of the opposition parties. Chamberlain then asked if he saw any reason why a Prime Minister should not sit in the House of Lords. Churchill just stared out of the window, and for once, was silent. The last peer to have been Prime Minister had been Lord Salisbury, whose history Churchill knew well; Salisbury had done nothing to prevent Churchill's father from resigning in December 1886.

This was the moment his career had prepared him for, Churchill said. He had learned from his many mistakes since 1910, but had lost none of his self-confidence, and remained determined and decisive, two qualities Attlee admired. In *The Gathering Storm*, written much later, Churchill suggested that Chamberlain 'evidently had in his mind the stormy scene in the House of Commons two nights before, when I had seemed to be in such heated controversy with the Labour Party'. He did not remember the precise words Chamberlain used, but he implied that the sharp exchanges in the Commons 'might be an obstacle' to Labour agreeing to work with him. Churchill did confirm his silence, which 'certainly seemed longer than the two minutes which one observes in the commemorations on Armistice Day'.

According to *The Gathering Storm*, Halifax then ruled himself out:

as a peer, it would be difficult for him to be a wartime Prime Minister. Andrew Roberts and Roy Jenkins both suggest that Churchill's version of events was less than accurate: Halifax was behaving evasively. Halifax had inherited his title from his father in 1934. Being a member of the House of Lords did not mean he had to be ruled out; it would not have proved too difficult to return him to the Commons by fashioning a by-election, and neither the Tories nor Labour would have objected, Roberts and Jenkins argue. The problem would not have been insurmountable.

Halifax had told several friends that he was prepared to take over, but the drama of the Norway debate made him pause, Roberts suggests. Halifax himself said that with Churchill in charge of the war, 'I should be a cypher.' When Butler tried to find Halifax in a final attempt to thwart Churchill, he was told the Foreign Secretary had gone to the dentist. Halifax developed acute stomach pains, too, which did not augur well for how he would cope with the top job. But Jenkins suggests that Halifax may not have been so ill; one of his nicknames was the Holy Fox and, being more fox than holy, he hoped Churchill would get into 10 Downing Street, only to fail after a few months. Halifax would then be able to take up the reins of power without any fear of being undermined.

In *The Gathering Storm*, Churchill projected himself as calm. His pulse was not racing.

I took it all as it came. But I cannot conceal from the reader of this truthful account that as I went to bed at about 3 a.m., I was conscious of a profound sense of relief. At last I had the authority to give directions over the whole scene. I felt as if I were walking with destiny, and that all my past life had been but a preparation for this hour and for this trial.

Before going to sleep, he spoke to his son on the phone, and told Randolph, 'I think I shall be Prime Minister tomorrow.' His warnings

> were now so terribly vindicated, that no one could gainsay me. I could
> not be reproached either for making the war or with want of preparation
> for it. I thought I knew a good deal about it all, and I was sure I should
> not fail. Therefore, although impatient for the morning, I slept soundly
> and had no need for cheering dreams. Facts are better than dreams.

The morning of 10 May started dramatically. Ten minutes after midnight, the Luftwaffe attacked Belgium. Its orders were to wipe out the Belgian air force, which had far fewer planes than the 1,375 the Germans could muster. The first day proved to be no triumph for Göring's crack pilots, however.

Hitler's move against Belgium almost cheered Chamberlain, who glimpsed a final chance to save himself; he believed the attack had totally changed the situation. Chamberlain rang Attlee and told him the crisis demanded continuity, which meant that he should stay on in Downing Street.

'Not at all,' Attlee replied sharply. Chamberlain should make way as soon as possible. Later that morning, Attlee told Brendan Bracken that he could serve under Halifax.

Roy Jenkins points out that the military calamity was never going to deflect the Labour Party from its beloved procedures. The National Executive Committee was preparing to meet in Bournemouth: Attlee and Greenwood wanted to consult it before reaching a final decision about joining any coalition. They promised Chamberlain a reply by the afternoon of 10 May.

Attlee and Dalton shared a taxi to Waterloo. Their conversation makes it clear that Attlee was sure there would be some sort of coalition. Dalton behaved nervously and said he wanted a serious role. Attlee reassured him, saying 'it was out of the question you should play second fiddle to anyone'. Dalton deserved a department of his own. The senior Labour men took the 11.34 a.m. train to the south coast.

The National Executive Committee of the Labour Party met at 3.30 p.m. Attlee and Greenwood had little trouble persuading it to agree to a coalition and were given freedom to negotiate the terms. Ninety minutes later, Chamberlain's private secretary rang Attlee to ask if Labour had reached a decision. Attlee said Labour would serve in a coalition government, but not under the man who had brought back no peace with no honour. Attlee did not plump either for Halifax or Churchill, but stayed neutral. According to Dalton, 'the last blow which dislodged [Chamberlain] was struck by us at Bournemouth'. Dalton had also learned that Bracken had told Macmillan it was as hard to get rid of Chamberlain as it was to prise a leech off a corpse.

Chamberlain went to see the King and recommended that Churchill become Prime Minister. By 6 p.m., Churchill finally had achieved the great office that it had been his ambition to achieve ever since Lord Randolph took him to see debates in the House of Commons, half a century earlier. When Attlee got back to Waterloo, a car from Downing Street was waiting for him. The Labour leader was driven to meet the new Prime Minister.

Attlee once observed that it was strange how Harold Laski, a professor of politics, possessed no gift for the actual business of politics. Laski now proceeded to prove Attlee's observation had been an astute one. Laski was patronising when Attlee and Greenwood announced that Chamberlain had resigned, saying 'it was as though the cook and the kitchen maid had been telling us that they had sacked the butler'.

Attlee's memories of Gallipoli influenced him over the next twenty-four hours. He remembered how 'vital decisions' had been delayed because of the 'long-drawn-out bargaining between the Conservatives and the Liberals over the formation of Asquith's coalition in 1915. I was resolved that I would not, by haggling, be responsible for any failure to act promptly.' Churchill had been distressed by that haggling, too, so they made fateful decisions fast: Labour would have seven seats in the Cabinet; Attlee would become Lord Privy Seal and, in effect, Churchill's deputy. Attlee had always wanted a small War Cabinet, and Churchill agreed. Lord Simon, who had been one of the appeasers, was made Lord Chancellor outside the War Cabinet, where 'he will be quite innocuous', Attlee wrote. So the War Cabinet consisted of two Tory appeasers, Halifax and Chamberlain, two former pacifists, and Churchill.

Attlee insisted on a number of concessions. He objected to Churchill's demand that Chamberlain become Leader of the House. They compromised, but Churchill insisted that Chamberlain remained in the War Cabinet; perhaps this was out of loyalty, or maybe because Chamberlain had urged George VI to send for Churchill.

Amery's diary reveals that Chamberlain fought to stay on as Chancellor. With Chamberlain proving obdurate, Amery phoned Salisbury. The man pushed by Churchill into the swimming pool at Harrow when they were teenagers talked to the grandson of the Prime Minister who had accepted Churchill's father's resignation in 1886. Amery persuaded Salisbury to phone Churchill and, with all the authority of a Tory grandee, insist that the new Prime Minister did not indulge Chamberlain. In this particular crisis, Churchill seemed to lack something he had hardly ever been accused of lacking – spine. Salisbury was successful, and Churchill duly informed Chamberlain that he would not become

Chancellor. Still, he could remain the Tory leader and become Leader of the House. Attlee decided not to quarrel with Churchill on this; he had already won the main point.

On 11 May, there were detailed negotiations about who should get what ministry. Attlee and Greenwood met Churchill in the morning and agreed on many appointments with little fuss. Those first meetings, with their easy give and take, set the tone for the whole of the relationship between Attlee and Churchill during the war. As well as seven members of the Cabinet, Labour would have one of the three crucial defence posts. Churchill wanted Bevin to become Minister of Labour and, having consulted his trade union colleagues, Bevin accepted. Halifax remained Foreign Secretary, while Eden became Secretary of State for War. Churchill's second-in-command from the First World War, Archibald Sinclair, took the Air Ministry and Herbert Morrison became Minister of Supply. Attlee reassured Dalton that he was 'well in the picture', but Dalton remained anxious until Churchill rang to offer him the post of Minister of Economic Warfare. Churchill apologised for being curt, but they had to deal with matters of life and death. The curtness did not stop Dalton from calling Churchill 'a grand man' in one diary entry. Amery wanted the job of Chancellor of the Exchequer and was disappointed to be offered the post of Secretary of State for India. William Jowitt, who had attended preparatory school with Attlee, became Solicitor General.

The coalition had to satisfy difficult constituencies: Parliament, to which the government had to account; the Tory Party, which distrusted Churchill; and the Labour Party, whose grandees felt that Attlee was not up to the job. Lord Taylor noted that Attlee had to put up 'with the extraordinary utterances of Harold Laski in public and private'. Laski had been elected to Labour's National Executive in 1937, so his sneers could not be ignored. Finally, the coalition had to also satisfy the British public, which did not always possess the bulldog spirit of legend.

Churchill found his first few days as Prime Minister 'peculiar. One lived with the battle, upon which all thoughts were centred and about which nothing could be done.' At the same time, he had to form a government, so there were 'the gentlemen to see' and a balance to keep between the parties. He and Attlee had to work out how sixty to seventy ministers could be 'fitted in like a jigsaw puzzle'.

When he wrote about all this later, Attlee referred to two of his interests: cricket and psychology.

> The problem of getting a Cabinet to work together is a profoundly difficult one, one which is to a very great extent veiled by the tradition of Cabinet secrecy and Cabinet responsibility. A good leader must understand human nature, and particularly the human nature of the particular group of men he has as his lieutenants, in relation to the particular stresses and strains of the day. He must also have good tactical judgement – know what issues to exploit in the House of Commons, how to make the most of them, and which ones to go easy on. You can't conduct a full-out dialectical battle on the floor of the House of Commons from the beginning of a parliamentary session to the end, with everything full out the whole time.

A good leader, Attlee stated, must be able to respond quickly and

> must be equally capable of holding himself on a tight rein, and making sure that in the interests of getting off to a flying start he will not compromise the opposition's case. In cricketing language, he has to be ready and willing to go out and hook one of his eyebrows over the

pavilion: but he has also got to move over and let a fast one go by the off-stump without nibbling at it, whatever the barrackers say.

Some of the most difficult conversations centred on Labour's wish to exclude the so-called guilty men, the appeasers. But old feuds must be forgotten, Churchill advised, and persuaded Attlee that this was not the moment for vengeance. The government had to be united.

Attlee reported to Labour's National Executive Committee on Monday morning and spoke stirring words. 'We have to fight for the freedom of the human spirit,' he urged committee members. Hitler was threatening to destroy what the British prized above all else, Attlee warned. 'Life without liberty is not worth living. Let us go forward and win that liberty and establish that liberty on the sure foundation of social justice.' It was a sign that he was fighting for a better future. In his autobiography, he wrote that though he was not yet formally Deputy Prime Minister, 'it was part of my work to relieve the Prime Minister of as much detailed administration as possible.'

Reactions to the coalition were not universally positive. Sir Basil Liddell Hart, who had acted as an occasional adviser to Churchill during the 1930s, and who had been asked by Chamberlain to prepare schemes for reorganising the army, grumbled that the new Cabinet 'appears a group devoted to "victory" without regard to its practical possibility'. He labelled Churchill a 'rogue elephant'. Sir Maurice Hankey, still at the centre of events eight years after his fact-finding mission to Germany, branded the war 'perfectly futile'. On 17 May, however, Dalton reported that Macmillan had said that Churchill was boasting about his government being the most broad-based Britain had ever known.

Churchill may have been vitriolic about socialism, but he never questioned Attlee's loyalty. 'We are in as partners, not hostages,' Attlee noted. It has often been argued that Churchill ran the war while Attlee concentrated on domestic policy, but this is untrue. Attlee contributed much to the military decisions in 1940 and 1941. The disputes on India and on socialism were shelved – for now.

Writing after the war had been won, Churchill was effusive in his praise of the Labour leader.

'During this time Mr Attlee acted as my deputy and did the daily work. His long experience in opposition was of great value,' Churchill wrote. Attlee was 'a colleague of war experience long versed in the House of Commons. Our only differences in outlook were about socialism, but these were swamped by a war soon to involve the almost complete subordination of the state. We worked together with perfect ease and confidence during the whole period of government.' Attlee's efficiency meant that Churchill only came to the House 'on the most serious occasions'.

According to Countess (Margaret) Attlee, the Labour Prime Minister's daughter-in-law, there was another reason why Attlee was loyal. In a 1997 interview in *The Independent*, she said that her husband, the second Earl Attlee, never took the Labour whip in the Lords when he succeeded his father. She added, 'I have always believed that Clement was a Conservative with a conscience. He was not a tremendous left-winger and that was the family tradition.' Attlee's cousin, Helen Rogers, offered some more personal history. 'He was known as Bolshie Clem in the family. It was seen as rather amusing that he became a Labour MP. The rest of the family voted Tory and it was quite a surprise that Clem went the other way.'

Churchill asked Attlee to work out of 11 Downing Street, which would allow the men to keep in constant contact. Initially, the War Cabinet met every day and Churchill would refer to himself as the

Minister of Defence, although such a post was never actually created. Attlee was on the Defence Committee and sometimes chaired it. He managed Churchill and believed that Churchill talked more frankly to him than to anyone else. Attlee usually returned home to Stanmore at weekends to spend time with his wife.

Churchill's anxiety manifested itself in one surprising way. Despite being a supreme orator, he distrusted the spoken word. He told General Hastings Ismay that any instructions he gave had to be issued in written form. Churchill would 'not accept any responsibility' for anything that was not written down.

On 13 May 1940, Churchill asked Parliament for a vote of confidence, giving a speech where he uttered the famous words: 'I have nothing to offer but blood, toil, tears and sweat.' The speech was also a defiant clarion call for victory. 'But I take up my task with buoyancy and hope,' he said. The black dog of his depression was for now well muzzled. No one voted against Churchill, but only Labour cheered at the end of his speech.

With the three principal parties now in a coalition, the question arose of how to carry on normal business in Parliament. Only the four Independent Labour Party members and one Communist refused to support the government. Attlee devised a solution that showed the 'practical illogicality which is one of the virtues of the British character'. Hastings Lees-Smith, briefly a Labour minister, took on the duties of Leader of the Opposition, though he was very much for the war, while Labour members not in government continued to sit on the opposition benches. Hitler should have surrendered in the face of such skulduggery.

A famous cartoon by David Low, published on 14 May, depicted Churchill, sleeves rolled up, marching forward followed by Attlee, Bevin and the rest of the government. The caption read: 'All behind you, Winston.' The Cabinet would need to be resolute, as 13 May had proved a disastrous day for the French, the failure of whose army would have made Napoleon weep.

Wars trigger emotional responses. When Britain fought to recover the Falklands from Argentina in 1982, the chances of General Leopoldo Galtieri landing on Dover beach were never great, but we still avidly followed the progress of the war. We admired the efficiency of the Royal Navy as it sailed to the south Atlantic; we watched in trepidation as Argentine planes bombed our ships; we mourned the loss of Lieutenant-Colonel H. Jones at Goose Green. Imagine, then, the intensity of feelings in 1940, when there was a good chance of a Nazi force coming ashore at Dover, and when the French Army and the British Expeditionary Force were suffering one military reverse after another.

On 14 May, the once not quite pacifist Attlee turned into one of Dalton's bellifists and suggested a counter-attack on German railways. The next day, Churchill was woken up by a phone call from the French Prime Minister, Paul Reynaud. 'We have been beaten; we have lost the battle,' he told Churchill. 'Surely it can't have happened so soon?' Churchill responded. It had, though. German troops had smashed through one supposedly impregnable obstacle after another. Crossing the River Meuse allowed them to attack the undefended rear of the Allies and advance to the English Channel without too much opposition. French counter-attacks were half-hearted at most, and essentially useless.

May and June saw Churchill make five visits to France in a desperate attempt to stiffen the sinews of the French; Attlee accompanied him on two of these trips. For the leading members of the government to fly into a country on the verge of collapse was extraordinarily risky, but both men felt they must do everything they could to bolster the morale of the French leaders. Churchill obviously enjoyed the adventure. Attlee did not mind it either, it seems.

Attlee was one of the strongest advocates of the decision to bomb German industry. On the night of 15 May, the Bomber Command sent 100 planes to attack the Ruhr. To help the RAF, Attlee even invoked the example of Milton's *Samson Agonistes*. Samson lost his formidable powers when Delilah cut his hair, but he begged God to give him one more chance to destroy the Philistines and deliver, as the RAF was about to do, 'winged expedition'. The poem could have been written for the occasion as Samson arrived with his 'invincible might':

> To quell the MIGHTY of the Earth, th' OPPRESSOR,
> The brute and boisterous force of VIOLENT men
> Hardy and industrious to support
> TYRANNICK power, but raging to pursue
> The RIGHTEOUS and all such as honour TRUTH;
> He all their ammunition
> And feats of war defeats
> With PLAIN HEROIC MAGNITUDE OF MIND
> And celestial vigour arm'd,
> Their armories and magazines contemns,
> Renders them useless, while
> With winged expedition
> Swift as the lightning glance he executes
> His errand on the wicked, who supris'd
> Lose their defence distracted and amaz'd.

France was not the only victim of the Nazi advance. In 1937, Hendrikus Colijn, the Dutch Prime Minister, had assured Churchill that he only needed to make a phone call to unleash a torrent of water that would drown any invaders. In the event, the button that would flood the dykes failed to stop the Germans from seizing all the locks and canals. The Netherlands surrendered on 15 May.

The next day, Churchill flew to Paris with General Dill, chief of the Imperial General Staff, and Ismay, Churchill's deputy as Defence Minister. French General Maurice Gamelin explained that the Germans had broken through on a 50km front and had advanced 60km from Sedan. When Churchill asked when and where Gamelin proposed to attack the German Army's flanks, Gamelin shrugged, 'Inferiority of numbers, inferiority of equipment, inferiority of method.' The French had committed all their forces and had no reserves left.

'I admit that was one of the greatest surprises I had in my life,' Churchill said. Experienced generals always kept some forces in reserve. Gazing out of the window, he saw French officials hurling official documents on bonfires: the Germans were expected in Paris and Parisians were fleeing the city. Churchill went to the British embassy and told Dill to assemble the War Cabinet, with Attlee in the chair.

Churchill knew that Air Chief Marshal Hugh Dowding, the head of the RAF, had circulated a memo warning that he needed at least fifty-two squadrons of planes; he was already down to thirty-six. Dowding said the War Cabinet must assure him that

> not one fighter will be sent across the Channel however urgent and insistent the appeals for help may be. I believe, that if an adequate fighter force is kept in this country, if the Fleet remains in being, and if Home Forces are suitably organised to resist invasion, we should be able to carry on the war single-handed for some time, if not indefinitely.

Churchill rejected Dowding's warnings, and urged the War Cabinet to send six more squadrons of fighters; even in desperate moments

Churchill took care to bring his colleagues with him. The War Cabinet agreed. Churchill's beloved Raj now played a part in making sure the Nazis would find it hard to understand British plans. General Ismay dictated the message about the six extra squadrons in Hindustani, as he had arranged for an Indian Army officer to wait in his office in London. (There is a touching naivety here in the assumption that the Nazis could not find anyone who spoke the language.)

Churchill flew back to London to report on his visit to Paris. Jock Colville noted that the Prime Minister seemed cheerful. On the night of 17 May, aware that France was being overrun, Churchill left Attlee to examine what would happen when Paris fell, 'and the problems that would arise if it were necessary to withdraw the BEF (British Expeditionary Force) from France'.

In this critical situation, Attlee's calm was remarkable. He went home to Stanmore and inspected his garden on 18 May. The daffodils were doing well. Flowers were a luxury the country could no longer afford, however, as every vegetable would be vital. Attlee decided to uproot the daffodils and plant potatoes. As Violet could not manage the garden, he handed its maintenance over to the local allotment committee, of which he was chair.

The next few days saw Churchill's mood swing, as it often did. On 17 May, Colville wrote that Churchill 'was full of fight'. Two days later, however, Colville noted, 'I have not seen Winston so depressed.' Churchill was unusually 'very inconsiderate to his staff'. These mood swings did not affect Dalton's view of Churchill, who for him was 'the man, the only man, we have for the job'.

Monday 20 May proved a frantic day. Churchill sent a message to President Roosevelt, assuring him that Britain would never accept 'a shameful peace or surrender'. Then the War Cabinet summoned a conference of all those who might be needed to arrange an emergency evacuation of the BEF from France. Attlee, with his experience of Gallipoli, was a key figure. In the midst of the crisis, Attlee attended a memorial service for George Lansbury at Poplar Town Hall. Attlee would be glad that his old comrade would never witness the devastation that Luftwaffe bombers would soon wreak on Lansbury's beloved East End.

In the 1930s, little thought seems to have been given to how war might change civilian life. Chamberlain now made a real contribution. He was asked to draft proposals for additional powers the government might need if Hitler seemed likely to invade. Chamberlain was in his element when it came to property and finance. For a sick and disappointed man, he worked fast. He consulted properly with Attlee as well as with other ministers and the proposals reflected the influence of the Labour Party, and particularly that of Bevin and Attlee.

The first issue was 'control over persons'. Staff needed to be provided 'not only for the factories and workshops making munitions of all kinds, but also for any other work that is required in the national interest'. Bevin, as Minister of Labour, should have the power to direct any person over the age of thirteen to perform any services required, and to decide how much people should be paid and their conditions of service. He could not give all his directions personally, so he would employ national service officers drawn from staff at the Ministry of Labour and the wider civil service. Bevin could also employ trade union officials. Giving union men power was a real change; sharing power would be the norm throughout the war.

Chamberlain's proposals allowed the government to control wages and profits. He suggested the introduction of an excess profits tax, something which Attlee, author of pamphlets against profiteers, fully supported. Banks would be ordered to cooperate with each other and with Whitehall, roughly on the lines of the Railway Executive Committee, which allowed the government to seize control of the railways in the event of war. The Cabinet also stared at the worst. If there was an invasion and a breakdown of bureaucracy, the system of regional commissioners would continue to function. If that failed, the military would take control.

On 22 May, Churchill returned to Paris to be greeted by General Weygand, who had replaced Gamelin as French commander-in-chief. Weygand was a colourful character, a man rumoured to be the illegitimate son of a Mexican princess and possibly Leopold II, King of the Belgians. As Leopold was Queen Victoria's cousin, this would link Weygand to the British royal family. He had also been one of Marshal Foch's chief aides during the First World War. Weygand proposed that the French First Army and British forces should strike south, while another force headed north to cut off the Germans about 80 miles northeast of Paris. The attack never happened. Three days later, the British commander General John Gort, despairing of the French, decided his only option was to make for the coast and evacuate as many troops to Britain as possible.

While Churchill was in Paris, Attlee introduced the Emergency Powers Defence Bill, which was based on Chamberlain's proposals. The unwritten British constitution worked fast. Between 2.36 p.m. and 6.09 p.m., the Bill was passed in the Commons and the Lords, then given royal assent. 'Our ancient liberties are placed in pawn for victory,' Attlee told the nation in a broadcast that night. The war concentrated power in Whitehall as never before.

With France teetering on the edge of defeat, many appeasers felt their moment had come. On 24 May, Halifax suggested that Mussolini should be asked to explore an arrangement with Hitler. Chamberlain backed the idea. Halifax met the Italian ambassador and flattered him into cooperation. The ambassador promised to inform 'Signor Mussolini that His Majesty's government did not exclude the possibility of some discussion of the wider problems of Europe'. Halifax said,

> This I told His Excellency he could certainly do, for plainly the secure peace in Europe that both Signor Mussolini and we desired to see established could only come by the finding through frank discussion of solutions that were generally acceptable and by the joint determination of the great powers to maintain them.

When Halifax reported back to the War Cabinet on 25 May, Churchill and Attlee reacted furiously. Attlee warned the Holy Fox that 'if the public got wind of the fact that the government was putting out peace feelers to the Fascists, morale would hit rock bottom.' The 'Unholy Fixer' might have been a better nickname for Halifax than the Holy Fox.

Military failures triggered psychological consequences, argued James Randolph, a writer on cavalry of all things. He highlighted a characteristic he called 'mental speed-up' or 'mental mobility'. Randolph's article in *The Cavalry Journal* for January–February 1940 was, he claimed, the first attempt at a comprehensive study of an essentially psychological subject. The Germans, faced with the problem of making their treaty army (limited by Versailles) of 100,000 as efficient as possible, had developed mental mobility tests and used them to select pilots, officers and tank drivers. The results had been 'as startling as the barbarian conquest of Rome'. The allegedly impregnable Fort Eben-Emael in Belgium 'was taken within thirty hours by parachutists and Bahnbrecher, or combat engineers'. The wooded hill region east of Sedan had been considered impassable for a modern army, but the German Panzers smashed their way through it. Randolph commented, 'The blitzkrieg moved too fast for the Allies to keep track of it, much less stop it. The Germans did not waste time coding and decoding radio messages … Before the Allies could use the information, it was obsolete.' By the time the Allies had decided how to respond to a move, the Panzers had sped off somewhere else. Randolph fleshed out the details of why the French Army collapsed before the German onslaught. 'Mental mobility, the ability to put the blitz in blitzkrieg, appears to have been Germany's secret weapon,' he wrote.

The collapse of France left Churchill temporarily dazed and he became even more inconsiderate to his staff. Clementine warned him against being disliked by his colleagues and subordinates: 'It seems your private secretaries have agreed to behave like schoolboys and take what's coming to them.' She continued, 'Higher up, if an idea is suggested to you … you are supposed to be so contemptuous that presently no ideas – good or bad will be forthcoming.' She had herself noticed 'a deterioration in your manner' and urged him to combine 'urbanity, calmness and if possible Olympian calm'. She could not bear it if people only admired him; she wanted them to love him too.

Attlee knew that when Churchill was fatigued it was not only cigars and cognac that helped him recover; he needed to speak and speak. 'We used to let him get it off his chest, and not interrupt,' Attlee said. He chaired meetings crisply, so letting Churchill vent his feelings must have sometimes tried his patience. He had the good sense, however, to know that Churchill needed to express himself this way.

On 28 May, Churchill told the members of his Cabinet they needed 'to maintain high morale and to show confidence in our ability and inflexible resolve to continue the war'. This was the day when Belgium surrendered. Dalton's diaries give the fullest account of the Cabinet meeting and unintentionally reveal that Attlee understood Churchill better perhaps than any other colleague.

Churchill reported on the last week and was 'quite magnificent', Dalton wrote; 'he gives a full, frank and completely calm account of events in France. When the Germans broke through on the Meuse, French morale for the moment collapsed.' The French had been hypnotised by the Maginot Line, a complex combination of massive concrete fortifications, decoy houses that concealed gun emplacements, bunkers, observation posts and a narrow gauge railway system. De Gaulle had been one of the Maginot Line's fiercest critics and was now being proved all too correct as the German Army blitzkrieg-ed round it. The French had become so demoralised that General Billotte, commanding French forces north of the Somme, had issued no important orders for four days. Then he was killed in a motor accident and was succeeded by General Georges Blanchard. The French had failed to push northwards from the Somme; 'we were in grave danger of being surrounded,' Dalton wrote.

British forces were falling back on Dunkirk, which Dalton wrote 'was under a great pall of black smoke, to which our ships were adding artificial smoke so as to screen our embarkations from the air'. The RAF was performing superbly 'and the Germans were suffering immense losses in the air, as on the ground, in their attempts to interfere with the embarkation'. The RAF's apparent superiority cheered Churchill and the Cabinet. 'It was clear that we had killed off most of the best Nazi pilots, unless, which seemed unlikely, they had been holding some of their best in reserve.'

Churchill had to prepare the British public for bad news. Dalton quoted him saying 'that what was now happening in northern France would be the greatest British military defeat for many centuries'. France might soon collapse, but Churchill stressed the positive: 'It might indeed be said that it would be easier to defend this island alone than to defend this island plus France.' He added that if Britain held out alone 'there would be an immense wave of feeling, not least in the USA which, having done nothing much to help us so far, might even enter the war'. Roosevelt would, of course, never hear such criticism.

At the end of the meeting, ministers cheered and patted Churchill on the back. Dalton told Churchill to buy the David Low cartoon, which Churchill agreed would be a good idea. 'He is a darling,' Dalton wrote. At 7 p.m., Churchill told the House that the whole Cabinet had 'expressed the greatest satisfaction when he had told them there was no chance of our giving up the struggle'. The appeasers had been silenced.

Due to his experience of Gallipoli, Attlee helped to draft the plans for the evacuation from Dunkirk. Attlee 'never took so gloomy a view' as General Gort, the BEF commander; Attlee thought most troops could be got safely off the beach and ferried back to Britain. On 29 May, Churchill noted that 'we sent modified instructions on the lines of Attlee's suggestions to get General Gort to get the last 40,000 troops out of Dunkirk'. Two recent films, *Dunkirk* and *Darkest Hour*, both ignore Attlee's part in the evacuation and so reinforce the false myth that he contributed nothing to military operations. Attlee realised that evacuating troops would not be the only problem; much vital military equipment would have to be left behind. German newsreel cameramen later drooled over the abandoned British tanks, trucks and heavy guns.

Churchill and Attlee flew to Paris to meet Reynaud and other French leaders on 31 May. He would never forget that meeting, Attlee said. Pétain, the hero of Verdun in the 1914–1918 war, looked dejected, like some 'old image'. Reynaud's memoir, written after the war, noted that Pétain was still fuelled by the fierce fires of ambition – the original French comment is ruder – despite being an old man. In Attlee's eyes,

Admiral François Darlan, the commander-in-chief of the French Navy, seemed 'a bluff sailor'. Paris was turning into a ghost town, as people fled south.

Attlee said that 'Churchill made a magnificent speech in indifferent French'. Churchill's words provided a momentary fillip to the French, and Attlee then added a few words of his own, 'indicating the solidarity of Britain'. The British were now fully aware of the terrible danger they faced and understood that 'in the event of a German victory everything they have built up will be destroyed.'

The coalition government was working well. Churchill encouraged Reynaud to invite Bevin to Paris to meet French union leaders. 'Mr Bevin was showing great energy', and under his leadership, Churchill noted, 'the working class was now giving up holidays and privileges to a far greater extent than in the last war'.

The chiefs of staff now produced a memo whose coy title was set in dramatic capitals: BRITISH STRATEGY IN A CERTAIN EVENTUALITY. That eventuality was the surrender of France. The chiefs investigated 'the means whereby we could continue to fight single-handed'. They assumed that the United States would 'give us full economic and financial support, without which we do not think we could continue the war with any chance of success'.

Three factors would be decisive, the chiefs argued. Morale must be maintained and imports had to make it possible 'to sustain life and to keep our war industries in action'. In addition, the British Empire needed to help. Then the country could resist invasion. The chiefs believed there were 'good grounds for the belief that the British people will endure the greatest strain, if they realise – as they are beginning to do – that the existence of the empire is at stake. We must concentrate our energies primarily on the production of fighter aircraft and crews.'

Factories essential to fighter production 'should have priority and be defended'.

One of the unanswered questions of the war is whether Hitler allowed the Dunkirk evacuation because he hoped to make some accommodation with Britain, or whether his generals committed a tactical blunder. As small and big ships continued to ferry troops away from the beach, the War Cabinet grew anxious about the French: might France make a separate deal with Hitler? In the end, 338,226 troops were evacuated from Dunkirk, including some 100,000 French soldiers.

On 4 June, Churchill told the Commons: 'We must be very careful not to assign to this deliverance the attributes of a victory. Wars are not won by evacuations. But there was a victory inside this deliverance.' He trumpeted famous defiance: 'We shall fight on the beaches; we shall fight on the landing grounds; we shall fight in the fields and in the streets; we shall fight in the hills; we shall never surrender.' Dalton for once praised Attlee, noting that he 'is a very good General Staff officer'.

On 11 June, Churchill flew to France again in another attempt to stiffen resistance. He travelled to Briare near Orleans but, according to Ismay, the meeting there felt like a funeral reception. When Churchill promised that Britain would support the French come what may, Pétain mocked '*c'est de la blague*'; it was a joke. Churchill at least managed to get Admiral Darlan to promise not to hand over the French fleet to the Nazis.

Only a day later, Churchill flew back to Britain, but that evening, Reynaud phoned him to ask if he would return and talk again with the French government, which had now moved to the old cathedral town of Tours as the Nazis continued their advance.

Churchill flew back to London the next day. The sheer danger of going to France became clear when his Flamingo aircraft had to dive low after the pilot spotted two Luftwaffe planes machine-gunning fishing boats.

On 13 June, Attlee wanted a statement 'to hearten the people of France'; Churchill would have to issue this in person. Escorted by Hurricane fighters, the two men flew to Tours, taking huge personal risks. They planned to continue on to a meeting at Concarneau, yet again with the aim of bolstering French resolve, but the French cancelled the meeting.

The following day, German troops goose-stepped down the Champs-Élysées. Churchill's generosity, his deep sense of the dramatic and of history now combined and he proposed an extraordinary idea: a declaration of union between Britain and France. Rather surprisingly, Attlee agreed. The two men and Liberal leader Archibald Sinclair now prepared to meet Reynaud to persuade him to accept the union, which would mean that every citizen of France would become a citizen of England. But if such a revolutionary union were to ever happen, it must happen quickly. The first plan was to meet in Bordeaux. Then the leaders decided to meet at sea off the coast of Brittany. Churchill, Attlee and Sinclair arranged to go by special train from Waterloo to Southampton and then board a cruiser. But as they waited in the train, Churchill's private secretary rushed over from Downing Street with a message that stated the meeting with Reynaud was impossible.

The French version of these events is also dramatic, if somewhat depressing. Reynaud told de Gaulle that if there was going to be a union, '*il faut le faire grand et vite*'; it had to be done grandly and quickly. Reynaud knew that Pétain opposed the idea. The old hero of Verdun was ambitious to become the leader of France, even if a German victory meant it would only be a much diminished France that he would be in charge of. Pétain persuaded many of his colleagues that Britain would never hold out against the Nazis – so what was the point in meeting the British leaders? Dalton said that Reynaud's mistress did not help matters, either, as she said the offer of union was 'only a trick to make France a British dominion'.

De Gaulle still flew to Bordeaux with the document offering union, but he stayed there for only eighteen hours before heading back to Britain. He confirmed that the French leaders had declined the offer as they thought Britain was bound to be defeated. On 16 June, de Gaulle met with Churchill. Roosevelt was pressing Churchill to send more planes to France, but Churchill refused to do so, and de Gaulle backed Churchill's decision. The two men would have an often difficult relationship, but in 1940, Churchill was sensitive to de Gaulle's situation. 'Under an impassive demeanour he seemed to me to have a remarkable capacity for feeling pain,' he wrote. The France he loved was lost, de Gaulle knew.

The Second Armistice at Compiègne on 22 June marked the surrender of France. Vichy became the capital of unoccupied France and Pétain assumed the title of Chief of State of Vichy France. George Orwell wrote:

> The sort of peace that Pétain, Laval & Co. have accepted can only be purchased by deliberately wiping out the national culture. The Vichy government will enjoy a spurious independence only on condition that it destroys the distinctive marks of French culture: republicanism, secularism, respect for the intellect, absence of colour prejudice.

Orwell then quoted Shakespeare: 'If England to herself do rest but true', and added,

> She is not being true to herself while the refugees who have sought our shores are penned up in concentration camps, and company

directors work out subtle schemes to dodge their excess profits tax. It is goodbye to the *Tatler* and the *Bystander*, and farewell to the lady in the Rolls-Royce car. The heirs of Nelson and of Cromwell are not in the House of Lords. They are in the fields and the streets, in the factories and the armed forces, in the four-ale bar and the suburban back garden; and at present they are still kept under by a generation of ghosts.

Orwell wanted to see the war won, but even more he wanted to start on 'the task of bringing the real England to the surface'. He could be said to have anticipated Attlee's vision of a more equal Britain. 'There is no question of stopping short, striking a compromise, salvaging "democracy", standing still. Nothing ever stands still. We must add to our heritage or lose it, we must grow greater or grow less, we must go forward or backward. I believe in England, and I believe that we shall go forward.' Orwell might be far to the left of Churchill, and indeed of Attlee, but his tone was distinctly Churchillian.

The Vichy government still controlled the considerable French Navy, the same force that Admiral Darlan had promised never to hand over to the Germans. With seven battleships, it was the largest navy in Europe after the Royal Navy. Despite Admiral Darlan's promise, Churchill feared that the French would surrender their warships to Hitler. This would make Germany's navy, the Kriegsmarine, an even more formidable fighting force.

The War Cabinet had been ready to declare union with France, but only three days later, it agreed to try to sink the French fleet while it lay at anchor at its base at Mers-el-Kébir, off the coast of French Algeria. Churchill had little difficulty in persuading his colleagues to order the attack, with Attlee being very much in favour. On 3 July 1940, the French refused to surrender. In the brief naval battle that followed, 1,297 French servicemen died; one battleship was sunk and five other ships were damaged. In response, France mounted air raids on Gibraltar and severed diplomatic relations.

In explaining the situation, Churchill and Attlee worked in tandem. Destroying the French fleet had shown, Churchill told a silent and solemn Commons, that the War Cabinet 'feared nothing and would stop at nothing'. When he finished speaking 'there occurred a scene unique in my own experience. Members stood up and cheered; members on both sides of the House. Until then it was from the Labour benches that I received the warmest welcome when I entered the House.'

As well as Orwell, the novelist J. B. Priestley became an important voice. In his 7 July BBC *Postscript* broadcast, Priestley told listeners about 'the two most heartening and inspiring things I've seen this week'. One of these was a duck and her ducklings on the Whitestone Pond in Hampstead. Priestley was delighted by the 'minute ducklings, just squeaking specks of yellow fluff', and saw them as symbols of hope and the energy of life to set against the 'death-worship' of Nazism. The other 'heartening and inspiring' event concerned Churchill. Priestley was watching the Prime Minister explain the decision to sink the French fleet when Churchill, despite the gravity of the situation, gave Ernest Bevin a dig in the ribs and grinned at him. Priestley found it inspiring that, though burdened by great responsibilities, Churchill could still express humanity and humour.

For his part, Attlee broadcast to the nation and expressed his profound regret at the sinking of the French ships. The country was engaged, however, in 'a war of nerves' with Hitler. At the end of June, Attlee called for Britain to publish war aims. Failure to do so would give the impression the country was fighting a conservative war in defence of the status quo, while the Nazis had a clear strategy. It would take Roosevelt to push Churchill into making Britain's war aims more comprehensive than simply beating Hitler.

Soon after Dunkirk, the Luftwaffe started raids on Britain; Hitler could not launch an invasion unless Germany controlled the skies. Churchill was incredibly active during the Battle of Britain, a heroic tale that has been told often. His brilliant summing-up used the three-pronged rhythm he loved so much. 'Never in the field of human conflict was so much owed by so many to so few' is one of the enduring phrases of the war.

Attlee was less involved in that battle. He and the Labour Party, however, played a very useful role in supporting Churchill in the second mating dance of the period, this one with Roosevelt. Roosevelt's New Deal, a policy in tune with many Labour Party ideas, had used public spending to combat the recession after the 1929 Wall Street Crash and to lower unemployment. There were numerous informal contacts between Labour and some of Roosevelt's associates. Even the usually critical Harold Laski helped.

The war had to be fought on the home front, too. As Postmaster General, Attlee had recognised the importance of advertising, and one of the more charming developments in 1940 was the government's use of it. Some campaigns were nicely recorded in *Mum's the Word*; the slogan that is best remembered perhaps is 'Careless Talk Costs Lives'. There were commercial campaigns, too. Before the war, Kraft had boasted it made the finest processed cheese 'you could buy – the delicate uniform flavour added something to every cheese dish'. Hitler had seen to it, alas, that Kraft Cheddar cheese could not be produced. Undeterred, Kraft had found ingenious ways of making cheese dishes using virtually no cheese.

Harvey Nichols, the Knightsbridge department store, was equally imaginative, trumpeting that 'a sewing machine can be almost as much a weapon for victory as a spade'. It tugged at people's consciences, too, adding: 'Are you living a selfish life thinking selfish thoughts, spreading complacency and thoughtlessness? If so you are dangerously out of fashion.' Russian women were fighting in smocks and slacks, while German women were working alongside men building barges, Harvey Nichols continued. The moral was plain: a woman's place was in the army or the Auxiliary Territorial Service.

In Stanmore, despite her tendency to depression, Violet Attlee set a brave example by becoming the local commandant of the Red Cross. The Attlees had an air-raid shelter built in their garden, where they sent the children, but they themselves opted to stay in the house. They grew so used to gunfire that Attlee could sleep through the heaviest raid. They were not immune to the Blitz, though; all the windows in their house were shattered when a bomb landed nearby. Churchill became worried the country might run out of glass.

During the Blitz, Attlee visited the East End regularly. Toynbee Hall was bombed, as was Newell Street, close to where he had once lived. Attlee visited another street which had been demolished, where a man said, 'Do you know the fun of it? The Luftwaffe had destroyed Mosley's headquarters.' Another man said, 'Hello major, old Hitler's bombed me out of Eastfield Street and had bombed me out of Maroon Street but he's b***** not going to bomb me out of Stepney.' On one of his visits Attlee encountered a rich businessman, a staunch Tory, who was paying for a canteen that served free food. The businessman's chief assistant was someone Attlee knew; he had seen him in Spain fighting for the Republicans.

A bomb hit the Treasury and many were dropped on Horse Guards

Parade. One morning the windows in the Cabinet Room were blown out, but that did not stop the business of government. In October, Churchill made his ministers rehearse meeting in an underground shelter. Typically, Attlee took some poetry to read. He needed relaxation as Churchill noted that Attlee 'has a lot of work'. The powers of the police were one of the many issues he dealt with. There was anxiety about a Fifth Column and about enemy aliens. Some of these foreigners had fled the Nazis, but others might be spies.

On 28 August, as the Battle of Britain raged overhead, Churchill journeyed to Ramsgate, which had been heavily bombed. He responded emotionally and dictated a memo to the Chancellor urging him to establish a war compensation scheme. People and businesses that had been ruined by the Blitz needed help. The burdens must be shared. Attlee thought that this was only fair. The War Damage Act was, he said, 'one of the most remarkable legislative achievements of the war', and a year later the government had paid all the claims submitted up till then.

The means test had angered the poor in the 1930s. It had allowed all kinds of snooping to take place; the government sent inspectors to search kitchens to see if a household had anything other than the cheapest cuts of meat, for instance. A single piece of steak found in the larder could result in benefits being slashed. Attlee persuaded the Cabinet to change all this. He also persuaded Churchill to let him chair a War Aims Committee, which would begin to plan for a far more socialist future.

One Tory commented with some surprise to Attlee, 'What strikes me is that your chaps know their jobs.' What strikes one seventy years on is the amazing spirit of optimism. The RAF had not yet won the Battle of Britain, but politicians were already planning to build a new Jerusalem.

Attlee had little difficulty getting Churchill to agree to what he called his war aims.

War aims were all very well, but the fighting was going badly for Britain, especially in the Atlantic.

Churchill now pulled off a vital deal. Roosevelt agreed, though the United States was neutral, to give Britain fifty destroyers. On 2 September, in exchange for the ships, the United States was granted land in British possessions to establish military bases, on 99-year rent-free leases. The bases were to be in Bermuda, Newfoundland, the eastern Bahamas, the south coast of Jamaica, Antigua, the west coast of Trinidad and British Guyana. The deal allowed Britain to hand much of the defence of Bermuda over to the United States, thus freeing British forces to fight where it mattered more.

Britain was now standing alone, and the country would become even more isolated if Spanish dictator General Franco decided to join forces with Hitler. Attlee, as has been pointed out, thought that Churchill had judged 'the Spanish show' wrongly. Churchill, however, ultimately judged Franco rather well. He sensed that Franco disliked Hitler and hoped to encourage the Spanish leader to stay neutral. On 23 October, the two dictators met at Hendaye on the border between Spain and France. Hitler wanted Franco to declare war on Britain and to order an invasion of Gibraltar. Franco's daughter, María del Carmen Franco y Polo, revealed later in her memoirs that her father and Hitler did not get on well. Franco feared Hitler might have him kidnapped in order to force him to do his bidding. Franco nominated a general and two others to take control of Spain if this happened.

Franco was sensible to be anxious given Hitler's record, but this did not stop him making exorbitant demands himself. If he were to ally himself with Hitler, Franco wanted Morocco, half of Algeria and more.

Churchill paid tribute 'to the duplicity' of Franco in his dealings with Hitler. If the Spanish had taken Gibraltar, it would have been a disaster.

Mussolini did not want Hitler to have all the fascist glory and ordered the Italian Army into northern Greece. As had happened in classical times, Rome would conquer Athens again, Il Duce believed. But the Italians encountered fierce and unexpected resistance. Britain supported the Greeks and Churchill wrote that 'from his own heart His Majesty replied to the King of the Hellenes: "Your cause is our cause; we shall be fighting against a common foe."'

Attlee's contribution did not earn him much recognition from Cecil King, later chairman of IPC, which owned the *Daily Mirror*. The two men met for the first time in October. King was unflattering. 'Attlee is a man I should say of very limited intelligence and no personality,' King confided to his diary. 'If one heard he was getting £6 a week in the service of the East Ham Corporation, one would be surprised he was earning so much.' Such inaccurate estimates of 'limited' Attlee persisted through the war.

Churchill remained surprisingly sympathetic to Chamberlain, despite the fact that the man had accused him of lacking judgement and had tried to have Churchill deselected in his Epping constituency. The stress of his years as Prime Minister, his failure to deal with Hitler, and his failing health now forced Chamberlain to resign all of his positions. Nevertheless, Churchill asked the King for permission to send Chamberlain Cabinet papers, to which the King gave his assent. On 9 November 1940, Chamberlain succumbed to bowel cancer. Churchill believed the former Prime Minister had the comfort of knowing that Britain had at least turned the corner. In his tribute to the House, Churchill called him 'an English worthy'.

Gas now became a problem. In late November, Churchill said it was 'of the upmost importance that departments should accumulate a thoroughly adequate reserve of gas weapons as quickly as possible'. If the Nazi invader 'could not beat down our resistance in any other way he might well have recourse to gas and we must be in a position to retaliate at once and effectively'. Attlee took charge of the details of where to store gas safely and how to be able to use it as a weapon.

As 1940 came to an end, Churchill wrote that it had been 'the most splendid, as it was the most deadly, year in our long English and British story'. A 'quaintly organised' England had destroyed the Spanish Armada in 1588 owing to the poor leadership of the Spanish commanders, the great storm that scattered their galleons and the first Cecil to make his mark. Napoleon had also given up on his dreams of invading Britain. But 'nothing surpasses 1940', Churchill said. The soul of the British people had proved 'invincible. The citadel of the Commonwealth and Empire could not be stormed.' But there were still 'no lack of cares' that needed to be contended with. The main one of these was the Battle of the Atlantic, which would take far longer to win than the Battle of Britain.

In November, Roosevelt won an unprecedented third term, which delighted Attlee. He wrote to Harold Laski, who had excellent contacts in America, that the result was 'magnificent'.

Churchill, in his Generalissimo garb, was the key figure in dealing with the military. As we have seen, however, Attlee was often closely involved, and sometimes advocated surprisingly aggressive policies. Attlee regularly chaired the key Defence Committee, which met on forty occasions in 1940. It also met seventy-six times in 1941, twenty times in 1942, fourteen in 1944 and ten in 1945. Once again, Churchill and Attlee were comrades-in-arms.

CHAPTER 9

BLOOD TODAY, JAM
TOMORROW, 1941–1945

Aristotle once said, 'No great genius has ever existed without some touch of madness.' Some 2,500 years later, psychologists have discovered that individuals who work in creative fields are significantly more likely to have – or at least have a family history of – mental health issues such as schizophrenia and bipolar (Appendix Two examines this in greater detail). Writers, and Churchill was a writer too, were 121 per cent more likely to suffer from bipolar disorder. Also, they were nearly 50 per cent more likely to commit suicide according to figures presented in *Eminent Creativity, Everyday Creativity, and Health.*

Recent research claims that psychopathic traits can turn you into a serial killer – or a rather successful chief executive. A Prime Minister prone to depression and compensating bouts of manic energy, however, might not lead to calm and considered decisions being made during a crisis. 'I believe I had as much direct control over the conduct of the war as any man,' Churchill said, as he praised 'the fidelity and active aid of the War Cabinet'. It is telling that Churchill admitted he needed both these things in 1941 and 1942, even though Hitler seemed to have 'missed the bus', as Chamberlain had remarked.

One question which was being asked then was whether Churchill would be the best driver of the British bus. At different times, Beaverbrook, Halifax, Cripps and even Eden voiced doubts about his leadership. They were all aware of his mood swings. Attlee had been fending off challenges to his leadership from well before the coalition started, but Churchill was unused to it, as he had never led either of the parties he had joined.

Sometimes against Labour instincts, sometimes against the mood of the House, and sometimes even against his own instincts, Attlee defended Churchill; the mouse had become a fierce member of the Praetorian Guard. Attlee believed that Churchill had many flaws, but he nevertheless considered him a great leader, a man who expressed the defiant spirit of a defiant country. Attlee also had a definite domestic agenda: at the end of the war, Britain would become more equal than it had ever been. The dream of John Ball might edge closer.

At the start of 1941, the risk of invasion was less of a problem than the risk of starvation. There would be triumphs and disasters over the next four years. With the exception of India, Attlee and Churchill worked in perfect trust. Churchill was often abroad and had no hesitation in leaving Attlee in charge. As it happened, these absences gave Attlee better preparation for becoming Prime Minister than any other twentieth-century politician enjoyed.

The coalition had to grapple with many complicated issues, including America's isolationism and Irish neutrality. The German ambassador in Dublin, Eduard Hempel, encouraged Irish intransigence. The Taoiseach, Éamon de Valera, who had clashed with Churchill over the years, did not need much encouragement. He refused to let Irish ports be used to combat the U-boats, which made American help even more vital.

The coalition commissioned novelist Elizabeth Bowen to write a report on Irish attitudes. She concluded that 'the assertion of her neutrality is Éire's first free self-assertion ... Éire (and I think rightly) sees her neutrality as positive, not merely negative.' De Valera could never forgive the British for how they acted during Ireland's struggle for independence, and this rendered him blind to the evils of Nazism. To curry favour with Hitler, de Valera even banned Charlie Chaplin's satire *The Great Dictator*.

Historians have made much of the close relationship between Churchill and Roosevelt. Churchill was aware of the importance of remaining on friendly terms with the Americans and he devoted much energy to convincing, cajoling, even almost wooing the man in the White House. There was another strand to Anglo-American relations, though. In his essay on Roosevelt, Isaiah Berlin ignored Lansbury, Attlee and other Labour Party leaders, and enshrined the American President as the leading advocate of social welfare reform of the era. As they shared many similar views, it is not surprising that a number of Labour politicians enjoyed good relations with Roosevelt's administration. That would matter in the future when Attlee brought off a nifty coup.

Roosevelt did not offer much practical help at first. The US Navy did little to protect ships that were both supplying, and failing to supply, Britain. On 16 January, Roosevelt told his chiefs of staff that the navy should be prepared to help convoys that were bringing supplies to England, but though he had once been Assistant Secretary of the Navy, Roosevelt hardly galvanised his admirals into action.

Three weeks later, Churchill voiced his anxieties and hopes in a broadcast that was very much aimed at the Americans. Britain had to be prepared to meet gas attacks, paratrooper attacks and even glider attacks, but Hitler would never triumph as Britain could count on the empire and because 'the whole English-speaking world will be on his track', brandishing the swords of justice. He might 'tear great provinces of Russia', and 'spread his curse' throughout Europe, and even march 'to the gates of India', Churchill said.

It had to be hoped that at those gates, Hitler would not meet Gandhi, who was so angry at the British, and at Churchill personally, that he refused to support the fight against the Nazis. Gandhi had cause given how rude Churchill had been, calling him seditious and a half-naked fakir who 'ought to be lain bound hand and foot at the gates of Delhi, and then trampled on by an enormous elephant with the new Viceroy seated on its back'. It is a pity the two men never debated, because Gandhi had a nice line in repartee. When reporters asked him if he felt he had been undressed when he met George V in 1931, Gandhi replied that the King wore enough clothes for both of them. Churchill, however, had no time for Gandhi's humour. He was blind about India and Gandhi was more than was a little short-sighted about Hitler.

Churchill ended with a direct appeal to the United States: 'Put your confidence in us. Give us your faith and your blessing and under providence all will be well. We shall not fail or falter.' He added another phrase that would become famous: 'Give us the tools, and we will finish the job.'

The Americans might have the hammers, nuts, bolts and greasing oil, but millions of them just wanted to stay out of any fight between the Europeans. Churchill had to woo, woo and woo again. He often signed himself 'former naval person' when writing to Roosevelt because the President had been Assistant Secretary of the Navy.

For once, Harold Laski did something useful by publishing a book on the American presidency, a subject he knew well, as he had taught at

Harvard and Columbia. Woodrow Wilson had once said, 'The President is at liberty, both in law and conscience, to be as big a man as he can, as big, that is, as he can be within the limits imposed by a federal system, a division of powers, and a party organisation.' These were precisely the constraints Roosevelt now faced, Laski helpfully explained. Churchill pressed for Roosevelt to fight, but Congress resisted.

In February 1941, the *Washington Post* recognised how important Attlee had become and profiled him as 'Cautious Clem', a man who was carrying, as Churchill acknowledged, a heavy workload. Attlee saw that the way 'the British people stood up to the Blitz impressed the Yanks'.

The War Cabinet knew the 'submarine menace' could scupper all hopes of victory. Admiral Dönitz set his U-boats a target of sinking 800,000 tons of shipping in the Atlantic each month. Though Dönitz's target was never met, Britain went short of food, fuel and military supplies. To watch over 85,000 miles of sea required endurance and brilliant organisation. In *Britannia Has Wings*, Archibald Hurd pointed out that it was not possible to say, 'We will send one convoy from Avonmouth on Tuesday and ... one from Gibraltar on Thursday and then sit back with the comfortable feeling that everything had been done.' Huge logistical problems had to be overcome in the battle against the U-boats.

Roosevelt's first contribution was a cunning one. On 11 March 1941, he signed the Lend-Lease Act into law; it allowed him to lend or lease equipment to any country essential to the defence of the United States. Britain fitted that bill. One of the first items loaned was 900,000 tons of fire hose, which shows how effectively the Luftwaffe had made Britain burn. The country needed Lend-Lease desperately. In April, 616,469 tons of shipping were lost to the U-boats and the Luftwaffe. It had been sensible of Attlee to plant potatoes instead of daffodils.

Dig for Victory was a brilliant slogan for a brilliant campaign, which encouraged people to grow their own vegetables. Then an organisation that turned members of the public into social science researchers reported more than mere grumbling from the diaries of its volunteers. Mass Observation's first report, 'May the Twelfth: Mass-Observation Day-Surveys 1937 by over two hundred observers', was edited by a distinguished quartet: the documentary film maker Humphrey Jennings, the poets Charles Madge and Kathleen Raine, and the literary critic William Empson.

The Merseyside volunteers painted a grim picture. Some civilians had 'to sleep in fields on the outskirts of the city, isolated from their neighbourhoods and traditional institutions, such as the corner shop and the public house, which helped maintain morale'. Mass Observation believed in Karl Marx more than Attlee did and detected what the theorist had attributed to workers, 'a sense of alienation'.

In May, a Home Office report warned that morale had dipped to dangerous levels and 'the grimness of the people has a menacing note'. The report went on to say that 'the expressions of revolt do not come from the submerged tenth but from the average person.' The submerged tenth was presumably larger than the Fifth Column. In the rougher districts there had been disturbances and private cars could not travel safely in some areas. Mustn't grumble was not the mood, 'amongst the working class comment is more severe ... after an hour listening to the remarks one is left with a feeling of dread.' The grumblers were 'not slum-dwellers'. Attlee was almost certainly aware of these findings and worked on all kinds of practical issues. If the trains did not run properly and sewage overflowed, morale would dip even more, he knew. His own morale was never in doubt because he was already looking to the future, despite the poor military situation. 'We are even in the midst of war trying to build up social security for our people,' he announced.

Attlee's determination was remarkable, as the performance of the British forces in the late spring and early summer could have inspired a book on how not to wage war. On 10 April 1941, Rommel attacked the port of Tobruk. By 30 April, mainland Greece was under Axis control; three weeks later Germany invaded Crete by air. Rommel had forced the Allies to retreat to the Egyptian border by 25 May. By 1 June, all Greek and British forces on Crete had surrendered. Nevertheless, on 6 June in Chesterfield, Attlee praised Churchill's inspiring leadership, although he also spoke honestly about Crete.

When there is a domestic failure, cynical governments have been known to provoke wars in order to divert attention. The coalition now turned this ancient wisdom on its head. Ignoring military setbacks, it planned for a better Britain: blood today, jam tomorrow was the message. As Attlee had argued, the Labour Party was not being held hostage; they were partners. Labour was fighting for liberty, but also for the future. On 10 June, Greenwood announced that an inter-departmental committee under William Beveridge would study Britain's social insurance and allied services. It was Churchill who had hired Beveridge, some thirty-five years earlier, after the Webbs had recommended him. Attlee spoke of Britain's 'practicality illogicality'. A logical government would have devoted all of its energy to winning the war, but the coalition went beyond this. Setting up the Beveridge committee was a fine example of surrealism in Whitehall.

The coalition then had to react when the Nazis broke the Soviet–German pact of 1939 and invaded the Soviet Union on 22 June 1941. The initial success of his armies made Hitler think that he would succeed where Napoleon had failed 130 years earlier. Like Napoleon had done, Hitler assumed that the Soviet Army would crumble. Military opinion was with him. Most experts believed the Germans would smash the

Red Army, especially as Stalin had purged many experienced officers whom he feared were plotting against him.

Despite his many doubts about the Soviet Union, it was Attlee who announced to the House that Britain would help the Soviet war effort. Relations with Stalin then provoked the first major rift in the coalition. Attlee had complained about Stalin's invasion of Finland in 1939 and had no intention of letting him absorb Lithuania, Estonia and Latvia. The Labour leader threatened to resign. Churchill refused to accept the resignation. They carried on as before.

The mating dance between Churchill and Attlee had been one between two equals until Churchill became Prime Minister. With Roosevelt, the position was different. America had the world's strongest economy and vast resources; however, in 1939, its military was still developing. The US was planning initially to stay out of any conflict, but the situation was becoming increasingly complex. It was not only the isolationists. De Valera was making his not so passive hostility to Britain known to Irish politicians who were influential in the US Congress. American Nazis had staged a rally at Madison Square Gardens in New York in February 1939. Some 20,000 Hitler enthusiasts heard their leader Fritz Kuhn criticise Roosevelt, repeatedly referring to him as 'Frank D. Rosenfeld' and calling his New Deal the 'Jew Deal'.

Churchill wrote constantly to Roosevelt, explaining, charming, badgering. In August, the two men finally met at sea, in Placentia Bay off Newfoundland, amid conditions of great secrecy. They had met before in 1918 at a banquet, when Churchill was already famous while Roosevelt was a young Assistant Secretary of the Navy; Roosevelt remembered the meeting, but Churchill did not. Churchill hoped that Roosevelt would not only pledge aid, but would also warn the Japanese not to attack British possessions in the Far East. Roosevelt was not going to say anything which might provoke difficulties at home, however. On the first day, he asked Churchill for an overview of how the war was going. The next day the Americans came over to the British battleship, HMS *The Prince of Wales*, for the Sunday service. Churchill paid great attention to the hymns, choosing 'For Those in Peril on the Sea' and 'Onward Christian Soldiers'. Both were meant to prod the conscience of the President.

Roosevelt's conscience, however, came at a price. In return for American help, he insisted that Britain accept dramatic changes in the post-war world. America had, after all, once been a British colony and had fought for its independence, so Uncle Sam thought he understood about freedom fighters.

At the end of the meeting, the two men issued a 'Joint Declaration by the President and the Prime Minister'. The main points were simple. Neither the United States nor the United Kingdom sought territorial gains from the war. The interesting assumption was that, at some point, America would enter the war. Ideological and idealistic, the declaration promised all peoples the right to self-determination and committed both countries to global economic cooperation. Attlee, very much in charge back in London, called a War Cabinet meeting after midnight. At 4 a.m., Attlee cabled back additional provisions on social welfare, better conditions for workers and economic progress; these all reflected Labour policy. Attlee also brought 'freedom from want and fear' into the document. When Roosevelt accepted Attlee's additions with enthusiasm, Churchill did not object. He never bore a grudge against Attlee for pushing the declaration to the left.

The Joint Declaration also promised that aggressor nations would be disarmed, and aspired to a general disarmament after the war. Roosevelt wanted the United States to be the only country that did not disarm, but eventually agreed that Britain also could have a substantial military.

The Labour-supporting newspaper the *Daily Herald* coined the name 'The Atlantic Charter' for the declaration, a name Churchill used in Parliament on 24 August. The Atlantic Charter, Attlee felt, 'was as important as Magna Carta or the American Declaration of Independence'. He had always believed that war aims, which emphasised the positive, would appeal to some Germans. The RAF dropped millions of copies of the charter over Germany to tell people Britain did not seek a punitive peace. Twenty-two years after Versailles, the Germans were understandably sceptical.

The Atlantic Charter left one issue unresolved, one of the few on which Attlee and Churchill differed – the future of the British Empire. Roosevelt had persuaded Churchill to agree that all peoples had a right to self-determination, though Churchill easily lapsed into the belief that some more so than others. Robert Sherwood, Roosevelt's speechwriter, argued that the peoples of India, Burma, Malaya and Indonesia were asking whether the Atlantic Charter extended to them. Or was it, to put it bluntly, just for white people?

A few weeks later, in the House of Commons, Churchill claimed the charter was only meant to apply to states the Germans occupied, and certainly not to the blessed British Empire. He wanted the flag to keep flying over India, Hong Kong, Cyprus, Gibraltar, Bermuda, Jamaica and some ten other territories. He was an imperialist rather than a racist, but it was easy to confuse the two. Backstop Attlee had to reassure a group of students in London that the promises made in the charter would apply to all races. Again, Churchill raised no objections.

October saw three important events occur – one of which was two years in the making. On 2 August 1939, Albert Einstein had written to Roosevelt explaining that recent work in physics made it possible to envision a devastating new weapon triggered by a fission chain reaction. The not so minor difficulty was that one could not build an atomic bomb without uranium 235. Canada had a little, but the largest deposits were to be found in the Belgian Congo. Roosevelt made the puny sum of $6,000 available to commence research. In 1941, Britain was ahead of America in this field. On 1 October, Roosevelt proposed a joint atomic effort and Churchill agreed. As usual, their agreement was not detailed because they trusted each other. The ramifications would be enormous.

The second October event was a dinner Churchill gave in honour of Attlee in the House before the Labour leader headed to New York for the International Labour Conference. During the meal, Churchill praised Attlee unreservedly. The third event was a declaration by Attlee, who said, 'I have not in taking office altered my political faith.'

When he got to New York, Attlee told a large audience at Columbia University that Britain faced a shortage of manpower. Fighting the war required socialist planning. He visited an aircraft factory in New Jersey and the Navy Yard in Philadelphia, but was careful to say nothing that would upset Roosevelt, who was experiencing difficulties with the American Federation of Labour. Attlee could now use his once crippling shyness in an endearing way. On 20 November 1941, he told American reporters that press conferences were 'one of the things of which I am naturally frightened'. He was more personal than usual when speaking to the press. He told them of Churchill's extreme sensitivity to suffering. He had seen him visibly upset by the Luftwaffe's destructive bombing of London's East End. The personal approach went down only so well. Roosevelt, however, saw no way of providing any real military help.

The situation changed totally three weeks later on 7 December, when the Japanese attacked Pearl Harbor. Roosevelt had no choice but to declare war on Japan. Hitler then made a catastrophic mistake. He had not attacked the United States; his ally had. He could have kept his distance, but instead, he declared war on America. Churchill went to bed that night happy. He wrote, 'Satiated with emotion and sensation I went to bed and slept the sleep of the saved and thankful. One hopes that eternal sleep will be like that.' Churchill had good cause to sleep so soundly. Hitler had just ensured his eventual defeat.

As 1941 drew to the close, one letter shows how Attlee supported Churchill – and a degree of affection even.

11 Downing Street
Whitehall. SW1
20 December 1941

My Dear Prime Minister,

I was sorry to hear that you've had a stormy voyage. I hope you have had a better time in the later part of the journey.

Events in the Far East have rather disturbed public, press and M.Ps most of whom seem to have been oblivious of the danger of which we have been conscious for months. House was, therefore fractious and difficult …

There is also a good deal of apprehension about the defence of India with which is connected anxiety as to the political situation. This cannot be ignored as it transcends Party divisions. The Evening Standard and the Mail and other papers have now joined the Herald in demanding action of some kind on the Indian political situation.

We have reviewed the Far Eastern position in the Defence Committee and have done our utmost to reinforce. Earle Page [Australian politician and former Prime Minister] has been very persistent and the tone in Australia is very critical. I think that I have demonstrated to him that we are doing our best utmost in the circumstances, but he harps on the past.

The Russian Front and Libya are bright spots in a rather gloomy land-
scape, but we none of us have been under any delusions as to what Japan's
entry into the war meant.
   The general public will gradually appreciate the position. With all good
wishes for Christmas to you and the party,
      yours ever
         Clement Attlee

The tone was remarkably comradely, with Attlee even extending his good wishes to the Conservative Party. Attlee was also often generous. He would never try to imitate Churchill, as it was 'obviously futile to try to put on Saul's armour'.

Psychology is full of stage theories explaining how children develop, but only one major twentieth-century psychologist, Erik Erikson, developed a theory of the stages of development throughout life. By their fifties, human beings should have developed wisdom or be in despair. Erikson did not consider that a man at this stage of life should have real ambition to change things, as Attlee now did. To return to the point made by Steve Ely about Ted Hughes, Churchill at war in 1941 was not all that different from Churchill in 1910. Attlee, however, had lost his shyness and no one could intimidate him now. Clementine Churchill sensed that and said shrewdly, 'I admire Mr Attlee for having the courage to say what everyone else is thinking.'

On 22 December, Churchill arrived in America to spend Christmas at the White House. Four days later, he addressed a joint session of Congress. His sense of history came to the fore:

For the best part of twenty years the youth of Britain and America have been taught that war was evil, which is true, and that it would never come again, which has been proved false. For the best part of twenty years, the youth of Germany, of Japan and Italy, have been taught that aggressive war is the noblest duty of the citizen and that it should be begun as soon as the necessary weapons and organisation have been made. We have performed the duties and tasks of peace. They have plotted and planned for war. This naturally has placed us, in Britain, and now places you in the United States at a disadvantage which only time, courage and untiring exertion can correct.

'Five or six years ago,' Churchill lamented,

it would have been easy, without shedding a drop of blood, for the United States and Great Britain to have insisted on the fulfilment of the disarmament clauses of the treaties which Germany signed after the Great War. And that also would have been the opportunity for as-suring to the Germans those materials – those raw materials – which we declared in the Atlantic Charter should not be denied to any nation, victor or vanquished. The chance has passed, it is gone. Prodigious hammer-strokes have been needed to bring us together today.

Congress gave him a standing ovation.

Churchill was on his way by train to Ottawa as 1941 ended. When he arrived in Canada, he was asked how long it would take to win the war. 'If we manage it well it will take only half as long as if we manage it badly,' he replied. Managing it badly was a real anxiety.

Attlee wrote to his brother, Tom, that he was 'busy carrying the baby', while Churchill was in America. Attlee chaired the War Cabinet with skill and without the flourishes that were so much Churchill's style. For Churchill, a committee was an audience; for Attlee, it was a group whose ideas he absorbed and then usually got his way. Churchill was a shaman and a showman, Attlee recognised. 'He was the driving force, a great war leader.' But this did not mean there were never any disagreements between them, or that Attlee was unaware of Churchill's flaws, which, for now, he kept to himself.

After Pearl Harbor, the Japanese bombed Singapore, landed in southern Thailand and moved rapidly down the Malayan Peninsula. On 10 December, Japanese aircraft sank Britain's two main warships in the area, HMS *Prince of Wales* and HMS *Repulse*. A month later, Japanese troops reached Kuala Lumpur and on 27 January, Lieutenant-General Arthur Percival ordered the remaining 30,000 British troops in Malaya to retreat to Singapore. In just fifty-five days, the Malayan Peninsula had been lost.

The siege of Singapore began on 1 February. Fifteen days later, General Yamashita Tomoyuki and his aides went to the Ford Motor Factory to meet the British party who surrendered. Typically, Percival did not know the Japanese had nearly run out of ammunition. N. F. Dixon, in his wry *On the Psychology of Military Incompetence*, described the catastrophic mistakes made at Singapore: Percival pointed his heavy guns out to sea, so he was defenceless when the Japanese attacked from the land. The fall of Singapore was a major blow. Churchill wrote to Violet Bonham Carter that he was afraid 'our soldiers are not as good fighters as their fathers were'. Then, on 11 February 1942, two German battleships which had been bottled up in the French port of Brest broke out and brazenly sailed up the English Channel.

Churchill's morale sank to a very low level. He needed all of Attlee's loyalty and reassurance; he got both, especially when, on 23 January 1942, Stafford Cripps returned from Moscow where he had been Britain's ambassador. Churchill invited Cripps to join the government as Minister of Supply, but Cripps refused. Two weeks later, Cripps made a critical broadcast, comparing the situation in Britain to that in the Soviet Union. There seemed to be a 'lack of urgency' in Britain, Cripps commented, and it was as if the British were spectators, not participants.

A few days later, Churchill summoned Beaverbrook, who as usual criticised Attlee and even wanted him sacked. The Prime Minister had no intention of being dictated to, but he acted subtly, making Cripps an offer he could not refuse; he would become Leader of the House and a member of the War Cabinet. Churchill's biographer Roy Jenkins argues that, as some people had imagined Cripps could replace Churchill, this was a brilliant move. Attlee was promoted, too, formally becoming Deputy Prime Minister and Secretary of State for the Dominions.

The confidence motion is sometimes a sign of no confidence. On 28 January 1942, Attlee tabled the motion 'that this House has confidence in His Majesty's government and will aid it to the utmost in the vigorous prosecution of the war.' Attlee argued that such a vote

> does not imply that everybody who votes for it believes that every part of the government's personnel is the best that could possibly be had. If that were so, I am afraid you would never get a vote of confidence in any government, because in a healthy and self-confident House of Commons there must always be a very large number of members who are confident they could fill some, or all of the available offices, much better than their actual occupants.

Attlee's self-confidence in the confidence debate was evident. Everybody could not be satisfied. He continued,

> Of course, there is room for improvement, and it is only in totalitarian states that it has to be an article of faith with those who wish to keep

their heads on their shoulders that everything the government does is right and that the Führer for the time being can do no wrong. In this House we assume as an axiom that the government will make mistakes, and we are never disappointed.

The Labour MP Manny Shinwell interrupted to criticise. Attlee shot back: 'I do not mind criticism.' In a splendid put-down, he added, 'And I shall never lack it while the honourable member is about.' There was

a great reservoir of men in the Indies, Malaya, and elsewhere, but the mass of them are untrained and unarmed. Everybody knows that after our losses in France we were hard put to it to arm our regular troops, much less our Home Guard, for the defence of this country. Everyone will agree that that armament had to have priority. Secondly, we had to arm for the Libyan campaign. We had to build up our army.

Being a skilful parliamentarian, Attlee promised to study 'a number of excellent suggestions put forward in the debate'. The government could not adopt them all, because some of them 'contradict each other, but the value of a debate like this is not, I think, in delivering attacks on individuals but in its constructive suggestions'. He was gently ironic, too: 'I do think, however, that when attacks are made, and when it is suggested that there should be removals from the government, it would be nice to know who they are. It would be nice, too, to know sometimes who would replace them.' Attlee now offered a variation of Lloyd George's remark that Churchill should make himself an air-raid shelter. Attlee said, 'I do not think it is right to say that the Prime Minister tried to put up an umbrella over all his colleagues in the government. I think he was merely enunciating what is a perfectly sound constitutional doctrine – that members of the government have a collective responsibility.'

Attlee promised the House a further reply.

> I have asked honourable members to give the government a continuance of their confidence in the sense in which a vote of confidence is always understood in the House, not as one of meticulous approval of every individual and every action, but of general agreement with the government on their policy and faith in their determination to carry us through to success.

There was only one vote against, from the conscientious objector and Independent Labour Party leader, Jimmy Maxton, a Glasgow MP and Red Clydesider. Maxton was considered one of the greatest orators of the era, with Churchill describing him as 'the greatest parliamentarian of his day', despite their views differing radically.

Now in charge of Dominions, Attlee developed his ideas on India. With push that even Beatrice Webb would have approved of, he convened seven meetings of the Cabinet's India Committee in the next fortnight. The Cabinet, however, would not agree to Attlee's proposals – a promise of independence within the Commonwealth. By way of compromise, Cripps was dispatched to India to negotiate with political leaders there.

Attlee was earning international recognition by now. On 16 February 1942, the *Washington Post* reported that he was the kind of man who appealed to the British people, who were always inclined not to trust too much brilliance and were happy 'to chuckle over the idea of a socialist deputy acting as a brake on Tory Churchill's daring'.

Chuckling was apt, and there were instances of humour in the War

Cabinet. During one Cabinet meeting, Attlee reminded Churchill of Lewis Carroll's *The Hunting of the Snark*, which starts:

> The crew was complete; I included a Boots—
> A maker of Bonnets and Hoods—
> A Barrister, brought to arrange their disputes—
> And a Broker, to value their goods.

A billiard-marker, a banker and a beaver were also in the crew searching for the snark.

The snark was Stalin, of course. Churchill knew the poem well and recited a few lines. He forecast that he would eventually walk paw in paw with the Russian bear, but he resisted the idea of sending troops to fight alongside Stalin now. Paw in paw was playful and this Cabinet meeting was far from the only time Churchill acted playfully.

On 4 May, Churchill sailed for America again, leaving Attlee in charge at home.

On the night of 26 May, Rommel started his offensive in the north African desert and headed towards Tobruk. Churchill told Eden, 'If Tobruk falls, then I'm done for and must hand over to someone else.' When it happened, however, he did not quit.

With Tobruk lost, Churchill was now unable to claim that the British could instruct the Americans in the ways of war. In Cairo, British officials imitated the defeatist French two years earlier and started to burn documents, certain that Rommel's Panzers would soon reach the city. The novelist Lawrence Durrell, who served as a press attaché in the British embassy, said later that life in the city then was almost fun. You had a hot bath, drank whisky and pottered off to a brothel if you fancied it. You certainly forgot Rommel.

Churchill was at the White House on 12 June, and he and Roosevelt discussed a proposal to develop a new international organisation where states could negotiate. The League of Nations had failed, as had the Kellogg–Briand Pact, but some forum was necessary to handle conflicts, and it needed to have some powers. Attlee became one of the prime advocates for the creation of the United Nations.

Peace was not the sole item on the agenda; Churchill also produced evidence of British progress in atomic research. Roosevelt was convinced and began to consider an immensely expensive programme which became the Manhattan Project a year later. American scientists thought the research would be unlikely to produce a bomb during the war, but British scientists were more optimistic. The Allies would site research stations in Canada, which had sources of uranium 235, and was less vulnerable to reconnaissance. The three countries would pool information as part of their common war effort. Roosevelt put Prescott Bush, the director of the Office of Scientific Research and Development, in charge.

The vote of confidence at Westminster held on 2 July 1942 was more contested than the one in January. Keyes attacked the chiefs of staff and Aneurin Bevan delivered a speech as sharp as some of Churchill's, saying, 'The country is beginning to say he [Churchill] fights debates like a war and wars like a debate.' Bevan proposed using brilliant Czech, French and Polish generals. Critics argued that Churchill should not be both Prime Minister and Minister for Defence, and urged him to delegate the responsibly for running the war to a senior military figure. Churchill was eloquent in his own defence, saying he had stuck to his promise of blood, toil, tears and sweat. Sadly, now he needed to add 'muddle and mismanagement' to this list. He told the House it would take time for the United States 'to bring its gigantic forces to bear'. Churchill won the vote by 475 votes to twenty-five. It was a fine example

of democracy in action. The twenty-five MPs who voted against included Bevan and, of course, Maxton.

A week after the debate, Attlee sent Churchill a long memorandum
reviewing the military situation and, as it was critical, he did not circulate
it to the full Cabinet. He was not the only critic. Eric Dorman-Smith
was something of a maverick officer and a historian. He was deeply depressed by the tactics of the British Eighth Army, which always lagged
behind those of the Germans. Field Marshal Rommel had succeeded
because he was a brilliant and enterprising commander who led from
the front – unlike most British generals, Attlee commented astutely. He
sacrificed everything to mobility. Attlee likened Rommel's soldiers to
guerrillas, and felt the British Army needed something of that spirit.

Churchill travelled to Cairo on 4 August, and then on to Moscow
to meet Stalin, leaving Attlee in charge at home. Churchill told Stalin
about the Allied plans for an invasion of North Africa that he had drawn
up with Roosevelt. The Soviet leader reacted angrily when he discovered
there would be no second front in Europe. Sir Alex Cadogan, Permanent Under-Secretary of State for Foreign Affairs, said Churchill had
been delighted by his first meeting with Stalin, who then confronted
them with an aide-mémoire that was

> as sticky and unhelpful as could be. This threw rather a cloud on the
> party, which was not dispelled by the banquet the following night.
> Nothing can be imagined more awful than a Kremlin banquet, but
> it has to be endured. Unfortunately, Winston didn't suffer it gladly.
> However, next morning, he was determined to fire his last bolt, and
> asked for a private talk, alone, with Stalin.

At 1 a.m. Cadogan was summoned to Stalin's private rooms, where he found Churchill, Stalin and Soviet Minister of Foreign Affairs Vyacheslav Molotov

> sitting with a heavily laden board between them: food of all kinds crowned by a sucking pig [*sic*], and innumerable bottles. What Stalin made me drink seemed pretty savage: Winston, who by that time was complaining of a slight headache, seemed wisely to be confining himself to a comparatively innocuous effervescent Caucasian red wine. Everyone seemed to be as merry as a marriage bell.

The 'evening' broke up after 3 a.m. Churchill never minded having late nights. Despite his caustic tone, Cadogan sensed the talks had produced important results: 'I think the two great men really made contact and got on terms. Certainly, Winston was impressed and I think that feeling was reciprocated … Anyhow, conditions have been established in which messages exchanged between the two will mean twice as much, or more, than they did before.'

As soon as Churchill returned from Moscow, he summoned Attlee and Eden and told them Stalin was determined to fight on. On a lighter note, he dismissed the fantasy that the Russians were champion drinkers, and boasted that he had quaffed twice as much as they had. He had developed a rapport with Stalin that surprised him. He told the House on 8 September that Stalin was a 'great rugged war chief' as well as

> a man direct and even blunt in speech, which, having been brought up in the House of Commons, I do not mind at all, especially when I have something to say of my own. Above all, he is a man with that saving sense of humour which is of high importance to all men and all nations, but particularly to great men and great nations.

Accidents can be fateful. Just before he left Russia, Churchill had learned that William Gott, the commander of the Eighth Army, had been killed in a plane crash. Churchill chose Bernard Law Montgomery to take Gott's place, an excellent choice it would turn out. Montgomery both inspired his troops and behaved quite cautiously. He gathered a force of some 200,000 men – Britons and many from the empire, as well as Poles, Czechs and Free French – until he commanded a force double the size of Rommel's, and then trained his men to work together. This needed time, so he resisted Churchill's demands to attack quickly. On 23 October, the infantry went in with a 'light-foot', as the operation was called, in order not to trigger German mines; the engineers followed to clear a path for one line of tanks.

Ever the showman, Montgomery had Operation Lightfoot filmed, and newsreels showed him a few yards from the mines. Wearing his jaunty hat, Montgomery finally unleashed his 1,029 tanks against the 547 Panzers the Germans could muster. Luck favoured him. Rommel had been ill and flew back from Germany forty-eight hours too late. His instinct was always to go on the offensive, and if he had been in command from the start of the battle he would probably have attacked when Eighth Army was at its most vulnerable – which was when engineers were clearing the German mines. But Rommel's deputy lacked the field marshal's drive and sense of timing. Though he had fewer men and fewer tanks, Rommel still held out for nearly two weeks, but was then forced to retreat – inevitably towards Tobruk.

When it was clear El Alamein was the long-needed success, Churchill ordered church bells to be rung all over Britain. To his relief, he had achieved a great victory before America had become fully engaged in the war. As ever, Churchill found the words – again in his three-pronged rhythm: 'This is not the end, it is not even the beginning of the end, but it is perhaps the end of the beginning.'

The Nazi invasion of the Soviet Union, however, marked the beginning of the end for Hitler, though he did not yet realise it. The Battle of Stalingrad became symbolic for Hitler: he would humiliate the enemy by capturing the city the Soviet leader had named after himself. The Luftwaffe pounded Stalingrad into rubble, but not into submission. On 19 November, the Red Army counter-attacked the Romanian and Hungarian forces that were protecting the German flanks, broke through and surrounded the German Sixth Army. Hitler's defeat at Stalingrad proved a turning point of the war.

Given the many reverses in the first years of the war, it seems wildly optimistic that the coalition decided to plan for life after victory. One could argue that Attlee and Churchill remembered the liberal social legislation of 1910, and that both wished to develop those policies, though with different emphases. Back in 1910, Attlee had only been an 'explainer', cycling from village hall to village hall. But Churchill had been second only to Lloyd George in pushing through the reforms. In December 1942, the Beveridge Report was published, the greatest domestic achievement of the coalition. It argued that a 'revolutionary moment in the world's history is a time for revolutions, not for patching'. It highlighted the importance of social insurance, but that was only one part of a 'comprehensive policy of social progress'.

The state and the individual needed to work together. The state 'should not stifle incentive, opportunity, responsibility; in establishing a national minimum, it should leave room and encouragement for voluntary action by each individual to provide more than that minimum for himself and his family'. Beveridge opposed 'means-tested' benefits, and suggested a flat-rate universal contribution for a flat-rate universal benefit. Means-testing would only play a tiny part. Reconstruction would vanquish want, disease, ignorance, squalor and idleness, Beveridge hurrahed.

Every summer we should thank a now forgotten Conservative Chancellor, Sir Howard Kingsley Wood, whose impact on British life is still felt. As a backbencher, Wood introduced the Summer Time Bill of 1924, while as Postmaster General he, like Attlee before him, improved the telephone service.

Wood was concerned that Bevridge's report involved 'an impracticable financial commitment' and argued for publication to be postponed. Nevertheless, the Cabinet decided to publish the report on 2 December. The Ministry of Information found it was 'welcomed with almost universal approval by people of all shades of opinion and by all sections of the community', and was seen as 'the first real attempt to put into practice the talk about a new world'; in essence, a Labour world. But this brave new world required the war to be won first. In his message to the Labour Party at the start of 1943, Attlee said Labour had to be prepared to win the peace.

There were two instances of Attlee's loyalty. On 1 April, he said few Labour members would want to break the unity of the government. Ten weeks later, on 12 June, Attlee told the Commons that it was unjust to suggest that the Prime Minister alone was to blame when something went wrong.

The coalition agreement stopped Tory and Labour candidates from standing against each other at by-elections, and some Labour MPs felt they were missing opportunities. Between 1941 and 1943, the Conservative Party lost three safe seats at by-elections to independent socialist candidates. Normally, Labour would have contested those seats and would probably have won them. Attlee spoke in Alloa, Scotland on that subject on 10 July 1943. He conceded that some Labour MPs felt frustrated, but there had already been major changes. In the 1920s, unemployment had been seen as the fault of the unemployed who had some 'defect'. Now it was recognised the government had a duty to combat it. Education and the Poor Law had once been the only social services, but these services had been developed over the past twenty-five years. Attlee finished with a plea for people to find the energy needed 'if we are to win the peace'.

The electoral truce did not stop Gallup from carrying out polling, and this consistently gave Labour a ten-percentage-point lead. The country's mood was changing. Unlike Churchill, Attlee did not project grandeur. The scene in *Darkest Hour* when Churchill travels by Underground and listens to ordinary people urging him to fight on is touching, but total fantasy. Attlee, however, did not seem too grand to accept invitations to the first-night performances of many long-forgotten plays. His wife sometimes went when he was unable to.

At Easter 1943, Churchill gave Attlee, Violet and their children a tour of his air-raid shelter. Violet and Clementine had both survived depression and, in Clementine's case, she was also living with a man who often suffered from the condition. Violet and Clementine became firm friends. Each knew what the other had to live through.

On 11 May, Churchill was at the White House again, and angry that the Americans insisted on an invasion of southern France. The next day he raised another difficult issue: the Americans were reluctant to share the atomic information they were acquiring as the Manhattan Project got down to work. Churchill sent Attlee a telegram explaining that Roosevelt had finally ruled that an exchange of information on 'Tube Alloys' – the code word for the bomb – should be resumed and the project considered a joint one. This partnership was clarified in Quebec later in the year.

Later, Attlee complained,

It was really rather a loose agreement. Practically, Winston said to the Americans: 'You can have all the peaceful developments'; I think we could have claimed more. We had given a great deal through our experts ... no doubt it seemed a nice gesture not to bother about industrial use, or even insist on too much specific exchange on the military side. We were allies and friends. It didn't seem necessary to tie everything up.

Both men would come to regret that failure to be specific.

On 6 July 1943, Churchill quarrelled with Montgomery, Alexander and Alan Brooke. The military chiefs left around 2 a.m., and Churchill then turned on Attlee. It was a rare shouting match and almost inevitably about India. In the morning, Attlee noted, the row was all forgotten, but perhaps too soon: three weeks later Attlee discovered Churchill was sabotaging the liberal proposals Amery had made about India.

Nevertheless, a few days after the fourth anniversary of the coalition, Attlee argued for its continuation. 'There are those who pine for the joys of irresponsibility,' he said on 13 May, sniping at some in Labour's ranks. Electoral reasons made irresponsibility tempting, but Attlee stressed the need for the coalition to carry on and defeat the enemy. Then Britain could be rebuilt in quite a new way.

As D-Day approached, both politicians became spectators, a role Churchill hated; he was eager to travel to Normandy with the troops. King George VI told him that he also wanted to go, but as he couldn't, it would be unfair for the Prime Minister to make the trip while his King could not. The royal ploy worked; Churchill obeyed.

Attlee thought it was brave of Eisenhower to risk an invasion while meteorologists were predicting stormy weather. Attlee could not sleep the night before D-Day and sat up at the Admiralty where he followed the progress of the Allied flotilla. He then grabbed a short nap at 11 Downing Street and then went to the War Office as news came in of the landings on the Normandy beaches.

As well as the Beveridge Report, two White Papers had planned for an end of the war in ways that Attlee favoured. One, on employment policy, aimed to achieve a 'high and stable level of employment' after the war; the second envisaged a national health service. Yet little was done immediately by the coalition, which made backbench Labour MPs impatient. They began to push for the coalition to end as soon as possible.

On 3 July 1944, Attlee chided Churchill: 'I think you underrate the intelligence of the public and I do not share your belief.' The Canadian Prime Minister, William Lyon Mackenzie King, claimed in 1944 that Churchill bullied Attlee, but Attlee never accused Churchill of bullying and nothing in their correspondence suggests it ever happened.

Talking to author Francis Williams fifteen years after the war, Attlee pointed out how careful Churchill had been to carry his colleagues with him most of the time, and pointed out that the Prime Minister had sometimes backed down. On 15 June 1942, for example, the Nazis massacred 1,300 Czech civilians and destroyed two villages after British SOE agents assassinated a leading Nazi, Reinhard Heydrich. The Cabinet met to discuss a response. Churchill wanted to 'wipe out' three German villages, while Bevin argued that 'Germany responds to brute force and nothing else.' The Secretary of State for India, Leo Amery, wanted to bomb towns. But Attlee questioned whether it would be 'useful to enter into competition in frightfulness with Germans'. Morrison supported him. Three Cabinet members were in favour of bombing German civilians, while five were opposed. Churchill said that although his instinct was in favour of bombing, he would submit to the view of those against. Attlee was analytical about what had happened. Churchill did not always get his way, he said.

> He'd get some idea he wanted to press, and after we had considered it the rest of us would have to tell him there was no value to it. But you

needed someone to prod the Chiefs of Staff. Winston was sometimes an awful nuisance because he started all sorts of hares, but he always accepted the verdict of the Chiefs of Staff when it came to it, and it was a great advantage for him to be there driving them all the time.

By August 1944, the Nazis were retreating in Europe, which allowed Attlee to retrace some of the journeys of his youth. He flew to Bayeux, saw that the famous tapestry was intact, and then went to Caen, where a bomb had blasted a huge hole in the cathedral. He flew next to Gibraltar and Algiers, and then back to Naples, where he met Churchill. While Churchill swam, Attlee chatted to Lord Moran. It is extraordinary that they had never really talked before. Moran thought Attlee seemed nervous and judged that he had no self-confidence. But Moran did not suggest he was 'limited', as so many others had done. He also felt Attlee's behaviour suggested that 'there is a great deal more to him than this.'

When Attlee arrived back in London he wrote a foreword to *Cockney Campaign* by Frank Lewey, the new Mayor of Stepney. Lewey stressed the need to look after the troops who had suffered so much to achieve victory. Attlee was finding it harder to persuade the Cabinet to agree to post-war projects, but he was determined that this time military victory would also be a victory for working men and women.

In November, Roosevelt was elected for a fourth term, with Harry Truman as his running mate. Truman became Vice-President, but was allowed to do little.

Six months before the end of the war, Attlee wrote a critical, but careful, letter to Churchill.

'I am expressing much that is in the minds of many colleagues whether Conservative, Labour, or independent ... you should put confidence in your colleagues. In the days when you were a minister, would you have been as patient as we have been?'

Far from bullying Attlee, on 20 January 1945, Churchill promised to do better, stating that he was 'very ready to admit my own shortcomings when it comes to civil affairs'. He added, 'I note what you say as to my laxity in these matters [he meant civil affairs] and heavy and exhausting as is my present burden I will do my best to be better acquainted with these subjects in the future so as not to take up your valuable time in explaining them to me in the Cabinet.' This conjures up images of an entertaining scene where Churchill is flummoxed by details of domestic policy, and defers to Attlee to explain the intricacies of national insurance. Five days later, Churchill told Jock Colville that it was the fiftieth anniversary of his father's death. Colville noted how alike – and unalike – Churchill and his father were. Churchill had mastered his flaws largely, something his father had never managed to do.

On 4 February 1945, the Allies met at Yalta to thrash out the principles of the post-war settlement. Roosevelt ignored Churchill's advice to stand up to Stalin. American generals were warning it would take many months to conquer Japan, and could cost a million American casualties. So Roosevelt wanted Russian help in the Pacific. Stalin agreed to provide this help, but only for a price. He would gain Sakhalin, the Japanese Kurile islands and 'zones of influence' in Manchuria and North Korea. Churchill, however, was more alarmed that Stalin intended to establish a Soviet empire in eastern Europe. Still, Churchill came away from the conference believing that he had negotiated a workable deal with the Soviet leader, and that he could trust him.

When Roosevelt died of a sudden cerebral haemorrhage on 12 April, Truman inherited the White House at some disadvantage. Though he had chaired an important Senate Committee on military expenditure,

Truman had met Roosevelt alone only a few times. The patrician President never trusted the farm boy too much, so Truman had never been informed of the loose agreements between Churchill and Roosevelt. On entering what was now his own Oval Office, Truman told reporters, 'I don't know if you fellas ever had a load of hay fall on you, but when they told me yesterday what had happened, I felt like the moon, the stars and all the planets had fallen on me.' He was right to be anxious; he knew he had to make decisions that would shape the world.

On 22 April, the Russians entered Berlin. Hitler committed suicide on 30 April and many of his closest colleagues were captured. Admiral Dönitz, whose U-boats had inflicted so much damage on British shipping, became Chancellor just long enough to surrender unconditionally. Churchill had said his policy was victory at all costs and he had achieved this, with Attlee at his side. They were now comrades in victory.

Victory in Europe did not make the Irish more malleable, however. On 2 May, de Valera visited the German embassy in Dublin to sign a book of condolences for Hitler. Ignoring the atrocities Hitler had perpetrated, de Valera said that a refusal to sign the book would have been 'an act of unpardonable discourtesy'. Churchill was furious. In a broadcast, he stressed the syllables of de Valera's name in such a way as to conjure up the idea that de Valera was the devil. Britain had shown great restraint towards the Irish, Churchill claimed. 'We never laid a violent hand upon them, which at times would have been quite easy and quite natural.'

On 15 July, Attlee visited Berlin and was shown round by Hugh Lunghi, an old Haileybury man who was now a military interpreter. Watching Attlee chat to soldiers, Lunghi decided that the Labour leader was almost pathologically anxious to 'endear himself to the common people'. Lunghi was one of the many people who viewed Attlee as insignificant, though he admitted that Attlee possessed 'a nice wry smile that savours of shyness'.

In May, Attlee flew to the Azores and then on to Denver. From there he drove to San Francisco for a conference on setting up the new international organisation Churchill and Roosevelt had mooted in 1942. As Foreign Secretary, Eden led the British delegation. Though he was the Deputy Prime Minister, Attlee did not object to this as he and Eden were on friendly terms. Eden once said he had never seen Attlee behave in a politically partisan way while a member of the coalition government.

The question of whether the major powers would have a veto in the United Nations was controversial. Believing the veto would be rarely used, the British were in favour. 'Its subsequent use by the Russians was quite contrary to the spirit with which it was accepted,' Attlee wrote. At the time, though, Attlee spent time with Molotov, who was quite co-operative 'and used to echo the OK of the American and British. It is a pity that dropped later out of his vocabulary.' The two men went to visit a Kaiser shipyard, where the Liberty ships had been built. Molotov was amazed that the workers were paid the fabulous sum of $120, equating to £30 a week. A skilled Russian engineer would be paid around 160 roubles, worth $30.

Churchill celebrated Victory in Europe Day with gusto. He appeared on numerous balconies, including that of the Ministry of Health, one of the few ministries he had never ruled. Finally, he was cheered when he waved from the balcony of Buckingham Palace with the royal family. Attlee was still in San Francisco where 'we gathered together to celebrate in a room at the top of a skyscraper'. If Attlee waved to the public, he did not say so.

Churchill told the House of Commons the coalition was the 'greatest reforming administration' since the Liberal government of 1905–15; its leaders were all 'committed to this great mass of social legislation' and it was impossible to imagine any of them would renege on their pledges.

Victory in Europe Day, on 8 May, marked the fifth anniversary of the vote on the Norway debate which had brought Attlee and Churchill together. Victory would not have been achieved without their collaboration. As the old politics returned, the comrades became rivals, but rivalry would never turn them into enemies.

CHAPTER 10

THE 1945 ELECTION

ttlee flew back to Britain, knowing that he and Churchill must discuss the timing of the new general election. As had been the case in 1940, Attlee wanted to consult the Labour Party's National Executive Committee. Churchill hoped to continue the coalition until the end of the war with Japan, but his advisers urged him to call the election sooner as they were confident his popularity would deliver a Conservative majority. Under pressure from fellow Tories, Churchill offered Attlee two alternatives: an election immediately or one at the end of the war with Japan.

In a long letter on 21 May, Attlee again chided Churchill, gently reminding him that he had once said it would be 'a very serious constitutional lapse' to extend the life of the current Parliament. He quoted the speech Churchill had made during the last debate on the Prolongation of Parliament Bill. 'We must look to the termination of the war against Nazism as a pointer which will fix the date of the general election,' Churchill had said. The Prime Minister had always hoped, Attlee reminded him, 'that the long and honourable association of the parties' which had brought victory should be ended 'by common agreement and without controversy'. But now, Attlee continued, 'it appears to me that you are departing from the position of a national leader by yielding to the pressures of the Conservative Party which is anxious to exploit your own great service to the nation in its own interest'.

Attlee begged Churchill to reconsider the polling date. The Labour Party conference, however, had grown tired of the political truce and demanded an immediate election. When Attlee eventually acquiesced, Churchill reacted angrily.

On 23 May, Churchill resigned as head of the coalition and formed a caretaker government, with a sprinkling of a few independents. But the presence of these independents would not fool anyone, Attlee said. It was a Tory government, and this fact mattered, as 'it is precisely on the problems of the reconstruction of the economic life of the country that party differences are most acute'.

The date of the election was fixed for 5 July. Troops in Europe, the Middle East and the Far East would be voting, so it would be the most logistically complicated election ever held in Britain. It took place while the war was still raging, as Japan had not surrendered. Since Attlee's poetry has been a feature of this book, it seems fitting to recall a short poem by Admiral Takijirō Ōnishi, who commanded Japan's kamikaze pilots. Life was all too fragile a flower, so one could not expect its fragrance to last.

The pilots have to sacrifice their lives, Onishi explained, as 'there is only one way of assuring that our meagre strength will be effective to a maximum degree. That is to organise suicide attack units composed of Zero fighters armed with 250-kilogram bombs, with each plane to crash-dive into an enemy carrier.'

The Admiral's feelings were not that different from those in Laurence Binyon's famous lines that are still spoken on Remembrance Day.

They shall not grow old, as we that are left grow old
Age shall not weary them, nor the years condemn.
At the going down of the sun and in the morning
We will remember them.

The flush of victory and the pain of mourning the war dead left emotions running high. The politicians, who had worked so well together during the war, were not immune to the febrile atmosphere. A classic expression for getting divorced is 'untying the knot' – and Churchill and Attlee now had to untangle theirs. The ebb and flow of personal feelings was intense. The campaign started with heartfelt tributes; Churchill complimented Ernest Bevin, who had arranged demobilisation 'with much wisdom'. Like Bevin and 'other leaders of the socialist party', Churchill thought the country needed some form of national service, so that young men were ready and trained to 'play their part if danger calls'. The tone of the election changed completely, however, on 4 June. Historians have made much of the vitriolic speech Churchill gave that day. He warned that a Labour government would impose Gestapo-like controls on Britain. It has been claimed that Beaverbrook persuaded Churchill to launch this bombastic attack.

Attlee pointed out later that Beaverbrook was a classic example of a political paradox. A man who did not have the respect of the opposition rarely had the respect of his own side and would 'not get far in politics', Attlee commented; he certainly would not get to the top. Beaverbrook possessed many gifts, 'including a bold and colourful character – of the greatest political usefulness'. But he never achieved real political power because 'not enough of his own party – let alone chaps on the other side of the House – trusted him'.

Blaming Beaverbrook ignores the political situation in 1945. Churchill and Attlee had liked and trusted each other as they dealt with crisis after crisis during the war. Imagine a moderately happy couple who have resolved their conflicts and achieved great things. Suddenly, their friends and families force them to separate and fight each other. It was bound to be uneasy. Beaverbrook jabbed at an open wound.

Attlee coped rather better with the situation. In *The British General Election of 1945*, authors Ronald McCallum and Alison Readman compared the campaign to Attlee's beloved cricket. Attlee 'had the air of a sound and steady batsman keeping up his wicket at ease against a demon bowler who was losing both pace and length'. But although opinion polls still picked up something like a 10 per cent swing to Labour, this did not necessarily mean Churchill would be ousted as Prime Minister. Mass Observation discovered that many voters believed he would continue as Prime Minister regardless of the election result.

Churchill was unchallenged as leader of the Tory Party, but victory in the war had failed to silence Attlee's Labour Party critics. Harold Laski, who had become chairman of the Labour Party, advised Attlee to resign, as

> the continuance of your leadership is a grave handicap to our hopes
> of victory in the coming election … Just as Mr Churchill changed
> Auchinleck for Montgomery before El Alamein, so, I suggest, you
> owe it to the party to make a comparable change on the eve of this
> greatest of our battles.

Attlee famously replied, 'Dear Laski, thank you for your letter, contents of which have been noted.' Beatrice Webb's once-insignificant clerk had become a master of the laconic put-down, a skill that would serve him well over the next few years.

Churchill was the Conservative's star of the election campaign. The party's manifesto was personal: *Mr Churchill's Declaration of Policy to the Electors*. But the rival party manifestos had more similarities than one might imagine and repay studying in some detail. The manifesto began with Churchillian brio:

Ours is a great nation and never in its history has it stood in higher repute in the world than today. Its greatness rests not on its material wealth, for that has been poured out in full measure, nor upon its armed might, which other nations surpass. It has its roots in the character, the ability, and the independence of our people and the magic of this wonderful island.

Churchill's declaration made it clear 'children must always come first. We are dedicated to the purpose of helping to rebuild Britain on the sure foundations on which her greatness rests.'

But Churchill then took the first modest potshot at Labour. Since 1919, the country had experienced enormous material progress, which had to 'be accelerated not by subordinating the individual to the authority of the state, but by providing the conditions in which no one shall be precluded by poverty, ignorance, insecurity, or the selfishness of others from making the best of the gifts with which providence has endowed him'.

The Tories would guard 'our ancient liberties', while tackling 'practical problems in a practical way'. He warned against 'untested theories', by which he meant socialism. His problem was that the coalition had tested some of Labour's theories, and, as the reaction to the Beveridge Report showed, people very much favoured them.

The once-pacifist Labour Party had no military doubts; its manifesto declared, 'Japanese barbarism shall be defeated just as decisively as Nazi aggression and tyranny'. But Labour then sniffed an advantage: 'We must consolidate in peace the great wartime association of the British Commonwealth with the USA and the USSR.' The authors of the Labour manifesto then took their own potshot. Before 1939, the Tories had been 'so scared of Russia that they missed the chance to establish a partnership which might well have prevented the war'. In building the new United Nations, Labour was one step ahead, as it had 'a common bond with the working peoples of all countries, who have achieved a new dignity and influence through their long struggles against Nazi tyranny'.

Both manifestos agreed it would be hard to change from the wartime economy to a peacetime one. The coalition had imposed controls on labour, materials and prices. Churchill's manifesto said, 'We stand for the removal of controls as quickly as the need for them disappears,' but this would be done gradually. 'As long as shortage of food remains, rationing must obviously be accepted: the dangers of inflation also must be guarded against.'

Churchill was scathing in his criticism: 'We intend to guard the people of this country against those who, under guise of war necessity, would like to impose upon Britain for their own purposes a permanent system of bureaucratic control, reeking of totalitarianism.' The Tories offered 'sound plans for avoiding the disastrous slumps and booms from which we used to suffer, but which all are united in being determined to avoid in the future.' The word 'united' shows the continuing influence of the policies of the coalition.

Labour's manifesto recalled that at the end of the First World War there had been a short boom 'when savings, gratuities and post-war credits' became available, which 'created a profiteers' paradise'. The

Tories were still the profiteers' poodle; Labour would bite them where it hurt, in their bank balances. Parodying Churchill's tribute to pilots after the Battle of Britain, the Labour manifesto blasted the profiteers: 'Never was so much injury done to so many by so few.'

The problem each party had was that they had jointly produced the coalition's White Papers. Both had promised full employment and a national health service. A Conservative government would seek 'a high and stable level of employment'. Without steady work, 'there will not be the happiness, the confidence, or the material resources in the country on which we can all build together the kind of Britain that we want to see.' Labour was sceptical the Tories would ever introduce real reforms.

Churchill reassumed his old mantle of the reformer. In 1943, he had made a broadcast 'in which I sketched a four years' plan which would cover five or six large measures of a practical character, which must all have been the subject of prolonged, careful and energetic preparation beforehand, and which fitted together into a general scheme'. The Conservatives now presented many of the coalition's plans as their own, with a small nod to free enterprise. Homes might be desperately needed, but builders could hardly be allowed to build without supervision by the men from the ministry. 'Prices of materials must be controlled as long as supplies are short,' Churchill's declaration noted. Local authorities and private enterprise would both need subsidies.

The Tories committed to recruiting and training 'our building labour force as quickly as we can to repair the damage caused by the Blitz'. They hoped to build 220,000 new homes a year. New types of factory-made houses would help reach this target as they could be built faster than traditional homes. But the Tories were not the landlords' lackeys, Churchill's declaration stressed, stating that 'so long as there is a serious shortage of houses, rent control must continue on houses controlled at present.' Tribunals would fix fair rents, 'which seemed to provide the best solution of a long-standing problem'.

Labour tried to top these Tory promises. More houses were needed, as was 'a full programme of land planning and drastic action to ensure an efficient building industry that will neither burden the community with a crippling financial load nor impose bad conditions and heavy unemployment on its workpeople'. Only Labour would ensure that happened. It also endorsed modern methods and materials which would 'have to be the order of the day'. Rather like the factory-made houses Churchill had referred to.

Both parties planned a new national health service. The Tories said it would be made available 'to all citizens'. Everyone would contribute to the costs, and no one would be 'denied the attention, the treatment or the appliances he requires because he cannot afford them'. The proposed health service would cover all treatment, 'from the general practitioner to the specialist, and from the hospital to convalescence and rehabilitation'.

There was a little difference in the details. The Tories would allow 'wide play' to the preferences of individuals. 'Nothing will be done to destroy the close personal relationship between doctor and patient, nor to restrict the patient's free choice of doctor.' Labour, on the other hand, was content to promise that money would 'no longer be the passport to the best treatment'.

Both parties were in favour of mothers, passionately so. The Tory manifesto declared, 'Motherhood must be our special care.' They would build more maternity beds. 'Mothers must be relieved of onerous duties which at such times so easily cause lasting injury to their health. The National Insurance Scheme will make financial provision for these needs.' The state had to support families. Nursery schools should be encouraged. 'On the birth, the proper feeding and the healthy upbringing of a substantially increased number of children, depends the life of Britain and her enduring glory,' Churchill waxed lyrically.

Labour's manifesto promised children's allowances and better maternity and child welfare services. 'A healthy family life must be fully ensured and parenthood must not be penalised if the population of Britain is to be prevented from dwindling.'

Churchill then took another potshot: 'Our object is to provide education which will not produce a standardised or utility child, useful only as a cog in a nationalised and bureaucratic machine, but will enable the child to develop his or her responsible place, first in the world of school, and then as a citizen.' Academies would not produce apparatchiks. 'Many parents will be able to choose the school they like and to play their part with the educational authorities in the physical and spiritual well-being of their children.' He added, 'Above all, let us remember that the great purpose of education is to give us individual citizens capable of thinking for themselves.'

Labour promised to raise the school-leaving age to sixteen at the earliest possible opportunity. It would also subsidise milk for mothers and children, as well as fruit juices and food supplements. Perhaps one of the more eccentric promises was that socialism would produce more canteens and better British restaurants!

The Tories outlined detailed help for farmers – and more. Under them, there would be more, and probably better, forests, with better leaves no doubt. 'We must take care of our big trees, and make provision for their replacement.' Villages, cottages and farms would get a proper electricity supply, water and sanitation. The Tories were also for fish. Churchill's declaration enthused on the subject. 'Our fishing industry had to be restored. What we want now is fish, and this must be tackled by every conceivable method.' In the spirit of the coalition, the better

British restaurants that Attlee was promising would presumably serve the better fish that Churchill planned to provide.

There was not even much difference on coal. In 1911, Churchill had introduced policies to make mining safer. He had no intention now of letting coal mine owners run the mines. 'Coal is owned by the state, and is a wasting asset,' his declaration pointed out. He was concerned that the industry had fallen behind some of its competitors overseas. A new central authority would ensure that mine owners took advice from the men from the Ministry. Mines would have to amalgamate 'voluntarily if possible, but otherwise by compulsion'.

While not specifically promising cod in plenty, Labour said the country needed

> good food in plenty, useful work for all, and comfortable, labour-saving homes that take full advantage of the resources of modern science and productive industry. It wants a high and rising standard of living, security for all against a rainy day, an educational system that will give every boy and girl a chance to develop the best that is in them.

This demanded 'a great programme of modernisation and re-equipment'. Unlike the Tories, Labour was ready for drastic policies and for 'keeping a firm constructive hand on our whole productive machinery; the Labour Party will put the community first and the sectional interests of private business after.' Labour would banish dole queues, while the Tories would allow 'the Czars of Big Business' to go on the rampage. The price of economic freedom for the few was 'too high if it is bought at the cost of idleness and misery for millions'.

Planning was essential, even Churchill agreed. A national investment board would 'determine social priorities and promote better timing in private investment. There must be no depressed areas in the new Britain.' Labour agreed that Britain needed a thriving industry. 'Only so can our people reap the full benefits of this age of discovery and Britain keep her place as a great power.' It was very much thrust and counterthrust.

The main differences between the parties concerned the extent of planning. Churchill's declaration foresaw 'cooperation between industry and the state, rather than control by the state – a lightening of the burdens of excessive taxation – these are the first essentials'.

Labour did not shy away from its ambitions. It was a proud socialist party. 'Its ultimate purpose at home is the establishment of the Socialist Commonwealth of Great Britain – free, democratic, efficient, progressive, public-spirited, its material resources organised in the service of the British people.' Attlee had stated in *The Labour Party in Perspective* that the British people did not believe in revolution. Labour's manifesto echoed his caution: 'Socialism cannot come overnight, as the product of a weekend revolution. The members of the Labour Party, like the British people, are practical-minded men and women.'

Fruit was still hard to get in Britain, which may explain why some eager political copywriter compared businesses to bananas. Labour distinguished between 'basic industries, ripe and over-ripe for public ownership and management', and unripe enterprises which would have to accept 'constructive supervision to further the nation's needs'. Labour argued for public ownership of the coal, iron and steel industries and of the railways. 'Red' Churchill had proposed nationalising the railways decades earlier, of course.

Labour said it had played 'a leading part in the long campaign for proper social security for all – social provision against rainy days, coupled with economic policies calculated to reduce rainy days to a minimum'. The past behaviour of the Tories meant that if, unhappily, bad times were to come, and our opponents were in power, then, running true to form, they would be likely to cut these social provisions on the plea that the nation could not meet the cost. That was the line they adopted on at least three occasions between the wars.

Voting for minor parties might deny Labour victory, so its manifesto appealed for support from 'all men and women of progressive outlook'. Progressives must ensure 'that the next government is not a Conservative government but a Labour government'.

The Conservatives said they would 'bring into action as soon as we can a nation-wide and compulsory scheme of national insurance based on the plan announced by the government of all parties in 1944'. In return for a single consolidated contribution there would be increased benefits, including an old-age pension of 20 shillings for single people and 35 shillings for married couples. The new Ministry of National Insurance had been set up to prepare, administer and control this legislation. 'There must be no queuing up for sickness benefits by those who are entitled to them.'

Both parties flattered the nation. Churchill said the Tories stood

for the fullest opportunity for go and push in all ranks throughout the whole nation. This quality is part of the genius of the British people, who mean to be free to use their own judgement and never intend to be state serfs, nor always to wait for official orders before they can act.

The war had been paid for, the Tory manifesto stressed, 'only by the severest taxation pressing heavily on everybody, by borrowing on a vast scale to meet the passing crisis, by huge Lend-Lease supplies from the

United States and by generous gifts from Canada and elsewhere. All this cannot go on.' The state could only spend what it got by taxes or by borrowing. Taxes had needed to be raised but the 'present level of taxation drastically restricts the ability of the ordinary citizen to satisfy his personal desires. It is discouraging to his enterprise and his efforts to better himself by doing the bit extra, for so large a part of anything he gains to be removed by the tax-collector.' Churchill promised to reduce taxes 'in a way that will stimulate energy and permit free individual choice'. His finale was rousing. 'On a basis of high employment, initiative and hard work on the part of everyone, we can achieve our great Four Years' programme. It is well worth achieving.'

Fairly similar manifestos, which built on the work of the coalition, should have made for a gentlemanly campaign. It was not to be. Some Conservatives thought Churchill was not a sound party man; they did not like the warmth he showed to his former associates, the Liberals, never mind Attlee. Churchill could be wheeled out for grand occasions, but he was still too incalculable, even dangerous. He was not quite 'one of us', as it were.

Perhaps to prove that he was a true Tory, Churchill's attacks against Labour were sometimes exaggerated. As well as his vitriolic first election broadcast on 4 June, Churchill made much of a slip that Harold Laski had made, when Laski had boasted that the National Executive Committee would control the Parliamentary Labour Party.

Attlee was moderate in his replies. Churchill made much of the risks Labour would pose for freedom, Attlee remarked, but the Labour leader could remember a time when employers had been free to work little children sixteen hours a day; a time when women had slaved to make trousers at a penny and a half a pair. Only Parliament protected the public 'against the greed of ruthless profit-makers and property owners'.

Attlee also took a swipe at Churchill personally, claiming the Tory leader had never been a wage earner. For once, Attlee was not quite living up to his high moral standards. Nor was he accurate. Churchill had written for a living since reporting on the war in Sudan back in the 1890s.

The possibility of an electoral victory made Attlee energetic; he addressed seven or eight meetings a day, speaking without notes. Attlee's chauffeur, his wife, never failed to get him to these meetings on time. Unintentionally, 'this turned out to be something of an asset', as the press made great play of it. By contrast, Churchill usually travelled in a grand procession of expensive cars, like a mediaeval monarch touring his domains.

Attlee was pleased that he kept being told Labour was on its way to a great victory but, as a veteran of many elections, 'I did not allow myself to be too optimistic.' Packed meetings did not guarantee a triumph; Attlee knew that Churchill was hugely popular with voters and, in Attlee's opinion to a great extent, rightly so.

In the middle of the campaign, the former comrades had to link arms again. Churchill 'wisely in my view', Attlee noted, asked him to journey to Potsdam to meet Truman and Stalin. Attlee accepted. Laski again blundered and said that Attlee would be going only as an observer.

Attlee prided himself on the fact that most countries would be astonished that the two leaders in a hotly contested election could 'meet again on easy terms' and work together well. 'But we had so recently been colleagues that we experienced no difficulty.' Both men were wary of Stalin's ambitions; he was out to seize new territory and huge reparations. Attlee later said that the Soviets never responded to a generous offer with generosity.

In Potsdam, Molotov asked Attlee about the forthcoming election. It would be a close-run thing, Attlee predicted. Molotov assumed he was lying. Election results surely were decided in advance by some

British equivalent of the Politburo; the people could hardly be allowed to choose their leaders. Attlee noted the Russians were surprised at the way he and Churchill walked about without any guards.

At Potsdam, the leaders demanded the 'unconditional surrender' of Japan, but what was equally important was how post-war Europe would be governed. A Council of Foreign Ministers was agreed, consisting of the United States, the Soviet Union, Britain, China and France. None of these countries wanted to see a strong military Germany again and decided that the German economy would focus on agriculture and peaceable industries. Nazi war criminals would be put on trial. The conference accepted the transfer of the land east of the Oder and Neisse rivers from Germany to Poland. Truman received word of the successful atomic bomb test soon after he arrived at Potsdam; he told Churchill, but mentioned 'a new weapon' only casually to Stalin.

On 5 July, British voters went to the polls. 'Three weeks of suspense followed,' Attlee wrote, because the votes of troops overseas had to be counted. Having won the war, Churchill did not expect to lose the election. Seventy-six per cent of the civilian electorate voted, but out of three million service voters only about 60 per cent cast a ballot. Churchill told the King he expected a majority of between thirty and fifty seats; Labour's leaders were even more pessimistic, believing Churchill would win a majority of about seventy.

As the results of the election started to pour in, however, it became clear that the politicians, perhaps with the exception of Harold Macmillan, had got it wrong. As Macmillan fought to be re-elected in Stockton-on-Tees (a battle he eventually lost), he had sensed the changing mood:

> As soon as electioneering began in earnest I knew what the result would be ... I had little hope of success ... The election in my view

was lost before it started. Vast crowds turned out in flocks to see and applaud him [Churchill]. They wanted to thank him for what he had done for them. But this did not mean that they wanted to entrust him and his Tory colleagues with the conduct of their lives in the years that were to follow … Nor had they forgotten or been allowed to forget the years before the war … It was not Churchill who lost the 1945 election, it was the ghost of Neville Chamberlain.

The results were declared on the night of 26 July. As news of the Tory losses rolled in, the gloomy mood in the Downing Street annex grew darker. At one point, Churchill's daughter went to the kitchen where she found their housekeeper making honey sandwiches. 'I don't know what the world's coming to,' the housekeeper remarked, 'but I thought I might make some tea.' Churchill then went to Paddington of all places, drank more tea and told Attlee he was resigning. He wrote to his successor, 'My dear Attlee. In consequence of the electoral decision recorded today, I propose to tender my resignation to the King at seven o' clock this evening. On personal grounds I wish you all success in the heavy burden you are about to assume.'

Churchill turned to one of his assistants and said, 'Fetch me my carriage and I shall go to the palace and hand in my seals of office.' He was being ironic, as the 'carriage' was only his official Humber. 'They are perfectly entitled to vote as they please,' he said later. 'This is a democracy. This is what we've been fighting for.' But he admitted that 'it was distressing after all those years to abandon the reins of power.'

Someone commented, 'While you held the reins you managed to win the race.'

'Yes,' Churchill answered. 'I won the race – and now they have warned me off the turf.'

Attlee was astonished to win – and by such a large margin – Labour captured 393 seats while the Tories only took 197. When Attlee went to see King George VI, he and the tongue-tied monarch stood in silence. Attlee finally said, 'I've won the election.' The King replied, 'I know. I heard it on the six o'clock news.'

In Britain the transition of power is brutally swift: the voters decide; the removal vans descend. Attlee told Alfred Laker, who looked after him in his final years, following Violet's death, that Clementine had been very helpful when he and his wife moved into No. 10. Clem had much affection for Clementine.

In triumph, Attlee was courteous, even concerned. He 'knew my Winston', and realised that Churchill would feel desperately hurt. 'I felt sorry for the old boy,' Attlee said. He invited Churchill and Eden to return to Potsdam with him. When both men declined, Attlee took the new Foreign Secretary, Ernest Bevin, but kept Churchill informed of all the discussions.

Harold Macmillan wrote,

Attlee assumed the office of Prime Minister with typical quiet efficiency. He had to deal with very difficult problems following the war. He also had a team of remarkable figures ... But he was always completely the master and his quiet way impressed his personality not merely on his colleagues but on all parties in the House of Commons.

Macmillan attributed this to Attlee's absolute integrity and sincerity. He would need those qualities – and more. Churchill would have to be generous to forgive him.

Forgiveness does not come easily to some politicians. When Ed Koch lost the election to become Mayor of New York, he said 'the people have spoken ... now they must be punished'. After being ousted as Tory leader by Mrs Thatcher, Edward Heath sulked on the back benches for years. Gordon Brown was so angry at Tony Blair for capturing Labour's leadership that when Brown became Chancellor, he refused to give Prime Minister Blair the details of his Budgets until the very last moment. Such attitudes would have failed to impress Attlee, who wrote that next to character – or integrity – came judgement. He listed the qualities in this order because 'true judgement is found, in my view, only in men of character and men of character learned from their mistakes, which requires humility.'

To cope well with rejection requires emotional maturity, precisely what Churchill now needed to show in defeat. He managed it in public, but not in private. Clementine expected the two of them to cling together in misery, but they ended up having row after row. Attlee had to be sensitive – and not make Churchill's difficult situation even more difficult.

When the House sat to elect a Speaker on 1 August, Churchill received a huge cheer. The Tories sang 'For He's a Jolly Good Fellow', but Labour broke into a rendition of 'The Red Flag'.

In his first speech as Prime Minister, Attlee ignored the babble of his backbenchers and praised Churchill, saying, 'I think it is fitting that I should pay tribute to one of the greatest architects of our victory.' Attlee thought Churchill had contributed more to the Second World War victory than Lloyd George had to the Allied triumph in the First World War. 'My judgement may be affected by personal experience,' he admitted.

On 16 August, Churchill made what Clementine called a brilliant, moving and gallant speech. She was right, because it betrayed no bitterness. Churchill began by congratulating Labour, who faced, as he had done in the last months of office, 'an element of baffling dualism' as the government 'had to plan for peace and war at the same time'. He added,

How to set people free to use their activities in reviving the life of Britain, and at the same time to meet the stern demands of the war against Japan, constituted one of the most perplexing and distressing puzzles that in a long lifetime of experience I have ever faced.

Churchill discussed the work done at Potsdam, and turned to Bevin.

I am very glad that the request that I made to the conference, and which my right honourable friend – I may perhaps be allowed so to refer to him on this comparatively innocuous occasion – supported at the conference, that the seat of the council's permanent secretariat should be London, was granted.

One did not call a member of a rival party my 'right honourable friend', but Bevin was exactly that for Churchill, just as Lloyd George had been years before.

Churchill said the world's three leading powers now could not impose solutions alone. 'We British have had very early and increasingly to recognise the limitations of our own power and influence, great though it be, in the gaunt world arising from the ruins of this hideous war.' He then told the House that a friend from Zagreb had met an old lady. 'Poor Mr Churchill, I suppose now he will be shot,' she said. His friend reassured her that Churchill might just be condemned 'to one of the various forms of hard labour which are always open to His Majesty's subjects'. The anecdote went down well.

Harold Laski was the only socialist Churchill went for. Attlee had recently told the professorial pest that military experience showed him you did not always need to launch an attack by charging the enemy with trumpets blaring. So Attlee probably approved when Churchill asked, 'What precisely is Mr Laski's authority for all the statements he is making about our foreign policy? How far do his statements involve the agreement or responsibility of the Secretary of State for Foreign Affairs? We know that Mr Laski is the Chairman of the Labour Party Executive Committee.' Churchill then adopted his humblest tone. 'This is a very important body. I have been told – I am willing to be contradicted and to learn – that it has the power to summon ministers before it.' His tone became mocking. 'The House, the country and the world at large are entitled to know: who are the authoritative spokesmen of His Majesty's government?'

Results would show whether the new domestic policies worked. Churchill acknowledged that the trade unions had behaved heroically during the war. Now, however, he was worried.

> It does not say much for the confidence with which the Trades Union Council view the brave new world, or for what they think about the progressive nationalisation of our industries, that they should deem it necessary on what the honourable and gallant gentleman called 'the D-Day of the new Britain' to restore and sharpen the general strike weapon, at this particular time of all others.

Churchill added that 'we also have an immense programme, prepared by our joint exertions during the coalition, which requires to be brought into law and made an inherent part of the life of the people.' There were differences of emphasis,

> but in the main no Parliament ever assembled with such a mass of agreed legislation as lies before us this afternoon. I have great hopes of this Parliament and I shall do my utmost to make its work fruitful.

It may heal the wounds of war, and turn to good account the new conceptions and powers which we have gathered amid the storm.

Attlee was gracious and also called Churchill his right honourable friend. He said,

In the darkest and most dangerous hour of our history this nation found in my right honourable friend the man who expressed supremely the courage and determination never to yield which animated all the men and women of this country. In undying phrases he crystallised the unspoken feeling of all.

Churchill's place in history was secure, Attlee added.

The former comrades in arms would face each other across the House for the next ten years. There would be some sharp exchanges between them, but often their most vicious battles would be fought with others.

CHAPTER 11

THE MOUSE THAT ROARED, 1945–51

The *Mouse that Roared* was a marvellous comedy in which America lost a war to the Duchy of Grand Fenwick who just wanted the Americans to subsidise them. The start of Attlee's tenure saw what can only be called a lark.

Churchill decided to travel incognito and assumed the identity of Colonel Warden. The name was no accident for two reasons. He had used it during the war to flummox the Nazis and, in 1940, he had become Lord Warden of the Cinque Ports on the Channel – Dover, Romney, Hythe, Hastings and Sandwich. Since he was rather busy, there had been no moment for his investiture.

Churchill's colonel pretence required Attlee's cooperation. Mail for this fictitious colonel was often sent to Downing Street, even from Clementine. The new Prime Minister, who had been Postmaster General after all, made sure letters and telegrams were received and forwarded. There was a playful side to Attlee, too. Anne Blackman, whose father worked for Attlee, remembered going to the Prime Minister's official country house, Chequers, when she was young. Attlee and his wife loved games, including charades.

After spending the summer in Italy and France, Colonel Warden returned to England with fifteen canvasses. Energy was the cure for failure, as Churchill had suggested in *Painting as a Pastime*; he had finished an average of one painting a day. He felt he had spent a few weeks 'completely out of the world'. He had still not finished his war memoirs, which eventually ran to six volumes. Attlee was again helpful in getting Churchill permission to quote from official records, which were not usually released.

Churchill could have retired from politics. Yet it would be absurd to win the war and leave the world at risk of another global conflict. Stalin was being opportunistic and demanded all East European countries should come under Soviet influence. He had extracted from Roosevelt the promise that the Soviet Union would have 'zones of influence' in Manchuria and North Korea. Bizarre calculations were agreed. Romania would be 90 per cent Soviet influenced and 10 per cent British influenced; Greece the other way round; Yugoslavia and Hungary were to be influenced equally by both. No one seems to have defined how to measure the elusive influence.

Combatting communism was not the only reason for Churchill staying on. He had worked with socialists for five years, but he was still suspicious of the creed. He also persuaded himself that no one could replace him as Tory leader. Eden was the only real option, but Churchill lacked total faith in him and would lead Eden a not so merry dance for the next ten years. If his relationship with Attlee had been a mating dance, it would be appropriate to call Churchill's relationship with Eden a tease.

After the election, Attlee moved from 11 Downing Street to 10 Downing Street with little fuss thanks to Clementine's help. As Prime Minister he did not have to consult the Labour Party's National Executive Committee when he made appointments, and he gave two great offices to men who had always thought they could do better than him: Herbert Morrison became Home Secretary and Deputy Prime Minister, while Hugh Dalton became Chancellor. Ernest Bevin became the first, and so far only, lorry driver to head up the Foreign Office. Stafford Cripps took up the reins as President of the Board of Trade and Aneurin Bevan was appointed Minister of Health.

Attlee had often chaired the Cabinet in Churchill's absence, and soon after the election their differences in style were leaked in the press. 'When Attlee takes the chair, we keep to the agenda, make decisions and get away in reasonable time. When Churchill presides, nothing is decided, we listen enthralled.' Attlee did not hesitate to silence any minister who talked too much. Churchill was revelling in the irony. Attlee was 'ruthless', as his friend Lord Taylor had said. He did not waste words. Lord Taylor remarked that when a minister, upset at having been dismissed, asked Attlee why he had been sacked, he was just told, 'Not up to it.' Laconic in the extreme.

Japan, which still refused to surrender, was the first priority. Roosevelt had been warned that up to a million American lives might be lost in an invasion. This was too high a price for his successor. Truman approved dropping the atomic bomb on Hiroshima.

Sadako Kurihara had been a shopkeeper in Hiroshima when the Americans dropped the bomb on 6 August. In 1946, General Douglas MacArthur, whom Truman had appointed to govern Japan, censored Kurihara's first collection of poems, *Black Eggs*, because she wrote about the horrors of the bomb. The full volume of *Black Eggs* would not be published for forty years. MacArthur wanted to hide the truth about the devastation wreaked by the bomb, but failed, as the *New Yorker* reported what had happened in a series of classic articles.

Despite the death and destruction caused by the bomb, one of Kurihara's poems is actually an affirmation of life.

In 'We Shall Bring Forth New Life', she describes hearing a voice in the basement of a devastated building; it was the voice of a woman going into labour, crying out for help. A midwife suffering from radiation offered her assistance and, in the hell that was the aftermath of the bomb, the baby was born. New life into a shattered world. But the midwife sadly passed away covered in blood.

In Britain, Mass Observation found that people were horrified and frightened; a few people used the word 'devilish' to describe the bomb. Some were reminded of the Blitz and a number pointed out that the Americans had never been bombed, and so could not begin to imagine the devastation. A second bomb was dropped on Nagasaki on 9 August. Japan surrendered unconditionally on 14 August.

Eight days later, Truman sent Attlee a telegram, announcing curtly that he was ending Lend-Lease. Attlee and Dalton sent John Maynard Keynes to America to explain the calamity this would cause. Attlee kept a postcard in his papers from an American who warned that Harold Laski might ruin the deal. Laski was so much in the news that many Americans thought that he, not Attlee, was the Prime Minister.

To press Britain's case, Churchill travelled by train to New York, where he held talks with his friend, the financier Bernard Baruch. As a result of their discussions, Churchill telegraphed Attlee: 'I do not think [Baruch] will take any action against the loan.' Baruch considered 'the Russian situation makes it essential that our countries should stand together. He is of course in full agreement with me on that.' Churchill added, '[Baruch] spoke last night to me in the sense that he might urge that the loan should be interest-free – as a gesture of unity.' Attlee thanked him warmly 'for the friendly line you took'. Keynes only managed to negotiate a loan of $586 million and an even bigger line of credit – $3.75 billion. Despite his efforts and those of Churchill, Britain would have to pay interest over fifty years. But at least, at 2 per cent, the rate was low.

When he agreed the Atlantic Charter, Roosevelt had insisted that Britain grant independence to much of the British Empire. Truman made many of the same demands now. 'Our allies had very strong views about "the evils of imperialism,"' Attlee wrote. Much of the criticism was 'very ill-informed', but it was also very strong. Attlee remarked that it seemed perfectly natural to the Americans to absorb a continent, not to mention decimating the native population, yet a patchwork empire 'inhabited by various races at different stages of civilization appeared an example of colonialism and rank imperialism'.

When it came to atomic policy, there was little difference between the ex-colleagues. On 6 October, Churchill wrote to the new Prime Minister: 'I am much obliged to you for a copy of your letter to the President. I fully recognise the fearful gravity of the problem with which it deals.' He went on,

I thank you for consulting me about the draft message. I am in general agreement with the sentiments you express and feel with you the appalling gravity of the matter. However the message does not seem to me to make clear what in fact you want the Americans to do.

Churchill wondered whether Attlee wanted to tell the Russians. He doubted Stalin would agree to share atomic knowledge and recalled that his agreement with Roosevelt was almost

a military understanding between us and the mightiest power in the world. I should greatly regret if we seemed not to value this and pressed them to melt our dual agreement down into a general international arrangement consisting, I fear, of pious empty phrases and undertakings which will not be carried out.

He ended on a heartfelt note: 'I sympathise deeply in your anxieties.'

The letter ranged from the atomic to the personal. Churchill had come back from America 'much refreshed, but, unhappily with a cold which I am nursing attentively'. He was sorry he could not come to dinner with Clementine when the Attlees invited both of them. She told him the evening had been 'very agreeable'. Then Churchill switched back to politics; he would like to talk with Attlee and agreed that matters of atomic energy, including secret agreements with Belgium, Holland and Brazil, should not be made public.

Attlee and Churchill's relationship was complex: on domestic policies they disagreed, sometimes angrily; on foreign policy, they were rarely at odds; and on a personal level, they were friendly. When Churchill had to be hospitalised, Attlee went to see him. He also later gave him a copy of *As It Happened*, a gift that mirrored the one Churchill had made before the war when he presented Attlee with a copy of *Step by Step*. The leaders were more than cordial, although their followers were not. They longed for the hurly-burly of what they deemed 'normal' politics.

In December, finally, there was a major clash. Churchill tabled a motion of censure and started with an overview of the world now at peace. Relations with the United States were tense. Europe was in chaos. 'Fateful and difficult decisions await us in India.' Churchill did not blame the new government, accepting that 'the greater part was inherited'. Still, he asked, 'What would have been said if a Conservative or even a National Coalition government had been in office and had no better showing to offer than what we see at present?' It seemed perverse that the government should 'choose this moment ... to proclaim great new departures in political theory'. Socialism would divide the land and lead to bitterness. 'Can we afford an internal struggle of such a character at such a time?' The government was not allowing people 'to recover normal mentality'.

If Churchill had won the election, 'my first thought would have been to seek the cooperation of the minority, and gather together the widest and strongest measure of agreement over the largest possible area'. Instead, the government was deliberately 'trying to exalt their partisan and faction interests at the cost not only of the national unity but of our recovery and of our vital interest'.

Churchill said he had done his best 'to make easy and nationally united the course of foreign politics. The Prime Minister found it convenient to refer appreciatively to this in his speech to the American Congress.' Labour, though, could not be coaxed out of its addiction to controls and insisted 'upon keeping on for five years by legislation all the extraordinary controls, which even in the heat of war we only renewed from year to year, and rejected our friendly proposal for a two-year period; they showed that they were imbued with the spirit of faction. They showed a desire to humiliate their defeated opponents.'

'The Prime Minister has not sought in any way to embitter or inflame our proceedings,' Churchill stressed. Other ministers, however, were guilty of doing so. Churchill then warned that Attlee might 'have to hurry up and toe the line this afternoon'. Laski might summon him to appear before the Labour Party's all-powerful National Executive Committee to explain why he was not keen on humiliating the Tories. But Churchill could not stay hostile towards his recent deputy for long and added that 'Attlee does not need to grind his personal axe, and will probably be content if he can keep hold of it. We are, therefore, glad he is here and safely back.'

Paul Beards, Churchill's private secretary who had gone to work for Attlee in July 1945, made clear that the regard between Churchill and Attlee was still mutual. 'One night at Chequers, a year or two later, at dinner, the conversation turned to the war. One of those present supposed Churchill's part in the war had been much exaggerated.' Attlee turned around and said, 'There is one man that won the war, and that was Winston Churchill.'

India still divided the two men, though. Indian troops had helped to win the war. Attlee had chaired a special committee of the War Cabinet on India and had increased the number of Indians on the Viceroy's Council. Independence could not be delayed, he felt. Attlee summoned Archibald Wavell, the Viceroy, and received some bad, but not unexpected, news. Wavell saw no way of reconciling the aims of the Hindu-dominated party, the Indian National Congress, with those of the Muslim League. Attlee considered Wavell too defeatist and sent three Cabinet ministers – Cripps, Pethick-Lawrence and Alexander – to India. They recommended dividing India into three autonomous groups of provinces with a weak central government. But Congress rejected the proposal as it feared India would become 'Balkanised'.

Attlee decided a more charismatic figure than Wavell was needed. He chose Lord Mountbatten and gave him crisp instructions: 'Keep India united if you can. If not, save something from the wreck. In any case, get Britain out.' Choosing Mountbatten was inspired, Attlee later thought. Mountbatten demanded more authority than any previous Viceroy and, before finally accepting the post, made the government announce that British rule would end by July 1948.

Churchill was romantic about India but realistic about Stalin. On 5 March 1946, Truman was on the platform at Fulton in Missouri where Churchill had been invited to speak. Churchill was in gloomy, visionary mode. 'From Stettin in the Baltic to Trieste in the Adriatic, an iron curtain has descended across the continent,' he thundered, coining another famous phrase. Drawing parallels with appeasement, Churchill said that in dealing with the Soviets, there was 'nothing which they admire so much as strength, and there is nothing for which they have less respect than weakness, especially military weakness'.

Churchill argued for an even closer 'special relationship' between the United States and Great Britain – the great powers of the 'English-speaking world' – in organising and policing the post-war world. Stalin denounced the speech as 'warmongering' and condemned Churchill's comments about the 'English-speaking world' as imperialist racism. Attlee was urged to disassociate himself from Churchill. He refused to do so, but neither did he endorse Churchill's pessimistic vision of the future. Later, however, Attlee admitted that he had shared Churchill's fears.

On 20 April, Truman wrote to Attlee that the Quebec Agreement of 1943 did not oblige America to give Britain engineering plans to construct an atomic plant. The President was patronising and said that he felt it would be unwise for Britain to have one. Attlee was restrained in reply; his own views had not really 'begun to crystallise'. But he thought it 'essential that you and I should discuss this momentous problem together, so that we may agree what the next step should be and be in a position to take it before the fears and suspicions which may be developing elsewhere have got such a firm hold, as to make even more difficult any solution we may decide to aim at.' Attlee was trying to talk as an equal. In October 1941, he reminded Truman, Churchill had proposed 'that any extended efforts in this field should be coordinated or even jointly conducted'. Britain had shared its knowledge and 'we gave it in the confident belief that the experience and knowledge gained in

America would be made freely available to us.' The War Cabinet had let the Americans into every secret 'of research radar and jet propulsion'. As soon as the war ended, however, 'we were told that until new arrangements could be concluded the supply of information must be stopped'. The new President made Attlee wait until November for any meeting.

When he finally saw Truman, Attlee obtained a memorandum for full cooperation between Britain, Canada and the United States on atomic energy. A Combined Policy Committee would consider the arrangements for this purpose. After he left Washington, Attlee told Truman he had been very much reassured, but urged Truman to allow continuing cooperation with all proper security precautions: 'We believe that we are entitled, both by the documents and by the history of our common efforts in the past.' This time Truman did not reply to Attlee's letter. The snub from Britain's closest ally was unacceptable. As ever, Attlee was controlled in his response. He then took a decision that would shape Britain's nuclear future: Britain would make its own bomb. He later said, 'We had to hold up our position vis-à-vis the Americans …We had to look to our defence – and to our industrial future.' If he told Churchill what he had decided, the two of them kept it secret.

Churchill was finally invested as Lord Warden of the Cinque Ports on 14 August. Crowds cheered as he drove from Dover Castle, and he gave his V for Victory sign. Military bands played; units from all the services marched; the Barons of the Cinque Ports attended in velvet costumes. The Seneschal of the utterly obscure Court of Shepway called 'Oyez! Oyez! Oyez!' The bells of Dover that had been rung to announce victory over the French at Agincourt back in 1415 now rang out again. The flummery was fantastic. The daft pageantry appealed to Churchill's playfulness. He got into the spirit of the event, a respite from the state of the world. In *Savrola*, the novel he wrote as a young man, he let his hero fear that the world would crumble into nothingness. The fear seemed not at all fictional now.

In Zurich, on 19 September 1946, Churchill lamented that Europe was 'the home of all the great parent races of the western world', but it had been wrecked by 'frightful nationalistic quarrels, originated by the Teutonic nations'. These quarrels had pulped Europe to 'a vast quivering mass of tormented, hungry, care-worn and bewildered human beings'. Among the victors there was 'a babel of jarring voices; among the vanquished the sullen silence of despair'.

The remedy, Churchill insisted, was 'to recreate the European Family'. He envisioned a kind of United States of Europe, 'which would make life worth living'. But in order for this to be accomplished successfully, there needed to be 'an act of faith in which the millions of families speaking many languages must consciously take part'. His vision of the future did not mean forgetting the past; he still believed that the guilty must be punished. 'Germany must be deprived of the power to rearm and make another aggressive war … But when all this has been done, there must be an end to retribution.' Quoting the man who had been his father's bitter political rival, he said,

There must be what Mr Gladstone many years ago called a 'blessed act of oblivion'. We must all turn our backs upon the horrors of the past. We must look to the future. We cannot afford to drag forward across the years that are to come the hatreds and revenges which have sprung from the injuries of the past.

Churchill then teased his audience: 'I am now going to say something that will astonish you. The first step in the recreation of the European family must be a partnership between France and Germany.' Time was short, though, because of the atomic bomb, whose 'use by several war-ring nations will not only bring to an end all that we call civilisation, but may possibly disintegrate the globe itself'. When he delivered his speech, only one country had the bomb: the United States.

As had been the case during the war, the British Prime Minister needed to act adroitly when dealing with the American President. Attlee was arguably in a stronger position than Churchill had been as Prime Minister during the war, so he decided that he would not be bullied by Truman.

Attlee's position would not have surprised the authors of three still funny books: the Hungarian George Mikes, the Frenchman Pierre Daninos and the very English public school boys Walter Carruthers Sellar and Robert Julian Yeatman. All were amused by Britain's in-vincible, perhaps incorrigible, belief that it was still a major nation. One is too polite to boast, however, to Johnny Foreigner, who would never understand given his, or indeed her, unfortunate impediment of foreignness. Johnny 'Jackboot' Foreigner, the pro-Nazi journalist Me-defind, had claimed in 1939 that Britain's foolish pride and clinging to traditions could lead it to defeat. History had splashed egg on his face.

All three books also commented on Britain's obsession with the weather. In the spirit of *1066 and All That*, it probably stemmed from the fact that Queen Boadicea could not find her umbrella one day.

From late January 1947, Europe endured some of the coldest tempera-tures ever recorded. For some inexplicable reason, Britain can cope with dictators and wars against the odds better than it can with snow and ice. Roads and railways were disrupted. Power stations ran out of coal. Radio broadcasts were limited and television services were suspended. Some magazines were ordered to stop publishing, while newspapers shrank in size. Emanuel Shinwell, the Minister of Fuel and Power, was blamed and received death threats. He had to be placed under police guard. Better weather in March brought a thaw and – widespread flood-ing. What was worse was that a country which had stood alone against Hitler now needed help from foreign aid agencies to feed itself.

At the Scottish TUC conference on 24 April 1947, Attlee attacked Churchill. 'There was not a drop of policy in the torrent of irresponsible abuse.' Attlee then sniped, 'He sinned, no doubt in all innocence.' Attlee earned the headline 'Clem the Giant Killer', which made it clear Churchill was still a giant. Giving as good as he got, Churchill replied that if Attlee had to dredge up his record as Chancellor from twenty years earlier it showed the feebleness of his arguments. Their clash did not stop Attlee, three months later, writing to hope that Churchill had recovered from an illness.

Mountbatten had arrived in India a month before the Scottish TUC conference. 'Action this day' seems to have been his motto, as it was Churchill's in the war. Mountbatten quickly manoeuvred Congress into accepting the partition of the sub-continent along religious lines, while giving the Muslim League less than it demanded. He also brought forward the date of British withdrawal to 15 August 1948. In a memoir, Mountbat-ten's daughter Pamela described the strange mixture of protocol and per-sonalities in the fifteen months that followed. Nehru was a friend as well as the lover of Mountbatten's wife, Edwina. Pamela liked Nehru very much.

Churchill remained unreconciled to Indian independence and wrote to Attlee:

My dear Prime Minister,

I am much concerned to hear from my colleagues whom you consulted yesterday that you propose to call the India Bill, 'The Indian Independence Bill'. This, I am assured, is entirely contrary to the text, which corresponds to what we have previously been told were your intentions. The essence of the Mountbatten proposals, and the only reason why I gave support to them, is because they establish the phase of Dominion status. Dominion status is not the same as independence, although it may be freely used to establish independence. It is not true that a community is independent, when its ministers have taken the Oath of Allegiance to the King. This is a measure of grave constitutional importance and a correct and formal procedure and nomenclature should be observed. The correct title would be, it seems to me, 'The Indian Dominions Bill'. I should, however, be quite willing to support it if it were called, 'The India Bill, 1947' or 'The India Self-Government Bill'.

I am glad to hear you are considering such alterations.

He ended with warm wishes but, in the end, Attlee insisted on 'The Indian Independence Bill'. Churchill had lost one of his longest battles – to save the Raj. Pamela Mountbatten said Churchill never forgave her father for 'giving away the empire' and cut him dead at every Buckingham Palace garden party. There would be a final twist to the saga, however, which would have delighted Churchill.

In his 1982 biography of Subhas Chandra Bose, Major General G. D. Bakshi claimed that history needed to be revised – Gandhi and Nehru had played less of a role in winning Indian independence than was generally assumed. In fact, the decisive role had been performed by Bose's Indian National Army. Bose had been a young and charismatic Congress leader when Attlee met him in 1938. But a year later, Gandhi had Bose ousted from the Congress leadership. Bose was then placed under house arrest by the British after the outbreak of the Second World War, but managed to escape to Germany, where Hitler met him and offered some unexpected help. First, a 3,000-strong force of Indians captured by Rommel became the nucleus of a new Indian army willing to fight against Britain. Second, Hitler ordered a U-boat to take Bose to Madagascar, where he was transferred to a Japanese submarine bound for Sumatra. Bose revamped the Indian National Army, or INA, and formed a provisional government of Free India in the Andaman and Nicobar Islands, which Japan had occupied. Bose's ambitions came to a sudden end, however, when he died in a plane crash in Taipei in August 1945.

His death did not prevent the British from charging 300 of Bose's officers with treason, an offence that carried the death penalty. But by November 1945, these officers were being hailed as heroic patriots in India. Posters threatening death to '20 English dogs for every INA man sentenced' were pasted all over Delhi. In Banaras, a public meeting heard that if the officers were not spared, 'revenge would be taken on European children'. The *Deccan Chronicle* reported that 20,000 sailors in the Royal Indian Navy mutinied and there were also rebellions in the Royal Indian Air Force. Attlee told the House that calm was restored after a few days, though not before 208 people had died and over 1,200 had been injured, mainly in Bombay.

Bakshi claimed that when the then Governor of West Bengal, Justice P. B. Chakraborty, asked Attlee why the British had finally quit India, Attlee replied that there had been several reasons. According to Chakraborty, Attlee said the main reason had been 'the erosion of loyalty to the British crown among the Indian army and navy personnel as a result of the military activities of Netaji [Bose]'. Chakraborty added, 'Towards the end of our discussion I asked Attlee what was the extent of Gandhi's influence upon the British decision to quit India. Hearing this question, Attlee's lips became twisted in a sarcastic smile as he slowly chewed out the word, "m-i-n-i-m-a-l!"' Churchill would have been pleased.

In the 1945 election, Labour had promised a national health service.

The British Medical Association fought against the plan. But they were fighting a minister who believed in what he saw as a central plank of Labour policy, though Churchill had promised a scheme much like it. On 5 July 1948, the Minister of Health, Aneurin Bevan, officially launched Britain's National Health Service. He visited Park Hospital in Davyhulme, Greater Manchester and met the NHS's first patient, thirteen-year-old Sylvia Diggory, who had a serious liver condition.

By the day of the launch, 94 per cent of the public were enrolled with the NHS. The next day's *Daily Mirror* editorial noted, 'The National Health Service has got off to an encouraging start ... an example of how the nation can cooperate in a great enterprise.' Oddly, though, Attlee did not know how to enrol himself and his family.

In July 1949, Attlee drafted a speech for the NHS's first anniversary, stating that Britain's health service commanded the support of all the political parties. But Bevan wanted Labour to claim exclusive credit for the formation of the NHS. 'The party would be made to look foolish if their leader attributes parentage to all-party inspiration. Why should we stretch the truth to favour our enemies?' Ignoring the fact that Churchill had played his part in the NHS's inception, Bevan argued that the Tories had voted against at the Second and Third Readings of the Bill that had set up the NHS.

Attlee refused to omit his reference to Churchill.

Harold Macmillan wrote that Attlee faced many difficult problems. Churchill wrote to Clementine: 'I continue to be depressed about the future. I really do not see how our poor island is going to earn its living, when there are so many difficulties around us and so much ill-will and division at home.' Ill-will, division – and also extravagance. Attlee's government went on what Churchill saw as a socialist spending spree. Labour increased food and rent subsidies, and introduced a universal family allowances scheme, 'with a song in my heart', as Dalton put it. Free school milk flowed, while the Chancellor removed 2.5 million workers from the tax system altogether.

The historian, Correlli Barnett, has argued that winning the war deluded both Churchill and Attlee into believing Britain could remain a major power. John Maynard Keynes, now an economic adviser to the government, had pilloried Churchill back in 1926. In August 1945, he wrote a series of papers which might have been called *The Economic Consequences of Mr Attlee*. Keynes told ministers that Britain's world role was a burden 'there is no reasonable expectation of our being able to carry'. The country faced a 'financial Dunkirk'. It could not afford to have more than two million men in its armed forces sprawled across the globe. Britain might soon be in the same economic league as France, Keynes warned. Neither Attlee nor Churchill could reconcile themselves to such a disgrace. Chancellor Hugh Dalton cut spending on the armed forces, just as Churchill's father, Lord Randolph, had wanted to do in 1886. Labour's Herbert Morrison shrewdly judged, 'We are in danger of paying more than we can afford for defences that are nevertheless inadequate, or even illusory.'

America was the triumphant economic survivor of the war, but a generous one too. It devised the Marshall Plan, which Whitehall saw not as a bounty for long-term aid reconstruction, but rather as a short-term fix. A Cabinet Office memorandum viewed it as a way of covering 'our dollar drain'. It would meet the costs of embassies, gold payments to Persia, petrol for the troops in the Middle East and 'every conceivable thing'. It was a monumental waste of an opportunity. Britain's creaking industries did not get the Marshall Plan money they needed to help them to modernise. Keynes might have persuaded the government that this was folly, but he had died in April 1946. The French and German governments produced tenders where reconstructing industry and infrastructure were priorities. The British tender, historian Correlli Barnett sniped, 'resembled an Oxbridge economist's prolix prize-essay – with a tour of the world's economic horizon and Britain's place within it'. Pipe-smoking Clem and cigar-smoking Churchill also knew that the government had to subsidise tobacco – two-thirds of men smoked – and tobacco coupons were handed out with pensions. Timber and food also needed subsidies. But this would prove costly. However, there is no reason to suppose Churchill would have proved any wiser than Attlee when it came to spending Marshall Plan money.

As leader of a country deeply in debt, Attlee also had to deal with a crisis that Stalin now provoked. When American and British officials denied the Soviet Union more say in the economic future of Germany, Stalin blockaded Berlin. Truman ordered a massive airlift of supplies into West Berlin and persuaded Attlee to cooperate. On 26 June, the first British and American planes took off from bases in England and western Germany. It took a total of 272,000 flights over a period of 321 days to keep West Berlin going. The Soviets were portrayed as bullies, holding men, women and children hostage and threatening them with starvation. In conditions of bitter cold, Attlee flew to West Berlin to inspect the situation.

The Foreign Ministers of twelve countries met in Washington, DC on 4 April 1949 and signed NATO (the North Atlantic Treaty Organization) into being. Bevin was a prime mover. Article 5 stated that a military attack against any member would be considered an attack against them all. NATO in case of war; the United Nations in the hope for peace. Attlee told the historic opening session of the General Assembly of the United Nations, which was held in London's Westminster Hall, that the UN would not be merely 'for the negation of war but for the creation of a world of security and freedom which would be governed by justice and the moral law'. In May 1949, the Soviets ended their blockade of Berlin. The West had won the first round of the Cold War.

The UK's economy worsened, however, and the pound came under pressure. The Marshall Plan money had nearly run out. Devaluation became an option. But *The Spectator* magazine complained that this would avoid dealing with problems such as the 'squeezing out of the less efficient firm by the more efficient'. A weaker pound would also make imports more expensive. Churchill saw devaluation as a calamity caused by socialist policies.

Labour had been in power for nearly five years. A general election was scheduled for 23 February 1950. Rab Butler, the Tory appeaser with amnesia about appeasement, realised that the Conservatives must accept Labour's reforms in terms of the welfare state and the mixed economy. The Conservative Party manifesto – this time Churchill's name was not in the title – promised to 'maintain and improve the health service' and free 'the productive energies of the nation from the trammels of overbearing state control and bureaucratic management'. It marked a remarkable shift in Tory attitudes.

Attlee faced internal problems. Morrison led the Labour moderates, who were calling for 'consolidation', while Bevan and the radicals demanded more reforms, especially greater nationalisation. Time was also taking a toll, Attlee feared. The average age of his Cabinet was around sixty; some of them were sick, nearly all were tired. Exhaustion may have also affected Attlee, making him even more succinct than usual. Interviewed by Pathé News during the election, Attlee had so little to say that the interviewer was forced to ask, 'Have you anything to add, Prime Minister?' 'No, I don't think so,' Attlee replied. That was the end of that conversation.

The Representation of the People Acts of 1948 and 1949 had changed constituency boundaries, much to Labour's disadvantage. Eighteen seats in one of Labour's safest areas, inner London, had been reduced to nine. Postal voting was also being allowed for the first time and these postal votes were, according to Herbert Morrison, likely to be cast 10–1 in favour of the Conservatives.

On election night, Attlee hunkered down in 10 Downing Street and listened to the radio as news reports came in of heavy Labour losses. The final result – 315 seats for Labour, 298 for the Tories and 9 for the Liberals – left Labour with a slim majority and Attlee remained Prime Minister. Enoch Powell was one of the new Tory MPs. One can understand why Powell said later that all political lives end in failure. He had witnessed it as a young man when Attlee's once-brilliant government began to lose its grip.

After the election, Attlee wrote to his brother Tom about 'the distasteful business of reconstructing the government ... It always means relegating some good friends to the back benches.' Six ministers were dropped and the average age of Attlee's Cabinet fell to fifty-nine.

When Attlee had commanded a huge parliamentary majority, he had been extremely considerate of Churchill. He would prove less so when Labour's majority was fragile. The next two months saw the former comrades-in-arms at their most hostile. Attlee was under great stress. On 16 March, he asked Parliament to approve a White Paper on defence. Churchill asked him to substitute the words 'takes note of', for the word 'approved'. Such a step, Churchill said, 'might be regarded hereafter as to some extent committing us to sharing, albeit indirectly, in the government's responsibility'.

Attlee agreed, but in summing up the debate he made one of his sharpest attacks ever on Churchill, accusing him of making 'a number of cheap party points. He began by attacking ministers, not in very good taste, and I should not have referred to his attacks except that I think that one should always stand up for people who are attacked quite unjustly.' Attlee then said,

> I am looking forward so hopefully to some subsequent volume of the memoirs of the right honourable gentleman, so that perhaps we shall have the reasons, at present hidden from everyone, for some of his remarkable appointments, particularly his choice for First Lord of the Admiralty in the caretaker government.

Attlee then moved to the atomic bomb situation, a matter that both Labour and Tory MPs had raised. The United Nations was still considering the issue, Attlee told the House. 'I think that many people delude themselves if they think that one can get rid of the menace of the atomic bomb by some sort of Queensberry rules being applied to warfare.'

'Queensberry rules,' one MP interrupted.

'Yes, the Queensberry rules,' Attlee replied,

> which say that one must not hit below the belt. It all depends on the will to peace, and it is for this that we are working, and have been working. So long as these things exist. I do not believe there is an effective way without the will to peace. One will not get one's desire merely by outlawing a certain weapon.

Despite his attack on Churchill, Attlee said the debate 'has been one of the best on defence that I have heard in this House'. Churchill kept his word and did not press for a vote.

The new government had to confront two issues that have still not been fully resolved today: Korea and the costs of the National Health Service. When Japan surrendered, America seized much of its empire, of which Korea had been a part. In August 1945, in the best traditions of Western imperialism, two young aides at the US State Department divided the Korean peninsula along the 38th parallel. Unfortunately, the North refused to accept this division. On 25 June 1950, 75,000 soldiers of the North Korean People's Army poured across the 38th parallel. Truman decided it was a war against international communism: evil must be defeated just as the Nazis had been.

In London, however, two days after the war began, Attlee held a Cabinet meeting at which Korea was only the fourth item on the agenda. The Cabinet Secretary, Sir Norman Brook, remarked to Attlee, 'Korea is rather a distant obligation, Prime Minister.' 'Distant – yes,' Attlee replied, 'but nonetheless an obligation.' Attlee had no intention of letting the United Nations down even if it cost yet more money.

The Cabinet eventually agreed to a UN Security Council resolution urging countries to help South Korea. Attlee became even more concerned when Truman briefed the press in November 1950 that the US was willing to do whatever was necessary to regain the upper hand militarily, including using 'every weapon'. The United States would be prepared to destroy Russian bases in the Far East with nuclear bombs.

Attlee travelled to Washington in December.

As part of his research, Hugh Gaitskell's biographer Philip Williams interviewed Norman Brook, the Cabinet Secretary who accompanied Attlee to Washington. The visit began disastrously, with Attlee reminding Truman of the Quebec Agreement and the deployment of British troops in Korea. No use of nuclear weapons could be contemplated without British consent, the Prime Minister insisted. But Truman asserted that he would make the final decision. After fifteen minutes of negotiation, the two leaders had reached deadlock. Then they started reminiscing about the First World War.

Truman had volunteered and fought with distinction in France. He admired fellow volunteers and quickly discovered the details of Attlee's war record. Before long, both men were at the piano, drinking and singing war songs. The evening ended in complete amity. Attlee explained that he simply needed Truman to assure him he would not use the bomb without Britain's approval. Truman agreed, but both men saw that it would be best to say as little as possible about their deal. Truman did not want the world to know he had given Britain a veto over America's use of the bomb.

When Stalin threatened to respond to attacks in the Far East by attacking American bases in western Europe, Truman sent bombers with atomic weapons to Britain, a fact Attlee did not reveal to the Commons.

A few months later, American troops headed north towards the Yalu River, which marked the border between North Korea and China. Mao Zedong ordered Chinese troops to North Korea and warned Truman to keep his army away from the river unless he wanted a full-scale war.

Attlee was forced to update Britain's defence policy. His relationship with Churchill was perhaps at its most adversarial when, on 15 February 1951, Shinwell put a White Paper before the House. Churchill said the Tories could not give the proposals 'an unqualified vote approving the military methods and proposals of the present government in these affairs'. In the previous eighteen months, the government had made 'large changes of policy. The extensive rearmament programme now before us is the third version we have had.' Before Parliament rose for the summer recess, Shinwell had 'made very alarming disclosures to the House about the overwhelming Russian strength in Europe', Churchill noted, 'and also confirmed to a large extent the detailed assertions which I had made upon the Soviet armaments on land, on sea and in the air'. Shinwell, 'who, I have no doubt, is doing his best according to his lights, then proposed an interim expenditure of £100 million, and we separated without a division for the summer recess.' But when Parliament reconvened on 12 September 1950, the government had a new plan that required more money: £3,600 million spread over three years. 'The Prime Minister appealed to us on that occasion for national unity on defence,' Churchill said. The Tories voted for the Labour motion and the Bill passed in one day.

Attlee had not proved grateful, Churchill complained. Almost the very next day, the date for steel nationalisation to come into effect was fixed for 15 February 1951. Attlee was responsible 'in a degree unusually direct and personal', Churchill claimed. The government required more money due to its perpetual mismanagement. As a result, Churchill could not support the government wholeheartedly. Yes, he remained 'in principle in favour' of more military spending, but as these were 'entirely new demands', they needed new scrutiny.

The past had lessons to offer, Churchill suggested. On 22 October 1945, he had urged the government to speed up demobilisation to spare two or three million men 'the ordeal of standing about needlessly under arms at a time when they were not wanted, when no new dangers appeared upon us'. At least £1,000 million might have been saved. Instead, the budget had spiralled out of control and to no effect. The government had 'produced so few effective tactical units that when the Korean trouble broke out and it was necessary for us to send a token force – it took over three months to produce even a brigade group of good quality'.

The atomic bomb situation triggered the bitterest exchange between the two leaders. Given 'how far we were ahead, and how we were able to deal on equal terms with the United States, it is indeed depressing to feel that we have been outstripped by the Soviets', Churchill said. The situation was now acute, as the government had allowed the Americans to establish an atomic base in East Anglia. 'We have made ourselves the target, and perhaps the bull's eye of a Soviet attack.'

Attlee interrupted to say that Churchill

ought not to mislead the country on a matter like this. He knows perfectly well it was by his agreement, and the agreement of the government of which I was a member, that the development of the atomic bomb took place across the other side of the Atlantic, and it is utterly untrue to suggest there has been a failure to develop it here. It is entirely wrong of him.

Attlee's reply – and his unusual display of anger – makes one wonder if he had told Churchill something about the secret research developments in Britain.

Churchill blamed the Luftwaffe. The only reason Britain had not constructed an atomic bomb during the war was that 'we had not got a safe place here and the United States therefore had the facility and the credit of making it. At the end of the war we were perfectly free to resume manufacture. Is not that correct?'

'Certainly,' Attlee replied. Very unusually, he then made a personal attack connected with the fact that Churchill occasionally found it hard to hear. 'I am sorry if the right honourable gentleman cannot hear me. I said, "Yes."'

Churchill then asked, 'Then what is the complaint about what I have said – that in the five and a half years no success has rewarded our efforts in making it?'

Attlee sought to correct him. 'There has been successful development.

He is not producing any evidence whatever to show that, given the resources and possibilities over here as compared with the resources they have in the United States of America, we could have done more than we have done now.'

Churchill conceded, saying that 'with many of his arguments we on this side of the House will agree.' But Churchill claimed Attlee was too anxious to water down the British position and rob it 'of as much meaning and reality as possible by stressing various conditions'.

There was a final spat about forming a European army; Churchill wanted one but Attlee opposed the idea.

Attlee had other things to worry about. His government was thrown into crisis when Aneurin Bevan quit as Minister of Health, after Labour decided to introduce charges for dental care, spectacles and prescriptions. Bevan complained to Attlee, 'It is the beginning of the destruction of those social services in which Labour has taken a special pride and which were giving to Britain the moral leadership of the world.' Future Prime Minister Harold Wilson also resigned over the issue. *The Guardian* dubbed the 1950–51 administration the 'unhappy parliament'.

Attlee was forced to call a new election after less than eighteen months. Labour was tired and disunited; the Tory Chief Whip, Patrick Buchan-Hepburn, had also made clever use of the pairing system, an arrangement where an MP would not turn up to vote if an MP from the rival party was going to be absent. Buchan-Hepburn rarely agreed to such arrangements. Sick Labour MPs had to vote, and sometimes were brought into the Commons in wheelchairs.

The general election seemed to follow tradition. Labour's manifesto claimed that a Tory MP still thought 'in terms of Victorian imperialism and colonial exploitation. His reaction in a crisis is to threaten force. His narrow outlook is an obstacle to that worldwide cooperation which alone makes peace secure. He would have denied freedom to India, Pakistan, Ceylon and Burma.' Labour had achieved full employment for six years, the manifesto trumpeted. Full employment had 'never happened before. It has meant a revolution in the lives of our people.' The manifesto had a neat slogan: 'Under Labour – more jobs than workers. Under the Tories – more workers than jobs.'

Attlee was rarely boastful, but Labour's election manifesto awarded the party a number of plaudits: the countryside was flourishing; farmers had beaten all production records; and 'prices [for consumers] had risen much less than in most other countries. No one ever had to pay the doctor. Old people were cared for and 1.3 million homes had been built.' It is almost surprising that Labour's slogan was not the one Harold Macmillan devised a few years later: 'People have never had it so good.'

But the greater equality that Attlee had always fought for still lay some way off. Fifty per cent of Britain's wealth was owned by 1 per cent of the population. Labour said it would press for more social equality and equal opportunities for all, while the Tories would slash taxes and public services. Labour's manifesto warned that the Tories, 'with their dark past, full of bitter memories for so many of our people, promise no light for the future'. They would take the country 'backward into poverty and insecurity at home and grave perils abroad'.

The Conservative Party manifesto countered that no matter how 'well-meaning many of the present socialist leaders may be', their proposals were 'fatal to individual freedom'. Britain needed stable government. 'The attempt to impose a doctrinaire socialism upon an island which has grown great and famous by free enterprise has inflicted serious injury upon our strength and prosperity.' Nationalisation had proved a costly failure, the Tories claimed. Even trade unions were unhappy because of controls imposed by powerful and remote officials in Whitehall. The

Conservatives would build more houses than Labour – 300,000 in a year – because 'in a property-owning democracy, the more people who own their homes the better'. A Churchill government would also look after pensioners, including war pensioners, and ensure that the most pressing needs were met first. 'The care and comfort of the elderly is a sacred trust. Some of them prefer to remain at work and there must be encouragement for them to do so.' Food subsidies would continue, but would be simplified in due course.

The Tories promised to restore fiscal discipline. 'British taxation', Churchill complained, 'is higher than in any country outside the communist world. It is higher by eight hundred millions a year than it was in the height of the war.' The Tories would reduce the burden, miraculously without harming either housing or social services. Churchill would also ensure that the rearmament programme, which he backed, provided greater value for money. But Churchill did not propose to overturn many of Attlee's reforms. He even offered an all-party conference on the subject he had first raised forty-nine years earlier: reform of the House of Lords.

Labour won 13.9 million votes in the election while the Tories got 13.7 million. Paradoxically, more votes won less seats: the Conservatives finished with 321 and Labour 295. Churchill was now seventy-seven years old, but he had seen Gladstone become Prime Minister for a fourth time when he was six years older, so he did not consider himself ancient. King George VI, though, believed that Churchill was slowing down and toyed with the idea of suggesting that Churchill retire in favour of Eden. Churchill would have rather given up cigars.

CHAPTER 12

LEADERSHIP QUALITIES

Before considering Churchill's last government, it seems useful to examine both men's views on leadership after many decades at the centre of power.

Attlee insisted that a leader must have the respect of his own party, and also that of the other side: 'If he doesn't obtain the respect of his own party (and of the other side; I have yet to learn of a case in which a man who did not enjoy a great deal of respect from the opposition had the respect of his own party) he will not get far in politics. He certainly will not get to the top.' Beaverbrook was an obvious example of this.

'A man may rise to the top without judgement, but will not stay there very long,' Attlee said. 'Sir Anthony Eden is the best example of this I know.' Eden had health problems after 1950 and Attlee linked a good physical constitution with the ability to lead.

Judgement, at any rate when exercised over a long period in everyday practical politics, is rarely found in men who do not have a strong physical constitution. Only men of very strong constitution can stand up to the nervous and physical strain of prolonged argument, especially in time of crisis.

Both he and Churchill had shown that

> an equable temperament, a strong constitution, and freedom from any excessive appetite of any kind are the three most important bases of a good, sound judgement. A man who lacks one of them will not be in a position of political power long before coming a cropper, and bringing his party down into the bargain. Judgement is required in order to be able to deal with men and with matters of moment.

The next essential was the courage 'to make big decisions which may, even if they are the correct ones, make him look a fool, a coward, or a renegade, in the short, or even the long, term'.

After many difficult decisions about appointments, Attlee concluded that 'decisions about sacking people are often harder than those about policy. If he doesn't display courage, the chances are that he will never become the leader, or that if he does, he won't last very long.' Courage came with the quality Attlee knew he himself possessed – an ability to make up his mind quickly. A good leader 'must be ready to act swiftly however much he has sweated about what is the right thing to do. Grown men, who know the score, do not want their leader to be continually beating his breast, and advertising his agonies. They want decision and action.'

'Finally,' Attlee said, 'a man who wishes to lead in politics must, on balance, enjoy being a politician. By enjoying, I don't mean the excitement and the pleasure of it, but the much deeper satisfaction that comes to a man who believes that what he is doing does honour to himself and his friends and is of social value.' Attlee had now been a 'socialist agitator' for nearly fifty years.

Intrigue was a sign of failure, Attlee argued. Knifing and backbiting in politics were usually the consolation of 'politicians who have failed to get to the top. The kind of politician who leaks to the press, or gossips to the third-rate novelist, is, in my experience, usually just that intriguing, egoistically ambitious and a feuding kind of personality who fails to be accepted as a leader.' The intriguers usually became victims of intrigue, Attlee wrote. The indiscreet usually perished by their indiscretions. Politicians sometimes did get stabbed in the back, he commented, but more usually they self-destructed. Attlee made it clear that he saw politics as a test of personality, saying that 'if a man stays in them [politics] long enough, they nearly always reveal him for what he is, and he tends to get not only what he deserves, but to find in his fate the reflection of his own strength and weakness.'

Churchill did not write on leadership as directly as Attlee, but his writings are suggestive of how he felt about the subject. He certainly had heroes. During the 1914–18 war, he was impressed by Lawrence of Arabia; Richard Meinertzhagen, a civil servant at the Colonial Office, said Churchill's attitude toward Lawrence 'almost amounted to hero worship'. In 1936, Churchill unveiled a plaque in honour of Lawrence, and described him as 'one of those beings whose pace of life was faster and more intense than what is normal ... The fury of the Great War raised the pitch of life to the Lawrence standard ... In this heroic period he found himself in perfect relation both to men and events.'

Nelson and Napoleon were also inspirations. A bust of Nelson sat on Churchill's desk at Chartwell and one of his favourite films was *That Hamilton Woman*, starring Vivien Leigh as Nelson's mistress and Laurence Olivier as Nelson. A slightly larger bust of Napoleon rested on the desk, and was more prominently placed than that of Nelson. Churchill had always hoped to write a biography of Napoleon, but he never found the time. He hated it when people compared Hitler to Napoleon. 'It seems an insult to the great emperor and warrior,' he said, 'to connect him in any way with a squalid caucus boss and butcher.'

Churchill's last two heroes were members of his family. We have discussed the complexities of Churchill's love for his flawed father, Randolph. His admiration for John Churchill, the Duke of Marlborough, who won the Battle of Blenheim in 1704, was much simpler. In Churchill's bedroom, a portrait of his famous ancestor hung next to the bed, and Churchill's four-volume biography of Marlborough did much to rehabilitate the duke's reputation. Whig historian Thomas Macaulay, whose ode Churchill had recited as a schoolboy at Harrow, had criticised Marlborough because he abandoned James II for William of Orange. The American political philosopher Leo Strauss called Churchill's biography of Marlborough 'the greatest historical work written in our century, an inexhaustible mine of political wisdom and understanding, which should be required reading for every student of political science'.

As indeed the careers of both Attlee and Churchill should be required reading.

CHAPTER 13

CHURCHILL'S LAST
ADMINISTRATION, 1951–1955

When Churchill returned to 10 Downing Street, he was far from being the oldest man to head a British government. His fellow Old Harrovian Lord Palmerston had served as Prime Minister at the age of eighty, while Gladstone was still in office aged eighty-four. Churchill was almost certainly the only politician in the House who had heard Gladstone speak.

Churchill and Attlee had now been at the centre of British politics for half a century. Of the major players in the wartime coalition, only Eden, Morrison and Dalton remained politicians of any great importance. Churchill, who had first mooted a coalition fifty years earlier, offered Clement Davies, the leader of the Liberals, a Cabinet post, though his party had only won six seats. Reform was still on Churchill's mind and he toyed with the idea of changing Britain's first-past-the-post electoral system, which would produce more coalitions. Attlee disapproved of the idea, as he feared Labour would suffer electoral damage.

The Tory victory led Aneurin Bevan to offer a snide psychological analysis. Churchill was 'a man suffering from petrified adolescence.

He does not talk the language of the twentieth century but that of the eighteenth. He is still fighting Blenheim all over again. His only answer to a difficult situation is to send a gunboat.' In reality, Churchill was neither an adolescent nor petrified – he was terrified that time was running out due to the development of the atomic bomb.

Both he and Attlee felt a little like strangers in such a changed world. In their last years as leaders, both men concerned themselves mainly with foreign affairs, as well as with keeping their parties under control and under their own leadership. Many Tories were restless for change; the most impatient of these was the perennial heir, Anthony Eden. Churchill charmed, teased and delayed Eden for four years before finally giving him the keys of No. 10. The strain of waiting damaged Eden's health and, as Attlee suggested, impaired his political judgement. The matter of succession also concerned Attlee and the Labour Party. One reason why Attlee did not resign as leader was because he did not want Herbert Morrison to succeed him.

Churchill made virtually no attempt to reverse the sweeping changes in domestic policy that the 1945 Labour government had introduced. This so-called political consensus came to be known as 'Butskellism', a play on the names of Rab Butler and Hugh Gaitskell. It would have been more accurate if the consensus had been a play on the names of Attlee and Churchill, but no one seemed to suggest 'AtChurch' as an alternative – perhaps it sounded too ecclesiastical.

The only nationalisations Churchill reversed were those of road haulage and steel. Steel was a major issue, but it was hard to drum up much passion over the issue of who should own Britain's trucks. One wonders if Churchill would have acted as he did if Ernest Bevin, whom he had liked so much, had been alive. Bevin had been a lorry driver.

Churchill's major objectives were how to achieve peace and ensuring that Britain was not left behind in the atomic race. In Churchill's novel, *Savrola*, his hero had imagined a state of nothingness, and the development of the atomic bomb might now very well lead to the extinction of all human life. Churchill was surprised by how much atomic work Attlee had authorised after Truman had proved so uncooperative in 1946.

One early issue the government had to confront was the always tricky issue of MPs' salaries, which were still £1,000 a year. Attlee wrote to *The Times* to say he knew MPs who had been forced to resign because they could not afford to stay in the Commons; Attlee supported increasing salaries to £1,500. As the country's economic situation was weak, Churchill felt that such a pay rise was not possible, but he told Butler to find some accommodation. In the end, MPs received a £2 a day allowance for every day they sat in the Commons.

Despite much consensus, Churchill and Attlee still fought a number of parliamentary duels. Churchill usually was the more aggressive now. On a number of occasions he even relished the idea that he was about to best Attlee in one of their many confrontations in the House. But it did not seem to harm their personal relationship. For example, Churchill now recommended his literary agent to Attlee. They had shared a governess, a valet, an agent and, of course, a government.

Attlee had spoken of Korea as an obligation and had sent British troops there as part of the United Nation forces. Churchill continued the policy. The eventual armistice, signed in 1953, gave South Korea an extra 1,500 square miles of territory and created a 2.5-mile-wide 'demilitarised zone' that still exists today. There were also end-of-empire problems. Attlee had rejected demands for land redistribution in Kenya, and Churchill continued this policy, which led to the Mau Mau rebellion. It would be left to younger men like Harold Macmillan to give independence to the colonies more easily.

There were many times when the old comradeship proved strong. Attlee remained loyal. For example, he refused to attack Churchill during the 1952 pea souper drama when a thick fog mired London, resulting in the deaths of perhaps as many as 12,000 people.

The two men were deeply affected by the death of King George VI in February 1952, as the monarch had been a good friend to both of them. In his eulogy in the House, Churchill highlighted the fact that it was only due to good fortune that the royal family had not suffered serious injury during the war when a bomb landed in the courtyard of Buckingham Palace; typically the King never breathed a word about the incident. Churchill also spoke of the magical ties that existed between the Crown and the British people.

Attlee recorded his keen admiration for the 'duty, tolerance and historical insight' of both George V and George VI. He particularly admired the dignity and decency with which George VI had treated him after the landslide Labour victory of 1945. The King's outlook, he suspected, was 'that of a broadminded Conservative', yet he had helped Attlee to rebuild Britain's shattered cities and confidence after the war. At the coronation of Queen Elizabeth II, both men were present. Churchill felt it his duty to guide the new Queen. Attlee, always a monarchist, supported him in that.

Politics, never far from the personal, became intensely so when, in 1952, Eden married Clarissa Spencer-Churchill, the daughter of Jack, the Prime Minister's younger brother. Clarissa was no typical upper-class girl. She had studied in Paris and then, dissatisfied with her 'useless, dilettante academicism', had settled in Oxford. She was a pupil of the philosopher A. J. Ayer and made friends with Isaiah Berlin. Oxford changed her life, she said.

When war broke out, Clarissa returned to London to work in the

Foreign Office and the Ministry of Information. For a time she was a resi-
dent at the Dorchester Hotel and stayed in the foyer during bombing raids
while others fled to the air-raid shelter. After the war, she worked for the
film director Alexander Korda, and became an admirer of Orson Welles.

Clementine regarded the marriage as a potential disaster: Clarissa
was too independent-minded to make a good wife for a politician. But
Clementine got it wrong. Clarissa proved totally loyal to Eden, supporting him when Churchill refused ten times to resign and allow Eden to
become Prime Minister.

On 23 June, Moran noted that Churchill

> seemed played out – as he was at Cairo before the Carthage illness. I
> thought his speech was slurred and a little indistinct. Twice I had to
> ask him to repeat what he had said. He said the Foreign Office was
> very hard work. I asked him must he really carry the burden of the FO
> until the autumn? He said he must.

Moran felt Churchill was leading 'an impossible existence'. But Churchill was in no mood to listen to him. He merely grunted and picked up
some papers.

The strain of office contributed to Churchill's second and more
severe stroke in Downing Street, after dinner on 23 June 1953. Despite
being partially paralysed down one side, however, he presided over a
Cabinet meeting the next morning without anybody noticing anything
was wrong with him. But once the Cabinet meeting had ended, his
condition deteriorated. Moran feared that Churchill might not survive
the weekend.

As happened so often, Eden suffered appalling luck, as he was 3,000
miles away being treated in New England for a gallbladder problem.

Had Eden been fit, the Cabinet would probably have insisted that Churchill resign. But Brendan Bracken organised a conspiracy of silence, and the press merely reported that the Prime Minister was exhausted. Parliament was never told the truth. Churchill journeyed to Chartwell to recuperate. His will to do so was fierce. A week after the stroke, he astonished Moran by lifting himself upright from his chair. News of his illness had bumped the trial of murderer John Christie off the front pages, he joked.

Churchill returned in October 1953 with a speech at the Conservative Party conference in Margate. There is a nice moment, captured by a cameraman for the Pathé newsreels, when Churchill pauses for a drink of water, then smiles and improvises: 'I don't do that often.' It might not have been cognac but, once he had refreshed himself with the water, Churchill praised the house-building programme, the denationalisation of steel and road haulage, and the way Chancellor of the Exchequer Rab Butler had made Britain more solvent. One of the more controversial aspects of the speech was that Churchill backed the idea of a European army that would include troops from Germany, a proposal Attlee disliked. Western Europe could not be protected against the Soviets, Churchill argued, if the Germans were excluded.

After the conference, Churchill explored ways in which the Soviet Union might be made more amenable. He met with the Soviet ambassador to the United Kingdom, Yakov Malik. His aim, Churchill confided to Malik, was to 'build bridges, and not to create barriers'. To this end, he would persuade President Eisenhower to convene a meeting of the great powers. With time and patience they could make a historic deal to improve international relations. Churchill told Malik he hoped to create an atmosphere of confidence for at least three to five years. None of the great powers would benefit from another war.

Malik replied that, while Britain, the Soviet Union and other European countries had suffered during the war, the United States had not. Churchill argued the Americans had endured tough times during the American Civil War, but Malik retorted that this had happened 100 years ago. Churchill explained that his mother's family had fought with George Washington in the War of Independence, so he considered himself half-American. Malik asked whether one should still consider him more an Englishman than an American, which made Churchill laugh. Yes, he said.

In December, as he had promised Malik, Churchill met Eisenhower in Bermuda. The new American President said in his diary that Churchill seemed set in his ways, and thought the world's problems could be solved merely by the close cooperation of Britain and the United States. To Churchill's surprise, the President was ready to share atomic secrets, at least to some extent. In his Atoms for Peace speech, which followed the meeting with Churchill in Bermuda, Eisenhower said he hoped to solve 'the fearful atomic dilemma' by finding a way which meant 'the miraculous inventiveness of man would not be dedicated to his death'. A non-proliferation agreement would stop the spread of nuclear weapons, but could allow non-nuclear countries to develop peaceful uses of atomic energy.

In 1954, *The Times* commented that apparently fewer issues divided the UK's political parties than had been the case three years earlier. Churchill confirmed this view when he said that Labour and the trade unions 'had given the feeling that the government of this ancient kingdom has a stature and substance considerably above the ins and outs of party politics'. Attlee had contributed to that.

Churchill was now more willing to compromise. In September, he initially refused to debate testing the H-bomb in the Pacific. But when the Labour Party collected a large number of signatures in favour of ending the tests, Churchill changed his mind – although he worried that the Russians would learn too much from what might be said in the Commons.

Two months later, Churchill turned eighty. To celebrate, Parliament had commissioned a painting of him by Graham Sutherland. The unveiling was a major ceremony. Attlee gave a speech which lauded Churchill's achievements and ended with words from Tennyson's *Ulysses*: 'Old age hath yet his honour and his toil ... Some work of noble note, may yet be done.' Churchill replied graciously: 'I am most grateful to Mr Attlee for the agreeable words he has used about me and for the magnanimous appraisal he has given of my variegated career.' Being so friendly 'might damage my standing as a party politician', he added. Churchill promised to recover soon and resume normal hostilities. There was a party at Downing Street; Attlee and his wife Violet were the only Labour people invited.

Churchill hated Sutherland's portrait. Attlee also disliked it. To his brother Tom, Attlee wrote, 'I tell people it's lucky he did not depict the Old Man in plus fours with loud checks and one foot in the grave.'

In 1954, Attlee published his autobiography, *As It Happened*. It was full of praise for Churchill, though reviewers were much less fulsome in their praise for Attlee's writing, calling the book rather dull. The quality 'of not getting in a flap' served a Prime Minister well, but an author less so, Tom Hopkinson commented in *The Observer*.

One sensitive issue has been little discussed so far: immigration. Churchill tried in vain to get the Cabinet to restrict West Indian immigration. 'Keep England White' was a good slogan, he told the Cabinet in January 1955. Ian Gilmour, the Tory MP who was editor of *The Spectator* from 1954 to 1959, said Churchill told him that immigration 'is the most important subject facing this country, but I cannot get any of my ministers to take any notice'. Churchill would not have been surprised by the Windrush debacle of 2018.

Attlee was the most skilful cox of a parliamentary crew, according to Churchill's biographer Roy Jenkins, but it is hard to cox an eight when the rowers sit facing opposite directions. Labour was badly divided between the party's right wing, led by Gaitskell, and its left wing, led by Bevan. Many Labour MPs felt that Attlee should have retired after the 1951 election to make way for a younger man. Attlee had told Richard Crossman he wanted Bevan to succeed him but, then, Bevan openly called for Attlee to stand down in the summer of 1954.

In an interview with the *News Chronicle* in mid-September 1955, Attlee explained why he now wanted Gaitskell to succeed him. 'Labour has nothing to gain by dwelling in the past,' he said.

> Nor do I think we can impress the nation by adopting a futile left-wingism. I regard myself as left of centre which is where a party leader ought to be. It is no use asking: 'What would Keir Hardie have done?' We must have at the top men brought up in the present age, not, as I was, in the Victorian age.

Even the greatest Victorians slow down, and by 1955 Churchill had begun to flag. He decided the time had finally come to resign. Attlee was invited to the farewell dinner with the Queen and the Duke of Edinburgh on 4 April 1955, the night before Churchill quit as Prime Minister. Queen Elizabeth II offered to make him the Duke of London, but Churchill declined, preferring to stay in the Commons.

Attlee said Churchill had given 'leadership to this country when it needed it most', and he would go down in history 'as one of the greatest of Prime Ministers, his place is assured'. The two men continued to meet in private; Attlee said he liked hearing Churchill speak. The image is an endearing one: two old men, Winston smoking his cigar and Clem his pipe, as they reflect on the past.

In his first speech after resigning, however, Churchill remained combative.

> Fancy, at this time, when all hopes are centred on a forthcoming conference with Russia, when we know that the strength of Britain is that she seeks peace for its own sake and not merely to avoid the burdens or dangers for which duty calls; fancy, when the meeting of the Big Four at the summit holds the first place in all our thoughts and hearts, the Leader of the Socialist Party feeling himself compelled to try to gain popularity in his party and notes in the election by saying something which might give the impression to the Communist world that Britain is on the run.

Britain was also facing an election.

Though now seventy-two years old, Attlee led Labour in the 1955 election against his wartime friend Anthony Eden. It is not clear what Attlee would have done had Labour emerged victorious; he could hardly carry the country and then resign. But in the end Labour lost, with the Conservatives capturing 345 seats, while the Labour Party took 277 and the Liberals six. Eden had finally become Prime Minister.

'Attlee was very kind to me when I took my seat [in the new parliament],' Churchill told Moran. An MP spotted Churchill, who was not so steady on his feet, advancing up the floor, and shouted, 'Churchill!' People in the public gallery clapped, and MPs crowding the benches waved their order papers, cheering madly. Moran wrote, 'Where would he take his seat? It could only be the seat below the gangway alongside the Treasury Bench. It was from this seat he had warned the nation of its danger in the years before the war.' Playfully, Shinwell beckoned him to come over to the Labour benches. Attlee rose from his seat, took Churchill by the arm and led him forward towards the table. They shook hands. Attlee insisted that Churchill take the oath before he did; the whole House rose and applauded.

Herbert Morrison patted Churchill affectionately on the back. Churchill turned around and shook Morrison's hand warmly. Then Churchill signed the roll of members and waited for Attlee to do the same. The two men then walked in unison from the Chamber.

Comrades-in-arms nearly to the end.

As Prime Minister, Eden soon had to handle a crisis which he misjudged totally – Suez. He viewed Egypt's President Nasser as a new Hitler. Nasser was indeed a dictator who threatened a new Holocaust, as he had vowed to sweep the Jews in Israel into the sea, but Britain could no longer stand alone as it was not now a great power. Privately, Churchill said he 'would never have done it without squaring the Americans, and once I'd started I'd never have dared stop'. Attlee was mystified by Eden's actions, which were quite out of character, he felt.

Churchill sent Attlee a copy of his first volume of *A History of the English-Speaking Peoples* in April 1956. Attlee thanked him, writing, 'I'm glad that you did full justice to the Wessex Kings. What they did is often underrated.' He signed off: 'Yours ever, Clem.' Attlee reviewed the book favourably, but said it would have been more accurate to have called it 'Things in history which have interested me'.

Old suspicions cling to some people like barnacles, and Churchill and Attlee had both been wary of Russia's actions since the end of the First World War. In 1957, the Soviet Union launched Sputnik 2, which carried a dog named Laika into outer space. Laika was faring better than people living under Soviet control, Attlee commented wryly. The dog was being fed and had some chance of escape. Quite how Laika would free itself from its tiny space capsule, never mind survive, Attlee did not specify. In fact, Laika died a few hours after the launch of Sputnik 2.

At Christmas in 1957, the Attlees and Churchills lunched together. Churchill occasionally voted in parliamentary divisions, but never again spoke in the Chamber. Sixty-three years after he had first been elected, he entered the House for the last time. A day later, on 28 July 1964, the new Prime Minister, Sir Alec Douglas Home, a good enough bowler to have spun Butler out of contention for 10 Downing Street, led a delegation to Churchill's home. He presented Churchill with a resolution which had been carried unanimously by the House of Commons. It read:

> That this House desire to take this opportunity of marking the forth-coming retirement of the right honourable Gentleman the Member for Woodford by putting on record its unbounded admiration and gratitude for his services to Parliament, to the nation and to the world; remembers, above all, his inspiration of the British people when they stood alone, and his leadership until victory was won; and offers its grateful thanks to the right honourable Gentleman for these outstanding services to this House and to the nation.

Churchill was now old and ailing. He could not paint and had nothing left to write after publishing *A History of the English-Speaking Peoples*. Age did not make him less restless, however, and he took eight cruises aboard the yacht *Christina* as a guest of the shipping magnate, Aristotle Onassis. Once, when the yacht needed to pass through the Dardanelles, Onassis ordered that this be done at night; he did not want to disturb his guest with unhappy memories.

In retirement, Attlee professed his pride that the Tories had accepted changes which in the past they had branded 'heresies and silly socialism'. He was one of the signatories of a letter to *The Times* on 7 March 1958, which urged reform of the law that outlawed homosexual acts; Attlee had come a long way from the somewhat straitlaced young man he had once been. A. J. Ayer, Isaiah Berlin and many other notables also signed the letter. The Homosexual Law Reform Society then campaigned for the decriminalisation of homosexual acts in private by consenting adults.

When Harold Macmillan became Prime Minister in 1957, after Eden resigned, Attlee was still sharp enough to write a ditty.

> Hail to the splendid Mac
> Long live our glorious Mac
> What though we've got the sack
> Enoch and Peter got back

Attlee and Churchill differed on Europe more than they had during the war. Attlee had become, if not a Little Englander, then at least a wary one. In 1962, he spoke twice in the House of Lords against the United Kingdom's application to join Europe's common market. Britain had a separate parliamentary tradition, and if Britain became a member, common market rules would prevent it from planning its economy, Attlee argued. He pointed out that Britain's traditional policy had always been outward-looking, embracing the whole of the wider world, rather than just Europe.

Churchill had predicted he would die on the same day as his father – and he possessed the willpower to make sure he did. On 15 January 1965, he suffered another stroke, this time a severe cerebral thrombosis. He died at his home nine days later, aged ninety, shortly after eight o'clock on the morning of Sunday 24 January 1965. He had timed his death perfectly. It was seventy years to the day after his father's death. That afternoon, in the House of Lords, Attlee said Churchill 'had sympathy, incredibly wide sympathy, for ordinary people all over the world. My Lords, we have lost the greatest Englishman of our time – I think the greatest citizen of the world of our time.'

Alfred Laker went with him to the funeral.

I heard people criticise him for going to Churchill's funeral because he stumbled on the steps of St Paul's. If only they had known how very poorly he was at the time, but how determined he was to pay his last respects to the man who had been both his adversary and his friend.

Attlee had learned that a rehearsal was going to take place on the afternoon before Churchill's state funeral, but that he was not expected to attend the rehearsal as he was unwell. Attlee turned up. 'It was a bitterly cold day,' Laker said,

and he was kept standing around such a long time, that he returned to his flat in a condition bordering on collapse, I put his warmed slippers on him and wrapped a blanket around him by the fire, then tried to get him to take a sip of brandy. He refused so I put a surreptitious drop in a cup of hot tea. He must have known, but he drank it probably just to please me. He had a poor night's sleep but still insisted on rising early to be sure of being in good time. He was still as punctual as always.

In its obituary of Churchill, *The Guardian* pointed out that he had been in Parliament longer than Disraeli and for nearly as long as Gladstone. But these two Victorian political titans had never witnessed the dramatic changes in society that Churchill and Attlee had. Nor had they confronted a monster like Hitler. Had Churchill died before 1940, *The Guardian* commented, 'he would have been remembered as an eloquent, formidable, erratic statesman, an outstanding personage, but one who was not to be put in the class of such contemporaries as Lloyd George or even Arthur Balfour'. But Churchill had died 'the greatest Englishman of his time, full of years and honour'.

Unlike most eminent persons he can at his death be given at once his place in history; it is not likely that posterity, when it sees him in perspective, will change to any great extent the judgement of his contemporaries ... He was the man who had summoned back to life the spirit of liberty and hope in a world prostrate and stunned beneath the shock of the Nazi onslaught. He will hold a place such as no other Englishman has ever held in the folklore of distant peoples and remote places. He will be the symbol for millions of the power of the love of liberty and the love of country.

Churchill's body lay in state for three days in Westminster Hall. Mourners, including de Gaulle and Eisenhower, came to St Paul's from over 100 countries. The Prime Minister of Australia, Sir Robert Menzies, then the longest-serving Commonwealth premier, paid tribute to Churchill as part of the funeral broadcast.

The procession moved to Tower Pier where the coffin was taken on board MV *Havengore*. Naval ratings 'piped the side' and the Royal Marine band played the musical salute due to a former First Lord of the Admiralty: 'Rule Britannia'. As the boat carrying Churchill's coffin moved sombrely up the River Thames, dockers lowered their crane jibs in a salute.

The crane jibs might have dipped for Churchill, but Attlee's declining years proved to be a period when he became almost anonymous. In 1966, an aged Attlee was travelling third class on a train when a group of students, not recognising the former Prime Minister, tried to persuade him to join the Labour Party. Attlee merely responded by saying that he was 'already a member'.

On 8 October 1967, Attlee died peacefully in his sleep in Westminster Hospital. He was eighty-four years old and had been suffering from pneumonia. He was interred in Westminster Abbey in November. *The Guardian* wrote that the service 'epitomised Attlee's love of simplicity and directness'. His ashes were interred in Westminster Abbey, again in a simple ceremony. His obituary in *The Guardian* stated that he was 'not in the line of the great Prime Ministers'. But the newspaper commented in that day's leader column that 'when time affords a better perspective he will probably be seen as the extraordinary man that he was'.

Roy Jenkins ends his biography by calling Churchill the greatest human being to have been Prime Minister. That has been the general perceived wisdom for more than fifty years now. But the man who was not even a starter would spring a surprise more than twenty years after his death, when he was named the greatest Prime Minister of the twentieth century.

CHAPTER 14

THE LEGACY

There have been some revisionist attempts to downplay Church-ill's role in winning the war, but he will never be forgotten. Attlee deserves the same recognition for his wartime efforts, a point made by journalist Adam Gopnik in a recent *New Yorker* review of John Bew's biography. Gopnik commented that thousands of Che Guevera T-shirts had been sold, but he did not know of any Attlee shirts being snapped up. The left needed a history lesson, Gopnik opined. Che Guevera had believed in hatred as part of the class struggle, but had only helped make an already desperately violent and impoverished region yet more violent and impoverished. Attlee, on the other hand, had quietly and non-violently helped bring about a genuine revolution, achieving almost everything Marx had dreamed of for the British working class.

It was time to produce T-shirts with 'Clem' blazoned on them, Gopnik argued.

Although such T-shirts have yet to appear, Attlee's efforts seem to have been recognised within academic circles. In 2004, a survey conducted by MORI and the University of Leeds asked academics specialising in twentieth-century British history and politics to vote for who they believed to be the most successful twentieth-century Prime Minister. Churchill came in second place, followed by Lloyd George in third place, while Margaret Thatcher was fourth and Harold Macmillan fifth.

Attlee came first.

The survey was conducted with the support of the Political Studies Association and asked 139 academics to rate on a scale of 0 to 10 how successful or unsuccessful they considered each Prime Minister had been in office – with zero being highly unsuccessful and ten being highly successful. It seems fair to imagine that as all twenty Prime Ministers were highly competitive they would have been curious to know who ranked where.

One question included on the survey was: what characteristics does a Prime Minister need to succeed? Those interviewed were asked to pick from a list the three they considered to be most important. The results were as follows:

	PER CENT
Leadership skills	64
Sound judgement	42
Good in a crisis	24
Decisiveness	23
Luck	23
Stable parliamentary majority	20
Good-quality colleagues	18
Understands the problems facing Britain	16
Integrity	11
Practises Cabinet government	10
Charisma	9
In touch with ordinary people	8
Ruthlessness	6

Poor state of the opposition	5
Strong convictions/ideology	4
High-level ministerial experience	3
Understands world problems	2
Understands economics	1
Down-to-earth	1
Honesty	1
Patriotism	0

Academics were also asked to rank how successful or unsuccessful the Prime Ministers were in office.

	MEAN SCORE
Clement Attlee (Lab, 1945–51)	8.34
Winston Churchill (Con, 1940–45, 1951–55)	7.88
David Lloyd George (Lib, 1916–22)	7.33
Margaret Thatcher (Con, 1979–90)	7.14
Harold Macmillan (Con, 1957–63)	6.49
Tony Blair (Lab, 1997– to date)	6.30
Herbert Asquith (Lib, 1908–16)	6.19
Stanley Baldwin (Con, 1923–34, 1924–29, 1935–37)	6.18
Harold Wilson (Lab, 1964–70, 1974–76)	5.93
Marquess of Salisbury (Con, 1895–1902)	5.75
Sir Henry Campbell-Bannerman (Lib, 1905–08)	5.01
James Callaghan (Lab, 1976–79)	4.75
Edward Heath (Con, 1970–74)	4.36
Ramsay MacDonald (Lab, 1924–24, 1929–35)	3.73
John Major (Con, 1990–1997)	3.67
Andrew Bonar Law (Con, 1922–23)	3.50
Neville Chamberlain (Con, 1937–40)	3.43
Arthur Balfour (Con, 1902–1905)	3.42
Sir Alec Douglas-Home (Con, 1963–64)	3.33
Sir Anthony Eden (Con, 1955–57)	2.53

Anthony Eden was last by a long way, but then he lost a war that he should never have started. The 'jury' was a sophisticated one, but that did not stop it awarding the top four places to Prime Ministers who had all won wars, even if the Falklands was a small one. The authors of *Why War?* would not have been surprised that winning a war cemented a political reputation.

Books often end with reviewing what can be learned from their narrative. It's not easy to extrapolate conclusions from the collaboration of Attlee and Churchill; they worked together at a critical moment in world history, two remarkable men at a remarkable time. The many crises that have threatened peace since 1945 have been usually more local as the bomb has proved an effective deterrent to global conflict – so far. At the start, I mentioned the unlikely collaboration of Iain Paisley and Martin McGuinness. The peace that the Chuckle Brothers achieved in Ulster still holds firm today. That achieved by Attlee and Churchill's triumph over Hitler has also largely held, and Europe has remained largely at peace, with the exception of the Balkan War in the 1990s.

Churchill and Attlee had no specific formula for their successful wartime collaboration. They were good men who were also clever, creative and decisive; men utterly committed to defeating Nazi tyranny and ensuring the triumph of decency and democracy. So often, and far more affectionately than one might have expected, the two comrades-in-arms just kept 'buggering on', to use Churchill's phrase. Until, ultimately, they saved the world.

APPENDIX ONE

ATTLEE'S POETRY

It is worth making a few more of Attlee's poems available.
He wrote on holiday in 1907:

> While gazing seawards to the West
> I look for Islands of the Blest
> And mindful of the teeming slum
> Cry out 'On earth thy kingdom come',
> For sure with beauty everywhere
> The heart must needs breathe such a prayer.
> Nor need we priest within the shrine
> With broken bread and hallowed wine
> To show that Love is all God's plan
> And teach the Fellowship of Man:
> When man and earth and sky and sea
> Are in such mighty harmony.

The next year saw him turn to socialism.

On Socialism

Socialism

Surely some day we'll make an ending

Of all this wretched state of want and greed.

Children shall reap, glad cries forth sending,

In field where we have sown the seed.

All through the years mankind ascending

Leaves the outworn and seeks a higher creed.

In true fraternity, on love depending,

Society fulfils its highest need.

Man cannot rest until mankind is freed.

One of his most introspective sonnets dates from this period:

The Lonely Stream

My life is passing like a lonely stream

Winding through meadows flecked with white and gold

That farseen distant castled hills enfold

Yearnings and visions, memories of a dream

Like tributary brooks my friendships seem

Into the volume of the river rolled

So in my heart their added wealth I hold

But still my life is lonely like the stream.

Sudden a change in this calm life I see

The cataracts and shoals of Love are near

Life is a torrent and within my heart

The calling of another stream I hear

This is the waters meet, never to part
Love let us flow together to the Sea.

I have quoted an extract from the poem that Attlee wrote when Macmillan got to 10 Downing Street. The full text runs:

Hail to Our Splendid Mac

Hail to our splendid Mac
Long live our glorious Mac
What though we've got the sack
Enoch and Pete got back
Why should not we?

Hail to our fine new look
Though Selwyn Lloyd's forsook
Still we've got Henry Brooke
Surely he'll find a nook
Somewhere for me.

Had I but wed his niece
I might have stayed in peace
With several other geese
Is it Too Late?

Surely some Highland Scot
Or Yankee girl if not
Pitting my cruel lot
Might make a date.

On 29 June 1951, a young girl wrote to Attlee in poetry about having to spend an extra year at school. Attlee replied in kind, delighted to show off his own skills:

> I've not the least idea why
> They read this curious rule
> Condemning you to sit and sigh
> Another year at school...
> George Tomlinson is ill, but I
> have asked him to explain
> And when I get the reason why
> I'll write to you again.

He was Prime Minister at the time.

APPENDIX TWO

MADNESS AND CREATIVITY

Since the days of Aristotle, philosophers have debated whether madness is close to genius. Many great artists have suffered from some form of mental illness. Friedrich Nietzsche suffered a long-term breakdown, as did the ballet dancer Vaslav Nijinsky. Vincent Van Gogh is perhaps the most famous example of a 'mad' genius. He completed some of his most famous paintings while living in an asylum in Provence. The English painter Richard Dadd killed his father but was spared the noose. Dadd ended his days in Broadmoor, a high-security psychiatric hospital; this was the place for which that other painter, Churchill, was responsible during his time as Home Secretary. The American poets Ezra Pound and Robert Lowell spent some time in mental health hospitals, as did John Berryman.

Churchill was, in many senses, a genius, and he also suffered from a mild form of bipolar disorder. Critics complained that he came up with a hundred ideas a day, but the problem was that he could not always identify the four good ones.

Victorian polymath Sir Francis Galton claimed genius was hereditary. But twentieth-century psychologist Hans Eysenck argued that

Galton misread the evidence; Eysenck insisted that genius was due to a genetic anomaly: a combination of independent polygenes caused a quantitative leap in a person's brain. This was known as 'emergenesis'. Such a miracle made it possible for geniuses to develop some unlikely, even mad, creative associations but also to possess the critical acumen necessary to weed out the too bizarre and useless ones.

The Churchills, like the Freuds, offer some evidence that genius can run in families. It could be argued that the Duke of Marlborough and Winston Churchill were both geniuses, and that Freud's grandson Lucien was every bit as much a genius as Sigmund. Eysenck argued, however, in favour of the accidental nature of genius, which showed up in the unlikeliest families. Eysenck studied the backgrounds of the twenty-eight greatest ever mathematicians, as chosen by E. T. Bell in his *Men of Mathematics*, and found there was little evidence of mathematical ability in most of the men's families. Only the family of the eighteenth-century Swiss mathematician Daniel Bernoulli had any such history.

Galton's mistake, Eysenck believed, was that he had assumed genius followed a normal statistical distribution. Galton calculated that 400 people in every million were 'idiots' and that 250 achieved great eminence. Galton divided the idiots into 120 so-called 'light idiots', who were below average, and a further 280 'true idiots'. Galton believed the same statistics were true for people of genius.

Eysenck, however, argued that every group of one million people did not produce 280 true geniuses. True genius is exceptionally rare. If a genius is defined as someone who makes a lasting contribution to a field, then Newton, Einstein, Shakespeare, J. S. Bach, Beethoven and Rembrandt possessed genius. But history is also full of once-important writers and scientists whose work now seems dated. Galton's normal distribution may fit eminent men with high IQs and real talent, but genius is much rarer.

Eysenck claimed that surprisingly few arguments existed about who was and wasn't a genius. Before he died in 1997, Eysenck pointed out that the work of roughly 250 classical composers was still being performed in the modern era. But just sixteen composers accounted for half of all the classical performances. These are the true geniuses: Beethoven, J. S. Bach, Mozart, Haydn, Chopin and Verdi. But no one puts the German composer Georg Telemann in that league.

The fact that genius does not form part of a normal distribution is a key part of Eysenck's theory. It leads to his claim that genius is more or less a genetic accident, a freak or the result of what the geneticist Robert Plomin calls emergenesis. To understand that freak better, Eysenck suggests we need to look at three factors – cognitive style, psychiatric symptoms and our growing knowledge of brain biochemistry. It has been suggested MPs should be tested before they are allowed to sit on the green benches. It is not likely to happen.

BIBLIOGRAPHY

Books by Clement Attlee

As It Happened (London: Odhams Press, 1956)

Labour's Peace Aims (London: Peace Book Company, 1940)

Labour Shows the Way (London: Methuen & Co., 1935)

The Labour Party in Perspective (London: Victor Gollancz, 1937)

The Social Worker (London: G. Bell & Sons, 1920)

Poetry by Attlee

Many of Attlee's poems can be found in:

Harris, Kenneth, *Attlee* (London: Weidenfeld & Nicolson, 1982)

Burridge, Trevor, *Clement Attlee: A Political Biography* (London: Jonathan Cape, 1985)

Reviews and articles by Clement Attlee

Borough Councils 1921, *Fabian Tract*, no. 121

'The Pleasure of Books', *National and English Review* (1954), vol. 142, no. 851, pp. 17–21

Review of Churchill's *On the History of the English-Speaking Peoples*

Attlee's letters and correspondence

Attlee's private papers are in the Bodleian Library in Oxford as detailed in the references.

Biographies of Attlee and his family

Attlee, Peggy, *With a Quiet Conscience: Biography of Thomas Simons Attlee* (London: Dove & Chough Press, 1995)

Beckett, Francis, *Clem Attlee: Labour's Great Reformer* (London: Haus Publishing Ltd, 2015)

Bew, John, *Citizen Clem: A Biography of Attlee* (London: riverrun, 2017)

Burridge, Trevor, *Clement Attlee: A Political Biography* (London: Jonathan Cape, 1985)

Clemens, Cyril, *The Man from Limehouse: Clement Richard Attlee* (London: Webster Groves, 1946)

Dellar, Geoffrey (ed.), *Attlee As I Knew Him* (London: London Borough of Tower Hamlets Directorate of Community Services Library Service, 1983)

Field, Frank (ed.), *Attlee's Great Contemporaries: The Politics of Character* (London: Bloomsbury Continuum, 2009)

Harris, Kenneth, *Attlee* (London: Weidenfeld & Nicolson, 1982)

Jenkins, Roy, *Mr Attlee: An Interim Biography* (London: William Heinemann, 1948)

Radice, Giles, *The Tortoise and the Hares: Attlee, Bevin, Cripps, Dalton, Morrison* (London: Politico's Publishing, 2008)

Thomas-Symonds, Nicklaus, *Attlee: A Life in Politics* (London: I. B. Tauris, 2012)

Williams, E. F. and Attlee, Clement, *A Prime Minister Remembers: The War and Post-war Memoirs of the Rt Hon. Earl Attlee* (London: Heinemann, 1961)

Books by Churchill

A History of the English-Speaking Peoples (London: Cassell, 1956)

Lord Randolph Churchill (London: Macmillan & Co., 1907)

Marlborough: His Life and Times (London: George G. Harrap & Co., 1947)

My Early Life (London: Thornton Butterworth, 1930)

Painting as a Pastime (London: Odhams Press, 1948). Originally published during the 1920s in *The Strand*.

Savrola, reissue (Bath: Cedric Chivers, 1973)

Step by Step: Political Writings 1936–1939 (London: Odhams Press, 1939)

The People's Rights: Selected from his Lancashire and Other Recent Speeches (London: Hodder & Stoughton, 1910)

The River War: An Historical Account of the Reconquest of the Soudan (London: Longmans & Co., 1899)

The Second World War: The Gathering Storm, Their Finest Hour, The Grand Alliance, The Hinge of Fate, Closing the Ring, Triumph and Tragedy (London: Cassell & Co., 1948–54)

Articles by Churchill

'My New York Misadventure', *Daily Mail*, 4 January 1932

'The Dream', *Sunday Telegraph*, 30 January 1966

Books authored by and on the Churchill family

Churchill, Lady Randolph Spencer, *The Reminiscences of Lady Randolph Churchill* (Bath: Chivers, 1973). A memorandum of her early recollections is in the papers of Peregrine Churchill, Churchill's nephew.

Churchill, Peregrine and Mitchell, Julian, *Jennie, Lady Randolph Churchill: A Portrait with Letters* (London: William Colllins, 1974)

Churchill, Randolph S., *Winston S. Churchill, Volume II, Young Statesman: 1901–1914* (London: Heinemann, 1967)

Cohen, Michael J., *Churchill and the Jews* (London: Frank Cass, 2003)

Colville, John, *The Churchillians* (London: Weidenfeld & Nicolson, 1981)

—, *The Fringes of Power: Downing Street Diaries 1939–1955* (London: Sceptre, 1985)

Cornwallis-West, George, *Edwardian Hey-Days* (London and New York: Putnam, 1930)

Keppel, Sonia, *Edwardian Daughter* (London: Hamish Hamilton, 1958)

Leslie, Anita, *Edwardians in Love* (London: Hutchinson, 1972)

—, *The Marlborough House Set* (New York: Doubleday, 1973)

—, *Jennie: The Mother of Winston Churchill* (Maidstone: George Mann, 1992)

Rowse, A. L., *The Later Churchills* (London: Macmillan & Co., 1958)

Mather, John, 'Winston Churchill: His Hardiness and Resilience', paper presented at the fourteenth International Churchill Conference, 18 October 1997

Moran, Lord (Charles), *Churchill at War: 1940–45* (London: Constable & Robinson, 2002)

—, *Churchill: The Struggle for Survival 1945–60* (London: Constable & Robinson, 2006)

Sandys, Celia, *Churchill Wanted Dead or Alive* (London: HarperCollins, 1999)

—, *From Winston with Love and Kisses: The Young Churchill* (London: Sinclair-Stevenson, 1994)

Sebba, Anne, *Jennie Churchill: Winston's American Mother* (London: John Murray, 2007)

Soames, Mary, *Clementine Churchill* (London: Doubleday, 2003)

Memoirs and biographies of Churchill

Best, Geoffrey, *Churchill: A Study in Greatness* (London: Penguin, 2002)

Bibesco, Princess Marthe; Kean, Vladimir (trans.), *Sir Winston Churchill: Master of Courage* (London: Robert Hale, 1957)

Bonham Carter, Violet, *Winston Churchill As I Knew Him* (London: Pan, 1967)

Eden, Clarissa; Haste, Cate (ed.), *A Memoir: From Churchill to Eden* (London: Weidenfeld & Nicolson, 2007)

Foster, R. F., *Lord Randolph Churchill: A Political Life* (New York: Clarendon Press, 1982)

Gibb, Andrew Dewar (originally published as Captain X), *With Winston Churchill at the Front: Winston in the Trenches 1916* (London: Gowans & Grey Ltd, 1924)

Gilbert, Martin, *Winston S. Churchill, Volume III: The Challenge of War 1914–1916* (London: Minerva, 1990)

—, *Winston S. Churchill, Volume IV: The Stricken World 1917–1922* (London: Minerva, 1975)

—, *Winston S. Churchill, Volume V: Prophet of Truth 1922–1939* (London: Minerva, 1990)

—, *Winston S. Churchill, Volume VI: Finest Hour 1939–1941* (London: Minerva, 1989)

—, *Winston S. Churchill, Volume VII: Road to Victory 1941–1945* (London: Minerva, 1986)

—, *Winston S. Churchill, Volume VIII: Never Despair 1945–1965* (London: Minerva, 1988)

Jenkins, Roy, *Churchill: A Biography* (London: Pan, 2012)

Johnson, Boris, *The Churchill Factor: How One Man Made History* (London: Hodder & Stoughton, 2014)

Lee, Celia and Lee, John, *Winston and Jack: The Churchill Brothers* (self-published, 2007)

—, *The Churchills: A Family Portrait* (London: Palgrave Macmillan, 2010)

Lewis, David, *The Man Who Invented Hitler* (London: Headline, 2003)

Lukacs, John, *The Duel: Hitler vs. Churchill 10 May–31 July 1940* (London: Bodley Head, 1990)

Manchester, William, *The Last Lion: Winston Spencer Churchill – Alone, 1932–1940* (London: Little, Brown, 1988)

Marsh, John, *The Young Winston Churchill* (Bath: Chivers, 1995)

Morgan, Ted, *Churchill: Young Man in a Hurry 1874–1915* (New York: Simon & Schuster, 1982)

Pelling, Henry, *Winston Churchill* (London: Macmillan, 1974)

Ricks, Thomas E., *Churchill and Orwell: The Fight for Freedom* (London: Gerald Duckworth & Co., 2017)

Rosebery, Lord (Archibald), *Lord Randolph Churchill* (London: Arthur L. Humphreys, 1906)

Taylor, A. J. P. (ed.), *Churchill: Four Faces and the Man* (London: Allen Lane, 1969)

Other works

Adler, Alfred, *Individual Psychology* (London: Harper Perennial, 1999)

Amery, Leo and Barnes, John (ed.) and Nicholson, David (ed.), *The Leo Amery Diaries: Volume I, 1896–1929* (London: Hutchinson, 1980)

Amery, Leo and Barnes, John (ed.) and Nicholson, David (ed.), *The Empire at Bay: The Leo Amery Diaries, 1929–1945* (London: Hutchinson, 1988)

Bakshi, G. D., *Bose: An Indian Samurai – Netaji and the INA, A Military Assessment* (New Dehli: KW Publishers Pvt Ltd, 2016)

Balfour, Arthur, *The Mind of Arthur James Balfour: Selections From His Non-Political Writings, Speeches, and Addresses, 1878-1917* (Forgotten Books, 2018)

Barnett, Corelli, *The Verdict of Peace: Britain Between Her Yesterday and the Future* (London: Pan, 2002)

Beeton, Isabella, *Mrs Beeton's Book of Household Management*, reissue (London: Ward, Lock & Co., 1915)

Begley, George, *Keep Mum!: Advertising Goes to War* (London: Lemon Tree Press, 1975)

Bell, Eric Temple, *Men of Mathematics* (London: Penguin, 1953)

Berlin, Isaiah, *Mr Churchill in 1940* (London: John Murray, 1964)

Bew, John, *Realpolitik: A History* (Oxford: Oxford University Press, 2016)

Boothby, Robert, *Boothby: Recollections of a Rebel* (London: Hutchinson, 1978)

Bowlby, John, *A Secure Base: Parent-Child Attachment and Healthy Human Development* (London: Routledge, 2005)

Callum, R. B., and Redmann, Alison, *The British Election of 1945* (Basingstoke: Macmillan Press, 1999)

Cecil, Viscount of Chelwood, *All the Way* (London: Hodder & Stoughton, 1949)

Citrine, Lord (Walter), *Men and Work: An Autobiography* (London: Hutchinson, 1964)

Dalton, Hugh and Pimlott, Ben (ed.), *Towards the Peace of Nations: A Study in International Politics* (London: George Routledge and Sons, 1928)

Dalton, Hugh, *The Political Diary of Hugh Dalton: 1918–40, 1945–60* (London: Jonathan Cape, 1987)

Daninos, Pierre, *Les Carnets du Major Thompson* (Paris: Hachette, 1954)

Dixon, Norman F., *On the Psychology of Military Incompetence* (London: Jonathan Cape, 1976)

Eden, Anthony, *The Memoirs of Sir Anthony Eden: Full Circle* (London: Cassell, 1960)

Einstein, Albert; Stuart Gilbert (trans.), *Why War?: 'Open Letters' between Albert Einstein and Sigmund Freud* (London: 1934)

Eysenck, H. J., *Genius: The Natural History of Creativity* (Cambridge: Cambridge University Press, 1995)

Freud, Sigmund, 'Three Essays on Sexuality' in the Standard Edition of Freud's works edited by James Strachey: Hogarth Press originally published 1909. Amazon magnificently lists it as first published in 1676!

Freud, Sigmund, and Bullitt, William C., *Thomas Woodrow Wilson: A Psychological Study* (London: Weidenfeld & Nicolson, 1967)

Galbraith, J. K., *The Great Crash 1929* (London: Hamish Hamilton, 1955)

Ghaemi, Nassir, *A First-Rate Madness: Uncovering the Links between Leadership and Mental Illness* (New York: Penguin, 2011)

Gorodetsky, Gabriel (ed.), *The Maisky Diaries: Red Ambassador to the Court of St James's 1932–1943* (New Haven, Connecticut: Yale University Press, 2015)

Gosse, Edmund, *Father and Son: A Study of Two Temperaments* (London: William Heinemann, 1907)

Haffner, Sebastian, *Defying Hitler: A Memoir* (London: Weidenfeld & Nicolson, 2003)

Hitler, Adolf, *Mein Kampf* (Mumbai: Jaico, 2007)

Holman, Bob, *Good Old George: The Life of George Lansbury* (Oxford: Lion Books, 1990)

Hunt, Sir David, *On the Spot: An Ambassador Remembers* (London: Peter Davies, 1975)

Hurd, Archibald Spicer, *Britannia Has Wings!: The Fleet in Action: On, Over, and Under the Sea* (London: Hutchinson, 1942)

Iremonger, Lucille, *The Fiery Chariot: A Study of British Prime Ministers and the Search for Love* (London: Secker & Warburg, 1970)

Jenkins, Roy, *Asquith* (London: Collins, 1967)

Jennings, H., Madge, C., et al., *May the Twelfth: Mass-Observation Day-Surveys 1937 by Over Two Hundred Observers*, reissue (London: Faber & Faber, 2012)

Jones, Ernest and Freud, Sigmund; R. Andrew Paskavkas (ed.), *The complete correspondence of Sigmund Freud and Ernest Jones 1908-1939* (Cambridge, MA: Belknap Press, 1993)

Kahneman, Daniel, *Thinking, Fast and Slow* (London: Penguin, 2012)

Keynes, John Maynard, *The Economic Consequences of Mr Churchill* (London: L. & V. Woolf, 1925)

Kiszely, John, *Anatomy of a Campaign: The British fiasco in Norway, 1940* (Cambridge: Cambridge University Press, 2017)

Kurihara, Sadako; Minear, Richard H. (trans.), *Black Eggs* (Ann Arbor, MI: Center for Japanese Studies, 1994)

Laski, Harold J., *The American Presidency: An Interpretation* (London: Allen and Unwin, 1962)

Le Bon, Gustave, *The Crowd: A Study of the Popular Mind* (New York: Penguin, 1977)

Lewis, C. S., *A Grief Observed* (London: Faber & Faber, 2012)

Lewis, Michael, *The Undoing Project* (London: Allen Lane, 2017)

Magnus, Philip, *King Edward VII* (London: John Murray, 1964)

Marquand, David, *Ramsay MacDonald* (London: Jonathan Cape, 1977)

Mikes, George, *How to Be an Alien* (London: André Deutsch, 1946)

Milford, L. S., *Haileybury College: Past and Present* (London: T. Fisher Unwin, 1909)

Money, Chiozza, *Riches and Poverty* (London: Methuen & Co., 1906)

Morgan, Kenneth O., *Labour in Power 1945-1961* (Oxford: Clarendon Press, 1984)

Mountbatten, Pamela, *India Remembered* (London: Pavilion Books, 2007)

Middlemas, Keith, and Barnes, John, *Baldwin* (London: Weidenfeld & Nicolson, 1969)

Macmillan, Harold, *The Past Masters: Politics and Politicians, 1906-1939* (London: Macmillan, 1975)

Moorehead, Alan, *Gallipoli* (London: Aurum Press, 2015)

Morrison, Lord (Herbert), *Herbert Morrison: An Autobiography* (London: Odhams Press, 1960)

Olden, Rudolf, *Hitler the Pawn* (London: Victor Gollancz, 1936)

Orwell, George, *Collected Essays* (London: Secker and Warburg, 1961)

—, *Such, Such Were the Joys* (London: Penguin Classics, 2014)

—, *The Lion and the Unicorn: Socialism and the English Genius* (London: Penguin Classics, 2018)

Patterson, John Henry, *The Man-Eaters of Tsavo* (London: Macmillan, 1907)

—, *With the Zionists in Gallipoli* (London: Hutchinson, 1916)

Pelling, Henry (ed.), *The Challenge of Socialism* (London: Adam & Charles Black, 1954)

Pimlott, Ben, *Hugh Dalton: A Life* (London: Macmillan, 1986)

Powell, Sean-Andre W., 'How Did Winston S. Churchill's Experience as a Prisoner of War During the Boer War Affect His Leadership Style and Career?', MA thesis, University of Virginia, 1998

Rees, Nigel, *Sayings of the Century* (London: Allen & Unwin, 1984)

Reynaud, Paul, *In the Thick of the Fight: The Testimony of Paul Reynaud* (London: Cassell, 1955)

Roberts, Andrew, *The Holy Fox: A Biography of Lord Halifax* (London: Weidenfeld & Nicolson, 1991)

Rowntree, Benjamin Seebohm, *Poverty: A Study of Town Life* (London: Macmillan, 1901)

Shakespeare, Nicholas, *Six Minutes in May: How Churchill Unexpectedly Became Prime Minister* (London: Harvill Secker, 2017)

Skinner, B. F., *Walden Two* (London: Macmillan, 1948)

Taylor, Lord (Stephen), *A Natural History of Everyday Life: A Biographical Guide for Would-be Doctors of Society* (London: British Medical Journal Publications, 1988)

Ward, Roger, *The Chamberlains: Joseph, Austen and Neville 1836–1940* (Fonthill Media, 2015)

Wilkinson, Rev. Allix, *Reminiscences of Eton* (London: Hurst and Blackett, 1888)

Yeatman, R. J. and Sellar, W. C., *1066 and All That* (London: Methuen, 1931)

Articles

'Mr Chamberlain's Statement on Negotiations with Herr Hitler', *Bulletin of International News* (1938), vol. 15, no. 20, pp. 30–39

Aydemir, Omer, 'Aretaeus of Cappadocia', *Acta Neuropsychiatrica* (2007), vol. 19; no. 1, pp. 62–3

Gopnik, Adam, 'Never Mind Churchill, Clement Attlee is a Model for These Times', *The New Yorker*, 8 January 2018

Myers, Charles, 'Contribution to the Study of Shell Shock', *The Lancet* (1915), vol. 185, no. 4772, pp. 316–30

Randolph, James, 'Psychology and the Blitzkrieg', *Dalhousie Review* (1942), vol. 21, no. 4, pp. 462–70

Rasmussen, J. S., 'Party Discipline in Wartime: The Downfall of the Chamberlain Government', *Journal of Politics* (1970), vol. 32, pp. 379–406

Reynaud, Emmanuelle, et al., 'Relationship Between Emotional Experience and Resilience: An fMRI Study in Fire-Fighters', *Neuropsychologia* (2013), vol. 51, no. 5, pp. 845–9

Rutter, Michael, 'Resilience Concepts and Findings: Implications for Family Therapy', *Journal of Family Therapy* (2002), vol. 21, no. 2, pp. 119–44

Thompson, Dorothy, 'I Saw Hitler!', *Cosmopolitan*, March 1932

Watson-Smyth, Kate, 'Attlee was really a Tory, says his daughter-in-law', *The Independent*, 7 March 1997

INDEX

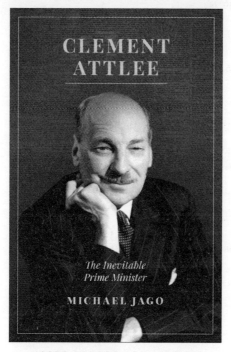

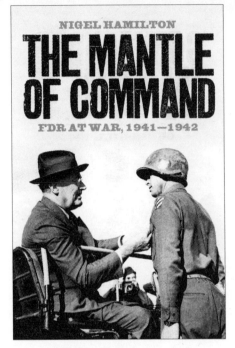

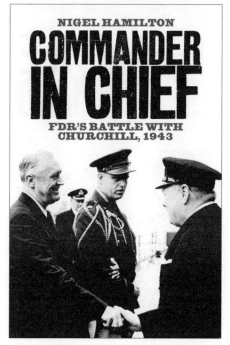

480PP HARDBACK, £25

In his masterly *Mantle of Command*, Nigel Hamilton made a powerful case for Franklin Delano Roosevelt as the brilliant war strategist whose towering importance to the Second World War is overlooked because of his early death. Now, in this second installment of his major trilogy, Hamilton reveals the remarkable truth – suppressed by Winston Churchill in his memoirs – of how Roosevelt battled with Churchill to maintain the strategy that would win the war.

Roosevelt knew the Allies should take Sicily but avoid a wider battle in the Mediterranean, building experience but saving strength to invade France in early 1944. Churchill seemed to agree at Casablanca – only to undermine his own generals and the Allied command, testing Roosevelt's patience to the limit. Seeking to avoid the D-Day landings, Churchill made the disastrous decision to push the battle further into southern Europe, almost losing the war for the Allies. In a dramatic showdown, FDR finally set the course for victory by making the ultimate threat.

Challenging seven decades of conventional wisdom about not one but two world leaders, *Commander in Chief* draws on extraordinary new archive material to delve further into the minds and actions of the men who led the Allied powers in the crucial year that decided the outcome of the Second World War.